Data Abstraction and Program Design

Rod Ellis

Principal Lecturer and Head: Division of Software Engineering
School of Computer Science and Information System Engineering,
Polytechnic of Central London

Pitman

PITMAN PUBLISHING
128 Long Acre, London WC2E 9AN

A Division of Longman Group UK Limited

First published in Great Britain 1991

British Library Cataloguing in Publication Data
Ellis, Rod
  Data abstraction and program design.
  I. Title
  005.1

  ISBN 0-273-03257-7

Reproduced and printed by photolithography
in Great Britain by Biddles Ltd, Guildford

Contents

Preface

The term *Object-based* is used to denote a common conceptual region shared by modern 'conventional' languages, such as MODULA-2 and Ada, and the Object-Oriented languages Smalltalk, C++, Eiffel etc. This region not only encompasses specifically linguistic concepts, of which data abstraction possesses a significance suggested by its prominence in the title of this book, but also an approach to software design without which these concepts lose much of their significance. In other words, these languages are not neutral in respect of the methods of software design with which they are utilised. Their features can be understood, and exploited successfully, only in the light of the design philosophy, in its various versions, that informed their development.

This book provides an introduction to object-based techniques of software construction. Its intended readership falls into two categories:

1. Software Engineering students in higher education who have completed their initial programming courses, probably in a language such as Pascal. The text introduces them to the concepts of 'programming in the large' and develops these along an Object-based trajectory. As such the book will form a useful basis for an academic course suitable for the second year of a software engineering degree programme.

2. Experienced software engineers who have come across references to Object-based techniques in the computer press, or by word of mouth, and who wish to update their knowledge in this area. The treatment in relation to this readership should enable the acquisition of a useful level of competence in some or all of the techniques dealt with, in conjunction with further reading selected from the Bibliographic Notes.

In writing a book with this objective two possible alternative approaches suggest themselves. The first, more radical approach, assumes no prior knowledge on the part of the reader and discusses Object-based concepts without reference to other, more familiar techniques. The second accepts that very few readers are likely to approach the subject with a mind innocent of programming experience and knowledge, and accordingly attempts to modify the 'mind-set' of its intended readership, by working from the reasonably familiar to the unknown in a gradual development.

This latter approach has been adopted for this book, in recognition of its intended readership. Thus the issues are developed through a progression from a Pascal context, through recognisable developments of Pascal, to the fairly remote areas of algebraic specification and Object-Oriented programming languages and techniques. The central, unifying theme of data abstraction is particularly useful in this context in providing a bridge from conventional to Object-based techniques.

Part of the motivation underlying its writing was the recognition of the difficulty that the average student (and the above-average student for that matter) has in coming to terms with the concept of 'programming in the large', or 'architectural' software design. This difficulty, which is endemic to the technology, is often exacerbated by the typical programming methodology course which, with its emphasis on 'programming in the small', or the detailed implementation of algorithms, provides a set of skills largely different from that involved in high-level, structural design. This emphasis induces a fascination with imperative detail that is extremely difficult to displace. The function of Chapter 1 is, accordingly, to get the reader to think in terms of 'programming in the large', or high-level design, to encourage an appreciation of the importance of defining software components in terms of their behaviour rather than their implementation, and to view success in this high-level design activity in terms of its outcome in supporting apparently mundane qualities such as modifiability and maintainability.

Readers who are experienced in software production may well find that Chapter 1 is preaching to the converted, and prefer to skip to Chapter 2. This interprets the criteria of good design identified in Chapter 1 in a more specifically software orientated context, articulated in terms of the vocabulary of modular software design. These ideas are not new, although their recognition in many works on software design seems fairly scanty.

Chapter 3 considers the support provided for the achievement of good modular design by conventional programming languages, for which Pascal is taken as the model. An examination of the deficiencies that this discussion reveals leads to an appreciation of the need for a new program structure — the data abstraction — the ubiquity of which, to program design, forms a core theme of the book.

Chapters 4 and 5 continue the discussion of language design issues by introducing two descendants of Pascal, MODULA-2 and Ada, from the particular standpoint of their support for the data abstraction. The aim of these Chapters is to convey the essential features of these languages whilst, particularly in the case of Ada, avoiding becoming enmeshed in detailed complexity.

The first five Chapters approach software design from an analytic viewpoint — *what* constitutes good design and how it can be reinforced by linguistic features. The next two Chapters consider design as a synthetic issue — *how* design is carried out as an activity so as to achieve the goals defined earlier, using the tool of the data abstraction.

Chapter 6 is a case study based on a well-known paper by Parnas, showing how the criteria introduced in earlier Chapters can be used to evaluate alternative approaches to design; and how information hiding, a quality closely related to the use of data abstraction, can be 'designed into' a system. Chapter 7 develops this idea but from a different standpoint — a consideration of the application and implementation domains — leading to an exposition of Object-Oriented Design.

A subsidiary theme is developed strongly in the second half of the book: software reuse, and its implications for design. The qualities of integrity and encapsulation conferred by the data abstraction provide the necessary syntactical support for reusable software components, but are not in themselves sufficient to ensure reusability. The nature of the requirements for reuse are discussed in Chapter 8 in a mainly Ada context, but leading to ideas going beyond Ada.

Chapter 8 can be seen as a bridge to two different facets of reuse. The first arises from the obligation of the writer or supplier of a software component to define clearly the semantics of its use. It is precisely those qualities of information hiding, of separation of interface from implementation detail, that make the communication of the semantics of these interfaces a critical issue — it is neither desirable nor, often, possible for the user of such a component to determine its correct usage by inspecting the code that realises its implementation. In Chapter 9 the necessity for formal, or mathematical, semantic specification techniques is discussed, as a precursor to an introduction to a particular formal technique — Algebraic Specification — which has found favour as the most appropriate for specifying components based on the data abstraction.

The second of these facets involves the deployment of a new programming paradigm — Object-Oriented Programming — which combines data abstraction and reuse in a way that both contrasts with and parallels the MODULA-2/Ada approach. Chapter 10 presents the major features of the Object-Oriented paradigm while Chapter 11 contains a comparison of the characteristics of a representative selection of Object-Oriented programming languages.

Finally, Chapter 12 reviews the contribution made by the data abstraction to modern approaches to software design and considers the tendency for convergence between the two models of exploitation within which the concept is found — a tendency that suggests a considerable unexploited potential.

Acknowledgements

The author would like to thank his colleagues for their forbearance during the gestation of this book, and particularly Mark Priestley for comments on Chapter 9. Thanks are also due for the helpful suggestions of the reviewers of the draft, particularly Gordon Blair of the University of Lancaster, and to John Cushion of Pitman for his patience and convivial encouragement.

To Liz, and Edward Gibbon

Chapter 1

The Design of Large Systems

1.1 Large Systems and Complexity

In this book we are concerned with the design of large software systems. There are many ways of defining what 'large' means in this context. To use the conventional, if probably the least satisfactory, yardstick, a large software system comprises something of the order of several hundred thousand to a million lines of source code. The unsatisfactory nature of this definition arises from both the vagueness — what exactly is a 'line of source code' — and also the slightly dated nature, of the terminology. Programmers are more used to thinking in terms of statements after all. It does convey, however, an impression of the order of magnitude of the physical manifestation of such a system as a very large body of text.

It may also be objected that the 'real' system is the machine-readable and executable object code version; but the design and implementation of software is a *human activity*, which results finally in a human-readable text — the source program. The generation of the executable form is, or should be, an automated process that requires no involvement on the part of the designer or implementor. So, with all its vagueness, we accept the definition above with its emphasis on the size, and therefore complexity, of the source text.

Even a slight experience of programming will have convinced the reader of the fact that the ease of understanding of a program or program fragment is adversely affected, in an all too dramatic way, by its size. Moreover, this effect is noticeable in numbers of statements counted in tens, rather than tens of thousands, with an all important threshold occurring, as noted by Brooks in *The Mythical Man-Month*, after *one page*. The difficulty involved in comprehending several hundred thousand statements, and correspondingly, in guiding the generation of several hundred thousand statements so as to realise a design, can easily be imagined therefore. So the question arises, how can the all too finite human mind span this kind of complexity? The answer is not a new one: it is by the use of *abstraction* — in other words, by the removal of inessential detail, by the removal of the trees obscuring the wood.

The key to abstraction lies in the ability to see a system as being composed of a small number of parts or components, each of which can be treated as a simple unit, the inner details of which need not be considered when viewing the whole system.

1.2   Abstraction and Design

The technique of abstraction is well-established in other, more mature branches of engineering. An aircraft wing, for example, is a highly complex structure. When viewed in the context of the predicted performance of the aircraft at the design stage, however, this complexity can be reduced to a few quantitative values: two constants that enable the calculation of the lift and drag of the wing over the range of speeds for which the aircraft is designed, and its weight and major dimensions, particularly including its volume (which normally determines the fuel capacity). Provided the designer of the wing manages, in 'fleshing out' its detailed design, to remain within the framework defined by these few values then the validity of the original predictions will be preserved. Another way of saying this is that, at the *level of abstraction* appropriate to performance calculations, the wing can be considered to *be* this rather small collection of values. Questions as to the airfoil section of the wing, its construction, control surfaces and so on are irrelevant *in this context* and need not be considered at the initial, high-level stages of design.

Abstraction is even more strongly established in electronic engineering with a theoretical basis that allows for any arbitrarily complex system component — an amplifier, say — to be replaced, for the purposes of the analysis of the complete system, by an *equivalent circuit*. An equivalent circuit consists of one each of the primitive circuit components resistance, capacitance and inductance, together possibly with a current or potential source. All specific details of the component in question are *abstracted away* as far as the rest of the system is concerned.

There are two notions involved in these examples of abstraction:

- the splitting up, or *partitioning*, of the design into discrete parts or components

- the ability to treat these components individually in terms of their effects on the rest of the system, whilst ignoring their internal structure. In these examples these effects can be captured by a small set of values.

1.2.1   Partitioning

When we consider design in these other areas of engineering the process of partitioning is a very natural one. An aircraft or a car can naturally be seen as a collection of components — integrated in the sense that the components fit and work together so as to enable the machine to achieve its designers' objectives. Moreover, the major components of a car such as the engine, the body, the transmission and so on, can be treated as single, monolithic objects at a high level of abstraction, or they may alternatively be viewed as being themselves composed of components populating a lower level of abstraction. For example, the engine is composed of the cylinder block, crankcase, crankshaft, connecting rods and pistons, cylinder head and valve gear, and so on. By choosing an appropriate level of abstraction we can reduce the complexity of the unstructured mass of basic, in the sense of 'having no components' components, that actually result from dismantling the car until no further dismantling is possible.

The process of design naturally follows the path from a high level of abstraction to lower levels — the car designer initially considers very high level 'broad-brush' factors such as the size and major features of the body, the position of the engine and so on. Once these major, high-level features have been determined then the filling out of the next level of detail may be undertaken. Then this process may be continued to successively lower levels until (literally) the nuts and bolts level is reached.

Common sense suggests that there is something wrong if the designer commences the task of designing a car by a detailed analysis of the instrument panel or the radiator grill. Not only does this offend against commonly held views on 'getting bogged down in detail' but also against the idea that over attention to one part of the design may well lead to an unbalanced final result.

Conventional engineering design techniques, then, suggest that success in the comprehension or design of large or complex systems is very dependent on the ability to consider these systems as comprised of components at various levels of abstraction.

1.3   Partitioning in Software Systems

Turning back to the consideration of software systems, with which we are concerned, it is clear that an important distinction between software and other forms of engineering is that the partitioning of a system into components is far less obvious. An aircraft, for example, is very clearly an assembly of sharply-distinguished components: the wings, tail, fuselage, undercarriage, engines etc. which have obvious and well-defined functions. The lack of any of these components is likely to result in an invalid 'system' — one that does not 'work'. With few exceptions that are only slight deviations from this pattern — and, even then, represent the extreme fringes of innovation ('flying wings' and so on) — this set of components forms the structural model within which the designers of *any* aircraft exercise their ingenuity.

By contrast, there are very few 'standard structural models' to be found generally in software systems, particularly at a high level of abstraction. It is true that many batch systems exhibit an input and an output component, but the rest is both application specific and also dependent on the inspiration of the production team involved. Perhaps more significant is the fact that in the one example where there *is* a generally-recognised standard partitioning, namely compilers, which are generally comprised of components that perform *lexical analysis, syntax analysis, semantic analysis* and *code generation*, there is considerable doubt as to whether this partitioning is a good one.

The software designer, then, does not work within the framework of a high-level structure of standard components. In the typical case a software system might be realised by *many different alternative* sets of components, any one of which would 'work', and it is the task of high-level design to determine the best partitioning from these alternatives.

1.4 Programming in the Large

The discussion above suggests that the major problem to be overcome in the design of largescale software systems is that of devising strategies for breaking down the design into a hierarchy of components. Also from the foregoing discussion it can be seen that the critical phase of this process is likely to be the initial one: the defining of the major components of the system at the topmost level of the hierarchy that form the *architectural* description of the system.

This high-level activity has become known as *programming in the large*, as contrasted with *programming in the small*, by which is meant the activity generally associated with the term *programming* — the translation of well-defined algorithms into some form of program structure expressed using a programming language. The term *programming* in the phrase *programming in the large* represents a deliberate attempt to get away from the idea that programming *means* 'writing source programs'.

Computer science students and, perhaps more surprisingly, professional programmers are often surprised at the lack of appreciation or importance given to 'programming skills' by software managers and the like. They are even more disheartened to learn that the writing of 'clever bits of code' is positively frowned upon in the gritty reality of the software industry. In other words, value is placed on programming in the large rather than programming in the small, for reasons that will be explored throughout this book. In simple terms this is simply a reflection of the fact that it is the largescale structure of a system (any kind of system) that is important — *it is the function of the high-level design to ensure that this is so* — to ensure that the internal details of individual components are relatively unimportant as compared with the architecture, the major high-level structure.

This guiding principle to design is known under various pseudonyms. The term *black box* approach is well-known in the world of electronics and has been borrowed by software engineers. It conveys the idea of components whose internal workings are hidden, and so inaccessible, with the complementary notion that what is important about such a component are the ways in which it interacts with other components over some well-defined interface: its *behaviour*. Recently, the term *mortar before the bricks* has been employed in respect of software systems to get over this idea that what is important is how the components fit together, rather than how each performs its particular function. The underlying theme is that the most important characteristic that a component may possess — given the satisfaction of minimal performance constraints — is that it may be replaced by an alternative version with no effect on the rest of the system. This reflects the inevitability of constant change throughout the operational life of any significant piece of software.

1.5 Evaluating Design

How then do we go about the job of the high-level design of a software system? The normal starting point is the agreed Requirements Specification that defines how the system will behave when it is used by its prospective users. But then, as we have seen, we are faced with many alternative designs that could satisfy the requirements, and apparently few guidelines as to how to choose between them — a blank sheet of paper (or VDU screen) in fact. Obviously, we want to choose 'the best' design — a possibility that depends on the existence of an objective basis for comparison between different designs.

The first question to be answered, then, is 'how can we tell a good high-level design from a bad one?' The easy 'answer' is to wait and see how the subsequent life of the design progresses — through detailed design, implementation and maintained use. But of course this is really no answer at all. What is required is to be able to evaluate a high-level design *before* it is too late to do anything about its shortcomings. Proving software puddings by eating them is a very expensive procedure. However, the 'wait and see' approach does suggest that it is possible to identify problems that are caused by failures in the high-level design of a software system when they occur during subsequent stages of its life. A consideration of these problems can lead to a characterisation of design faults whose absence can be regarded as indicative of good design. The following sections, therefore, describe characteristic problems arising from bad high-level design at the various stages in the life of a software system.

1.5.1 In Detailed Design and Implementation

The immediate objective of high-level design, programming in the large, is to be able to produce a 'mind-sized' model of the final system: to break it down into a manageable number of components. This model is then elaborated during the successive, detailed design phases. However, the success of these detailed design phases is dependent not just on partitioning into components. It is dependent on partitioning that produces components that can be treated as simple units, because their effects on the rest of the system are limited and may be captured by a small collection of information comprising a *behavioural* description.

If the high-level design fails to produce components with these characteristics then subsequent design tasks are hindered rather than helped by it. The inability to conceptually isolate components, and to have a clear view of the interactions between them, makes a proper understanding of the design impossible.

This effect will become more noticeable as the detailed design progresses, as inconsistencies and omissions are overlooked in the general confusion. The designer of a software component is far more likely to do a good job if he or she has a clear idea of precisely what the component is supposed to do. This may seem so obvious as to be hardly worth stating; it is the case, however, that very many software systems contain 'ragbag' components that have accumulated a large and unrelated set of functions that they perform. Often this is the result of design changes being made 'on the fly' during the implementation phase in conjunction with a bad structural design.

Distributivity

A different set of problems may also arise from bad high-level design. These are concerned with the practical realities of the software production process and in particular with the fact that, probably during the design, and absolutely certainly during the implementation ('programming') phases, the work will have to be distributed to several designers/programmers. It is simply impossible for one person to produce the volume of program code characteristic of large systems within the time that is normally acceptable, and thus it is inevitable that the work will be divided up between a production team, typically of anything from five to fifty members.

If work is to be progressed in parallel by a number of people then, making the reasonable assumption that each component is the responsibility of one person, it is clear that the components must possess a degree of independence so as to allow their separate development. If the structure is a bad one in which the components are insufficiently independent then each team member will constantly need to check up on what everybody else is doing, and be obliged to rewrite constantly to compensate for detailed changes made by others.

Testing

Testing, both of individual components, and larger assemblies up to full system test, is hindered by bad structural design resulting in components with a confused or badly-understood functionality. Both the devising of test data and the construction of test harnesses are affected, and the identification of bugs made difficult. Furthermore, a structure that fails to preserve adequate component independence will allow the modifications made to correct bugs when they are detected to proliferate to other components, causing new errors in consequence.

1.6   In Operational Life

Reliability

An unreliable software system continually throws up new bugs throughout its operational life. The cause of unreliability is a combination of inadequate testing, resulting from the kind of problems mentioned above, and a lack of independence between system components. This allows errors to migrate into regions remote from their original sites, often remaining undetected until a new combination of input data or usage reveals them. Both of these causes stem originally from bad high-level design.

Performance Aspects

So far nothing has been said about the likely effects of shortcomings in high-level design on the performance of the software system in question, including such aspects as speed and memory occupancy, and less tangible measures such as user friendliness. The short answer to the question as to the extent to which these are affected by high-level design is 'not at all'. This is, per-haps, an over-simplification. But it has been well established that attempts to base *high-level* design on the achievement of specific performance levels have invariably produced poor designs. In most kinds of software system unsatisfactory performance can be remedied by the 'tuning' of critical com-ponents. But the possibility of tuning is dependent on the ability to modify individual components without disrupting other parts of the system, which is dependent, in turn, on good high-level design. Given a good structure the achievement of specific performance levels is generally possible, but a bad structure can never be remedied.

Maintenance

The maintenance activity consists of the modification of an existing software system: either to cure errors ('bug-fixing') or to incorporate improvements ('enhancements'). The activity is traditionally bedevilled by the interdepen-dence of the system components arising from the inadequacy of high-level design. This interdependence is often poorly documented and apparently carefully hidden from the unsuspecting maintenance programmer, who all-too-often after a time-consuming search for a bug finds it and incorporates a modification to cure it, only to find that the 'cure' causes bugs to appear in some other part of the system. Similar problems occur when modifications are made in the course of the evolution of the functionality of the system, for change is endemic in any piece of software.

It is not unknown for this kind of problem to be so deep-seated in a badly-designed system as to make maintenance effectively impossible and to ne-cessitate a complete 'ground-up' rewriting.

1.6.1   Reuse

Mention of the enforced need for the rewriting of a software system may generate a distant ideal that is its opposite — the *reuse* of a software com-ponent — that is its incorporation in a system other than the one in which it was originally implemented. Reusable software has been used for many years in the form of 'compiler-planted' code such as input/output packages, intrinsic functions etc, and also a small but well-supported set of subroutine libraries, often concerned with computer graphics. The reuse of higher-level, application-oriented software components, however, is still in its infancy.

The motivation underlying this idea is not difficult to understand: software is legendarily expensive; if the investment in the production of a software component can be amortised over several systems that utilise it then the economics of software production begin to look somewhat more encouraging. The problem is that the functionality of a software component is normally heavily dependent on the environment in which it was designed, as the result, once again, of poor high-level design leading to a lack of independence.

It is also the case that software components are likely to be candidates for reuse only if they perform some well-defined function that is sufficiently general in its application so as to be relevant to many different contexts. Perhaps more importantly, only components that perform *well-defined* functions are likely to find application within a different environment if that function is *free-standing*: the kind of idea that is conveyed in other technologies by the phrase *plug-in* — a self-contained, integrated functional unit that performs a commonly-needed service. Again, these characteristics are critically dependent on high-level design.

1.7   Good High-level Design

We were led into this discussion of what characterises good high-level design by a realisation of the amorphousness, or plasticity, of software: virtually any partitioning into components can be made to work. It turns out that, except in a few very specialised applications, what constitutes good high-level design has little to do with the primary aim of satisfying the requirements specification, and everything to do with what might, in other areas of engineering, be considered secondary factors such as modifiability, maintainability, reliability, and so on. The justification for this view is based on the ever-changing nature of software. To talk of 'the' requirements specification is unrealistic. Requirements change constantly in response to user aspirations and experience, the effects of competitive products, new technologies and many other factors. The performance of a system at any particular point in its life can be seen as a cross-section across an evolutionary process of responding to these changing requirements. Thus the most important quality that a software design can possess is the ability to evolve systematically in a trouble-free way.

The discussion above leads to the conclusion that good high-level design results in a partitioning into components that exhibit two not entirely distinct characteristics. One of these is concerned with each component considered individually. The other is concerned with the relationships between components. These characteristics are:

- The possession of a well-defined, unified functionality. The touchstone of this quality is that such a functionality can be defined as the 'behaviour' that the component exhibits externally, without recourse to knowledge of its internal structure: *what* it does rather than *how* it does it, in other words.

- A high degree of independence as between the components. It is of course impossible for components to be completely independent, otherwise they would no longer constitute a system! What is required is the highest level of independence consistent with the satisfactory functioning of the system as a whole.

As noted above, these characteristics are related. A component is unlikely to have an adequate level of independence if its functionality can be defined only in terms of its internal structure (because the designers of components that interact with it will be obliged to use their knowledge of this structure in the design of *their* components). Again, a component that is intimately (that is, structurally) dependent on other components is unlikely to exhibit a well-defined, unified functionality. Although related, however, it is useful to continue the discussion in terms of two separate characteristics, for reasons that will be clarified in the next Chapter.

1.8 Summary

In this Chapter we have set the scene for an exploration of the principles of design relevant to large software systems. The universal engineering principle of abstraction has been related to software engineering, and the uniquely flexible nature of software has been found to necessitate a high-level design activity — programming in the large — concerned with devising architectural structure, a partitioning into components. The far-reaching effects of high-level design decisions have been considered and found to suggest criteria for evaluating programming in the large. These may be expressed in terms of the achievement of partitionings into well-defined, independent components.

So far the discussion has not addressed itself to the actual techniques that will produce designs meeting these criteria. Indeed it will be several Chapters before these techniques are discussed. For the moment we are concerned with *what* characterises good design rather than *how* it may be achieved. Perhaps surprisingly, an analysis of the former will provide a pathway to the discovery of the latter.

Following this analytical approach, the next Chapter relates the characteristics recently identified as being intrinsic to good high-level design more specifically to the realities of software construction — considering questions such as, for example, what does it mean for software components to be independent?

Chapter 2

Concepts of Modularity

In the last Chapter a discussion of high-level design, or programming in the large as it is known in the software context, led to the conclusion that good high-level design results in a partitioning into components that exhibit:

1. a well-defined, integrated functionality

2. a maximal independence

In this Chapter these criteria are interpreted in terms of modular software design, so that they may be more readily applied to the realities of software construction using conventional programming techniques and languages.

2.1 The Nature of Modules

The term *component* that has been borrowed from other areas of engineering is actually of only fairly recent use in software engineering. The established term, whose meaning roughly corresponds to that of component, is *module*. The term was originally rather vague — a wag at the 1969 Rome Software Engineering conference suggested in answer to the rhetorical question: "how big is a module", "1024 bytes" — but it has become considerably more precise recently. For the moment we will assume that it is simply equivalent to component and refine the meaning over this and the next few Chapters. Before looking further at how we can decide whether the breakdown of a software system design is a good one, or to put it in a slightly less clumsy

13

form, whether the *modular structure* is a good one, we need to clarify our ideas about the kind of entities that modules must be.

The important considerations here are the practical ones noted previously concerned with the parallel development of a system by different members of the development team. If this is to happen in an acceptably efficient way then each team member must be able to test his or her own module(s). In turn this means that modules must be individually compilable. The alternative, which would require the shuffling around of bits of source program between programmers, is too horrible to contemplate — although this does not mean that it has not happened! There are some quite far-reaching implications to be drawn here:

- modules must be well-formed syntactic units according to the rules of the programming language being used. (This is obviously a requirement imposed by the compilation system for the language.)

- the kind of communication between modules, which obviously affects the degree of interdependence, is determined by the nature of the language used and, particularly, the structures used to implement modules

Two concepts have become associated with the idea of modules, which correspond closely with the design criteria enumerated in the opening paragraph. They are:

1. *Module Coupling* — which corresponds to the criterion of independence — or rather to the reverse notion of *interdependence*

2. *Module Cohesion* — which corresponds to the criterion of possessing a well-defined, integrated functionality

They were first explored as such by Myers in *Reliable Software Through Composite Design*, on which a good deal of the discussion of them in the next two sections is based.

2.2   Module Coupling

Module Coupling is a measure of the extent to which modules are dependent upon each other in the sense of one module being affected by the *internal structure* of another. One way of illustrating this idea in action is to consider the extent to which the *designer* of a module would have to know about the internal structure of another module, in order to be able to design the new module so that it would work correctly with the other.

2.2.1 Content Coupling

The highest level of coupling can be seen when direct branches are made into and out of the code of another module. Clearly our designer would need to have a complete knowledge of the way in which the target module works, including the labels of the points to which control is to be transferred. He or she would also presumably have to plant the return jump back from the target module.

This level of coupling is so tight that the modules involved can hardly be considered to be independent in any real sense. A change to one, particularly the target module, will almost inevitably necessitate changes to the other — giving exactly the kind of pathological maintenance problems mentioned in the last Chapter. Again, the parallel development of modules linked in this way would require the constant consulting of the two programmers involved. The result would really be one large, messy module produced by two people, rather than two individual modules.

Fortunately, very few high level programming languages in current use will support branches, or jumps, between the kind of constructs that might be used as modules. This does not rule out assemblers of course, but thankfully few largescale software systems these days are written in assembler, even in the guise of Coral 66! (An in-joke, for which the author apologises.) This kind of direct branch coupling, called *Content Coupling* by Myers, possesses significance only in so far as it stands as the extreme limit in the range of degrees of coupling, perhaps as a reminder of precisely why modern programming languages prevent it.

Although content coupling is normally ruled out by the language used, a more diluted, and slightly more sanitised, version is still commonly to be found as what will be referred to as *Control Coupling*. Before considering control coupling in detail it would be appropriate to consider another dimension of coupling, that formed by the two possibilities of intermodule communication: shared variable and parameter.

2.2.2   Parametric and Global Coupling

In conventional imperative languages, of which Pascal forms both an idealised model and, in certain implementations, a practical example, communication between the modules of a program (note the assumption that
modules are sub-program structures) is achieved by means of either shared
variables or parameters.

Global Coupling

Shared variables are typically declared as *global* to the program units utilised
as modules in a block-structured language such as Pascal or are defined
in COMMON areas in languages such as FORTRAN. Communication via
shared variables is accomplished by the result of an assignment to such a
variable made within one module being accessible to all the other modules
that share it. All the modules that share such a variable may either read
from or, more importantly, write to it in a completely uncontrolled way.

When viewed in the context of module coupling it is clear that shared variable communication represents a high level of coupling. Each module that
participates in the sharing of COMMON or global areas must be aware of
how all the other participating modules use them and, as was noted above,
there is no possibility of any kind of discipline, like 'read-only' access, being
imposed. In the late sixties it was very common to find program designs
based on a large 'spine' of common areas, along which the subroutines were
arranged in a way analogous to the way the components in a computer
are arranged along a bus. This was particularly so in systems written in
FORTRAN and also assemblers, which often provided a FORTRAN-like
COMMON facility. The GINO-F graphics package, which achieved quite a
significant level of popularity in the UK and was still in use in 1990, was an
example of such a design.

This superficially pleasing arrangement was in fact frequently the cause of
disaster. In those long-departed days it was not uncommon for programs
to become short of memory (when 12K was a big machine), and programmers were imbued with the idea of saving space. One way of making your
own module apparently smaller was by utilising some of the common area
to hold local data — there were always 'unused' locations, or ones that
'wouldn't be used until the output phase'. The result was that eventually,
during enhancement or whatever, these 'unused' common areas would be

used, and of course promptly corrupted by the 'private' use made by some space-conscious programmer.

This kind of bug is extremely difficult to find, particularly in the absence both of the miscreant who perpetrated it, who had probably left by then, and the kind of software tools that are taken for granted now. This difficulty arises from the documentary problem with common or global data items: references to them in the program text — in assignment statements, say — give no clue as to their special status, except in the *very* unusual case of the highly disciplined programmer who comments every such reference. Consequently, the task of searching through a few thousand lines of program listing for references to globals is both time-consuming and boring, with a low success rate as a result. The task is made even worse by languages such as FORTRAN because it is not necessary for the variables in a FORTRAN COMMON block to be consistently named in each instance of the block.

To summarise: the use of global or common data items represents a high level of coupling, essentially because the intermodule communication that they support is too free, too uncontrolled and thus requires too much discipline and mutual awareness on the part of the communicating modules.

Parametric Coupling

Communication via parameters is, by contrast, a much more constrained affair, particularly in the more 'structured' languages. Parameterisation is associated with the *calling* operation, which is applied to program units commonly named *subroutines, subprograms, procedures, functions* and so on; we will use the term *subprogram* in this discussion. Subprogram declarations may incorporate *formal parameters*, which typically occupy a distinguished position at the head of the declaration, and which act both as local variables from the point of view of the subprogram but also support *parameter substitution* — the transmission of values into and/or out of the subprogram from its external, calling environment. An important feature of parameterisation in modern languages is the ability to restrict the transmission of values to one-way only: normally input or read-only from the point of view of the called subprogram.

By contrast with the use of global variables, parameterisation provides the *potential* for very low, or loose, coupling. This is particularly the case when *value* or *read-only* mode parameters are used, where the called subprogram receives only *copies* of the actual parameter values, and thus any modifica-

tion to the formal parameters is localised within the called subprogram —
there is no possibility of changes being propagated to the external, calling
module. Clearly, read-only mode parameters can be used only when it is not
required to export results from a procedural module, in which case input-
output or read-write mode parameters must be used. This is still a much
more controlled arrangement, however: the formal parameters of a subprogram are modifiable only by the subprogram during its call or invocation.
They form a well-defined and distinguished collection of variables whose
purpose is quite clearly involved with the communication of data into or out
of the subprogram. Furthermore, this communication is normally synchro-
nised with the *call* or *return from call* actions. To put it another way: the
designer of a module consisting of a subprogram that calls another, existing
subprogram knows exactly the extent to which his or her module is affected
by the call(s) to the other subprogram, provided that communication is restricted to parameter passing: only the actual parameters can be affected,
and only those substituting for input/output or output mode formal parameters. This provides a powerful contrast with subprograms linked by a large
set of global variables — any of which could be changed by a subprogram
with the appropriate visibility.

Consideration of the shared-variable/parameters axis shows, therefore, that
the use of parameterisation is a necessary condition for achieving low coupling. It is not a sufficient condition, however. It is quite possible to use
parameterisation in such a way as to require a high 'interface commitment':
in other words, to be dependent on a particular complex interface format,
which is still indicative of high coupling.

2.2.3   Interface Commitment

A high level of interface commitment may arise from one of two causes:

- the use of *control* parameters

- the use of *data structure* parameters

Control Parameters

It was suggested previously that the tightest form of intermodule coupling
is exhibited by direct branch, or content, coupling and also that a slightly

diluted and sanitised version exists. This version is the use of *control parameters* — i.e. one or more parameters whose values are not used as data to be transformed in some way but as selectors determining the sequence of execution that the called module is to perform. The typical structure of a module that provides a control parameter is that of a large case statement of the kind found in Pascal — the values of the control parameter corresponding to the various cases, each of which selects a sequence of statements (blocked into a compound statement in the case of Pascal). Such a module consists, in fact, of a collection of separate modules corresponding to the set of cases; this point will be returned to shortly.

The coupling involved in the use of control parameters is high because of the requirement that they place on external modules, or rather their designers, to understand the internal structure through which the paths of control selected by the control variable values are traced. It may be objected that this is merely a matter of documentation. The interface definition of the module should simply include the range of values for the control variable, together with a description of the function corresponding to each value. Complexity almost invariably arises, however, because it is very rare for the multiple functions discriminated by the control variable to need the same set of data parameters.

Let us consider an example, namely a *queue*. Queues are widely used in software systems, in operating systems for example; they are lists that impose a first-in first-out discipline. A queue has four essential operations associated with it:

1. **Initialise** the queue, that is, set it or reset it to an empty state

2. **Enqueue** an item, that is, enter it into the queue

3. **Dequeue** an item, that is, remove the item from the queue that has been there for the longest time and make it available externally.

4. **Test for Empty** a Boolean (true/false) value made available externally. Alternatively, a count operation may give the number of items currently in the queue.

A module that implements a queue with these operations will require four parameters, as follows:

- `control` an integer valued (see below) input parameter with values, say 0..3 corresponding to Initialise, Enqueue, Dequeue and Empty?

- `input` an input (value) mode parameter with the type of the queue items, to supply the item for the Enqueue operation

- `output` an output (variable) mode parameter with the type of the queue items, to make available the item exported by the Dequeue operation.

- `is empty` an output parameter of boolean type, to make available the result of the empty test operation.

It may be objected that two item parameters are unnecessary: one parameter would suffice for both the Enqueue and the Dequeue operations; this is true but represents bad programming practice and is, in fact, illustrative of the dubious nature of control coupling.

The use of control parameters, because they require the remainder of the parameter set to accommodate *all* the operations, inevitably causes complexity in the use of the parameters. Some will be unused in any particular operation (e.g. the boolean parameter in the two item transfer operations; no parameters are used in conjunction with the initialisation operation), whilst requiring the supply of dummy actual parameters for the sake of the syntactic correctness of the calls. At the risk perhaps of overstressing this point it is worthwhile showing a typical calling sequence to a module implementing a queue in this way

```
queue(2,in_item,out_item,is_empty); (* test for empty Q *)
if not is-empty
then queue(1,in_item,out_item,is_empty); (* get item in
    out_item *)
```

As can be seen, this kind of arrangement falls somewhat short of the ideal of low coupling. Both parties to a module interaction are committed to a reasonably complex interface, which is made intelligible only by comments, with a correspondingly increased possibility of error. This is exacerbated by the common use of integer values for those of control variables — it is fairly difficult to remember that '0 means initialise' while '1 means Enqueue' and so on, particularly while checking code rather than actually writing it.

At this point the experienced Pascal programmer may well be saying "yes but in a civilised language we have enumeration types so that the control values can be given meaningful names and the calls become self-documenting".

Unfortunately the use of an enumeration type in this way will increase the coupling of the relevant module to its environment: because the scope rules of Pascal and similar languages dictate that the declaration of the enumeration type must be global to both the module and the external calls made to it. The effect would be to require the module to trail a detached declaration around with it, destroying its status as an independent, integrated unit and doing considerable violence to the whole idea of a module.

This raises the question of the types of the parameters that constitute module interfaces. As we have seen there are strong objections to the use of user-defined types, in strongly typed languages like Pascal at least, because of the necessity for the type declarations to be external to the module — so that both the formal and actual parameters can themselves be declared. In fact this restriction is fortuitous because there are other good reasons for avoiding the use of user-defined, particularly structured, types.

Structured Type Parameters

It has been common practice, particularly in the operating system world, to use module interfaces with large, structured parameters. The typical example is the 'file header block' (FHB), which is often passed back and forth between operating system services and user programs. When the user program requests the creation of a file, for example, the operating system will pass back a FHB containing details of the file just created. In Pascal terms these structures are records — consisting of a number of fields of differing types: integer block numbers, character string names, and so on.

Normally, however, the language used is not Pascal, but a less strongly-typed language that permits different record structures to be supplied as the actual parameter corresponding to an unchanged formal parameter, the fields in such a structure being identified by their offset from the base address of the whole. This arrangement has proved to be a fruitful source of errors over the years. Inevitably the format of the FHB structure is changed in successive releases of the system and, equally inevitably, the custodians of the modules using the structure fail to notice or are not informed of the changes. The user modules, which 'unpack' the structure using the (out of date) offset information, then wrongly interpret the data, and the system 'falls over', to use the colourful term.

It is also the case that a read-write parameter effectively constitutes a global location as far as the calling and called modules are concerned. In languages that are unable to impose a read-only discipline on a large data- structure parameter, or indeed in any language environment where a field of such a parameter, and therefore the whole data structure, is required to be read-write, there is no protection against the possibility that a user module may corrupt the 'global' data structure.

The moral is that the use of data structure parameters implies a high level of coupling both because of the 'sub-COMMON' coupling that they entail, and because of the need of the user module (designer) to know their formats. It may be objected that the use of a strongly typed language would prevent this kind of problem, because the module calls would no longer compile if the format, and therefore the type, of the structure was changed. This ignores the fact that type checking even in Pascal is restricted to compile time. Normally modules are independently compiled, and so the matching of formal and actual parameters goes by the board — structures that occupy the same space can be passed willy-nilly.

Pointer-Connected Structure Parameters

Another possibility for the passing of complex data structures is the use of dynamic, pointer-connected structures rather than static structures such as arrays or records. Typical examples are lists and trees. Superficially the parametric interface commitment for such a structure is very simple: a pointer value that is the 'header' or 'anchor' of the data structure. This is passed as a parameter and then can be used as the 'keyhole' through which the traversal of the whole structure may be initiated.

In fact the underlying commitment is equivalent to that for the record structure that defines the format for each node in the structure. In loosely-typed languages the fields of such a structure may be remapped leading to exactly the same kind of problems as have been described in the context of static, record structure parameters. A further problem with dynamic structures is the requirement to mark the limits of the structure — to terminate a list, for example. Conventionally this is done by 'nil' value fields — but, of course, there are many alternative possibilities, whose existence represents yet more information that the user of a module with this kind of parameter must respect.

Unstructured parameters

We are led inexorably to the conclusion that low coupling implies the use of parameters with 'simple', unstructured types of the kind that are generally available — that is pre-defined or declared by default — such as integers or ASCII characters. The relevant point about these types is that their formats are, to all intents, fixed. Their use requires no *specialised* or *application specific* knowledge on the part of users because they are universal and unchanging: no bug correction or enhancement is going to change the ASCII character set, for example.

In addition to the types of the parameters we can also see that coupling, in the usual sense of the measure of how much the user needs to know, is also dependent simply on the number of parameters — the fewer, the lower the coupling. Finally, the ultimate in low coupling is provided, in languages that support the feature, by read-only or *value-mode* parameters. Here the reduction in coupling is more a matter of physical isolation, because a read-only parameter cannot cause the propagation of any effects, particularly erroneous ones, outside the module for which it is defined.

The reader may well be feeling by now that the discussion has entered a somewhat unreal stage. It is obvious that a module interface comprising a few read-only integer parameters exhibits a low level of coupling — but surely any attempt to design systems in which all interfaces are like this is quite impractical! Operating system designers did not invent file header blocks out of some wilful desire to produce unmaintainable systems after all — they exist because it is useful and indeed necessary to group information relating to entities such as files together — and how can this be done without using structures that provide this grouping? The answer to this question will be provided in the next Chapter.

2.3 Module Cohesion

The second criterion that was previously identified was a measure of the extent to which the function that a module carries out is a unified, integrated, well-defined one. The terminology that has become established to denote this idea is *module strength* or *cohesion* The advantages of high module strength both complement and, to a certain degree, are interdependent with those of low coupling.

The replaceability of a module, which is the key to avoiding problems both in parallel development and maintenance, is obviously highly compromised if it performs several unrelated activities. Modification will invariably be intended to affect a subset, typically of one, of these activities, yet all will be potentially involved if the module is replaced. By contrast, a well-defined 'single-function' module can be 'unplugged' and replaced with the minimum of disturbance to the rest of the system: provided, of course, that this cohesion is supported by a low level of coupling between the module and its environment.

Again, the implementor of a module is far more likely to perform the task well if he or she understands fully the intentions of the designer, and these are obviously much clearer if the functionality is well-defined and unified in some way. A further benefit of high module cohesion is that of improved error locating — if there is a clear relation between the overall functions of the system and the modules that comprise it then the pin-pointing of the source of a failure of functionality is made much easier. The contrast, i.e. systems in which modules have little cohesion, provide nightmares for maintenance staff who are obliged to spend large amounts of time searching through source files trying to find 'where it does ..'

Myers uses the term *strength* rather than cohesion: the author prefers the latter but it is, of course, a matter of taste. He gives a classification of module strengths, with names that in some cases seem rather less than obvious, but which provides a useful framework for discussing the concept. Briefly, Myers' classification is as follows:

- **Coincidental** is the lowest strength classification and is possessed by what have been inelegantly termed 'ragbag' modules previously in this text. In other words, modules whose components, or elements to use Myers' term, have no relationships other than their common home. Coincidental strength is often the result of the 'modularising' of an existing program whose design is simply incapable of being split into a good structure. Or, as has been suggested previously, the result of redesigning during the implementation process.

- **Logical** strength is possessed by modules whose elements have relationships that are derived from the application — in other words a module that contains 'all the XXXXX operations' where XXXXX is a feature of the application. Myers gives the examples of a module that performs all the input/output operations for a program or one that does all the editing of data. Logical strength, in practice, is low on the strength scale because the relationships derived from the application are not necessarily visible at the program level, and attempts to package them up invariably result in 'tricky code' that is difficult to understand and modify. Perhaps *superficial* strength would be a more illuminating term.

- **Classical** strength, apart from representing the pinnacle of Myers' inspiration in the way of names, is Logical strength with the additional constraint that the components are related in time. The characteristic examples of Classical strength modules are the 'program initialisation, open all files ..' or 'system shutdown, clean up, close files ..'. Classical strength is close to Logical strength, but, according to Myers, Classical strength modules 'are higher on the scale since they tend to be simpler'. Myers also makes the point that Classical strength modules are often unavoidable — most programs have a module whose functions are 'when an error condition occurs diagnose the error, correct it if possible and continue execution'. Such a module inevitably has Classical strength.

- **Procedural** strength is the analogue of Logical strength at the implementation level. In other words, a module with procedural strength has components that are related by the structure of the program's procedural sequence. Conceptually, and indeed practically on occasion, Procedural strength modules correspond to one or a connected set of boxes from the program flowchart.

  Myers places Procedural strength above Classical strength in his scale, but at a position that is still well below the ideal, which is described below. Interestingly, design methodologies based on the use of 'Structure Charts' would appear inevitably to generate Procedural strength modules, and thus, according to this classification, to fall short of ideal modular design. As we shall see in a later Chapter, this suspicion is actually borne out in practice.

- **Communicational** strength is possessed by a module with procedural strength, but with the added constraint that the module's elements share or communicate a common set of data between themselves. Obviously the effect of this common set of data is to bind together the elements in terms of their functions, and so Communicational strength is placed higher on the scale than Procedural strength. Also, it can

be seen in the light of the previous discussion that Communicational
strength may possess complementary effects on module coupling, depending on whether the common set of data is isolated from access by
other modules.

- **Functional** strength is the ideal of maximum module strength, derived
  from the concept of the mathematical function — which informally
  may be described as an object that produces a single, unified output
  value for every call, the output being a well-defined transformation of
  the input parameters, or arguments, to use the conventional mathematical terminology. Importantly, the results of calling a function are
  restricted completely to the value that it returns, the arguments being
  unchanged. Its elements, therefore, are totally integrated into the internal algorithm that produces the output value and are irrelevant to
  the outside world, so long as the output value represents the correct
  transformation.

  Like mathematical functions, modules with Functional strength may
  have no arguments. Unlike mathematical functions, Functional strength
  modules may return no value — thus having no effect at all on the
  program in which they exist. Myers gives the following examples of
  modules with Functional strength:

  - *Compute square root* which closely resembles the model of a math-
    ematical function, producing an output value for each value of its
    single input parameter.

  - *Obtain random number* (presumably by some such method as tim-
    ing an unpredictable hardware process) is given as an example of
    a module that produces an output with no input arguments.

  - *Write record to output file* is an example of a Functional strength
    module with no output value — the file is external to the program
    and so no effect is visible within the program.

Once again the reader may be struck by a sense of unreality — it is fairly
easy to see that modules that are like mathematical functions will be well-
defined in a way that has been identified as a desirable characteristic. But
surely it is quite impractical to think of basing an entire system on modules
of this type. Apart from any other considerations there is the problem
that, by their nature, Functional strength modules cannot possess *memory*;
in other words, a module that behaves like a mathematical function will

always produce a specific output value every time that it is called with a particular set of argument values — its behaviour cannot be modified by the sequence of calls that it has undergone. In turn this means that there are very considerable difficulties in implementing something like the Queue, which is defined in terms of the way its behaviour is dependent on its history.

Myers recognises that Functional strength represents a largely unattainable ideal and introduces a classification that is related to it but is lower on the scale. *Informational* strength, to use Myers' definition, is possessed by a module that "performs multiple functions where the functions, represented by entry points in the module, deal *with a single data structure*. In other words, this module represents the physical packaging together (into one module) of two or more modules having functional strength".

Myers gives the example of a module with two entry points corresponding to two functions, respectively "insert symbol into symbol table" and "search for symbol in symbol table". The two entry points deal with a single data structure, the symbol table, and each is equivalent to a Functional strength module. Informational strength thus seems to have the advantages of Functional and Communicational strength and might be thought to be higher on the scale, at least in view of its practicality, than Functional strength. Myers rejects this view, although perhaps not without some reluctance, because of the added complexity implied by the 'packaging-up' characteristic of this kind of module. Inevitably, this will provide the opportunity to 'intertwine', to use Myers' term, the code for each entry point, with the corresponding tendency to complexity and errors.

The reader may well be puzzled by the term *entry point*. Although its meaning is perhaps intuitively reasonably obvious it is not, after all, a term associated with modern programming languages and indeed the concept that it denotes is not a feature of Pascal, say. At the risk of leaving things slightly up in the air, it is proposed to delay a definition of the term until the next Chapter where the facilities of programming languages will be considered from the perspective of the criteria for modular design that have been introduced here.

2.4 The Principle and the Benefits

In the discussion of these two criteria, module coupling and module cohesion, it has been transparently clear which end of the scale is desirable in each

case. At the risk of stating the obvious, the criteria can be used to express
the principle of good modular design, thus: *in a good modular design all the
modules should exhibit* **low** *coupling and* **high** *cohesion.*

The benefits that flow from adherence to this principle are many, but may
be characterised under the following headings:

1. **Distributivity** — the independence and lack of interface commitment
   displayed by the modules allows for their separate development by
   members of the development team.

2. **Clarity** — the effect of high cohesion and lack of interdependencies is
   to clarify the specific role of every module in the system, with corresponding benefits in terms of the achievement of the system requirements and low error content.

3. **Localisation of Errors** — the clean nature of the interfaces, and
   the control over data flow that parameterisation provides, tends to
   prevent the propagation of errors outside the modules in which they
   occur. This is important not only to the integrity of the system during
   its operational life but also to the location of errors as they occur.

4. **Modifiability** — the ideal of the 'plug-in' module with black-box
   characteristics can be most closely achieved in this way. The hiding
   of the internal implementation of such a module means that it may
   be modified, or completely replaced, with minimal effect on the rest of
   the system.

5. **Maintainability** — the combination of clarity, localisation and modifiability provides powerful support for the maintenance activity. This
   is obviously a benefit derived from the other characteristics, but because maintenance is so frequently a largescale absorber of resources
   it is worthwhile emphasising this aspect of good modular design.

2.5   Summary

In this Chapter we have continued the analysis of the characteristics of good
high-level design, discussed in terms of the concepts of *module coupling* and
module cohesion, concluding with the general prescription that a good modular design exhibits low module coupling and high module cohesion.

As has been remarked, these concepts are not unrelated, but they differ significantly in their nature. Coupling is essentially a *syntactic* concept, which can be measured objectively by a consideration of program structure. An appropriate metric would determine the existence of global data, the number and nature of parameters, and so on. The process could be automated quite satisfactorily. Cohesion, on the other hand, is largely a *semantic* concept — it can be determined only in the light of an understanding of the *meaning* of the module in question. As such it is much less amenable to automatic measurement, and is an altogether less tractable idea. Perhaps surprisingly, a concentration on aspects of coupling will also produce useful insights into cohesion, and it is to the consideration of language characteristics in this context which we turn in the next Chapter.

Chapter 3

Language Structures and Modularity

3.1   Introduction

In this Chapter we initially investigate the extent to which it is possible
to achieve the ideals of low module coupling and high module cohesion in
programs written in a conventional programming language. The language
used as the vehicle for this investigation is Pascal, mainly because of its wide
popularity as a first programming language, and also because it provides a
representative model for a large class of languages.

The investigation will be based on the use of a particular program data
structure — the *push-down stack* or, more simply, the *stack*. The author
makes no apology for the very considerable lack of innovation displayed
by the exemplary use of the stack — it has the advantage of being a real
structure, albeit with comparatively few applications as compared with, say,
the queue, but which may be implemented in a manner simple enough to
avoid obscuring more important matters. It is also the case that the stack
has attained a unique position in the literature surrounding data abstraction.
Once having been introduced to it in this context, the reader will experience
a feeling of warm familiarity at each new instance in more advanced works.

3.1.1   The Stack

The stack, or *last-in first-out list*, is a structure that may be imagined to be the program analogue of a tube-like receptacle containing a spring. Objects may be pushed into the tube, against the pressure of the spring, and prevented from being expelled by some sort of catch arrangement at the mouth of the tube. The catch may be released momentarily so that one object, the object at the end of the tube, pops out.

In program terms, the stack is a data structure with two characteristic *associated operations*. The operations are known as *push* and *pop*, following the operations of the tube analogue, and respectively allow data items to be inserted into, and removed from, the data structure. The *stack discipline* imposed by the structure ensures that the item that is 'popped' is always the one that has remained for the *least* time of all the items that are in the structure. The stack may be seen, therefore, as in some sense the 'opposite' or complement of the queue. Stacks are used in algorithms for parsing nested structures such as bracketed expressions — the well-known 'Dijkstra's marshalling yard', for example, uses two.

In addition to the characteristic push and pop operations the stack also needs to be initialised — i.e. cleared to an empty state, and this produces in turn the need for an operation to test for the empty stack. Obviously a pop operation on an empty stack cannot be expected to produce a useful result.

The stack would appear to be an ideal candidate for implementing as a module — it is a self-contained, well-defined component. It might be expected therefore to provide a useful benchmark against which to measure the support given to modularity by a language.

3.2   Pascal Implementations of the Stack

3.2.1   Support for Modularity

The initial problem that we are faced with in devising Pascal implementations of a stack module is the fact that few Pascal systems support independent compilation , and thus it is impossible to have modules in any real sense at all. Many Pascal systems provide an 'include file' facility, which allows the source of a program to be drawn from several source files. These are not compiled independently, however, but merged together before compilation. For the moment, however, we shall ignore this drawback.

3.2.2   A Multiple Subprogram Implementation

The 'single-ended' nature of the stack — both push and pop operations affect the same end of the tube model — means that a reasonable approach to a Pascal implementation is to use a one-dimensional array as the basic data structure. As items are pushed into the stack they are stored in successive elements starting from the left-hand end of the array. When an item is popped it is taken from the rightmost of the occupied elements, which is then made available for overwriting by a subsequent push operation.

The only additional data structure that is required is a variable to hold the index of the 'last occupied element' in the array, a value conventionally called the *top of stack pointer*, abbreviated to TOS. TOS is incremented by the push operation and decremented by the pop operation. TOS is set to the value of the predecessor of the lowest array index by the initialisation operation, thereby indicating a non-existent last occupied element and thus an empty stack. This value is used in the test for empty stack. The value of TOS is used also in the supplementary test for full stack operation, which is necessitated by the fact that the underlying array must be of a fixed size.

As an aside we may notice the fact that the operations of the stack are quite unaffected by the nature of the items manipulated by it, although a Pascal implementation is obliged to respect the strong typing of the language in the declaration of the underlying array. In other words, a Pascal stack must be a stack of objects of some specific type.

The straightforward approach is to implement each of the stack operations as a separate subprogram that accesses the common data structure. An implementation adopting this approach is shown in Figure 3.1. It is assumed that the stack forms part of a larger program called **stack_user** that contains numerous calls to its operations.

3.2.3   Coupling

If we apply the criterion of module coupling to the implementation we see immediately that the stack is tightly coupled to the rest of the program because of the global declaration of the data structure — the array **stack** and the stack pointer **TOS**. It is quite clear that these declarations must be global to the subprograms that implement the operations. If they were located within, say, the **initialise** procedure, the scope rules of Pascal would prevent any access being made to the data structure from any of the

```pascal
program stack_user(input,output);

(**************** stack data structure *****************)

const    stack_size       = (* some suitable number *)

type     stack_range      = 1 .. stack_size;
         TOS_range        = 0 .. stack_size;(* allow for
                                                empty stack *)
         item             = (* the type of the items to be
                                                stacked *)
var      stack            : array [stack_range] of item;
         TOS              : TOS_range;

(************ stack operations **************)

         procedure initialise_stack;
         begin
                     TOS := 0
         end;

         procedure push (I : item);
         begin
                     TOS := TOS + 1;
                stack[TOS] := I
         end;

         function pop : item;
         begin
                     pop := stack[TOS];
                     TOS := TOS - 1
         end;

         function stack_empty : boolean;
         begin
                stack_empty := TOS = 0
         end;

         function stack_full : boolean;
         begin
                stack_full := TOS = stack_size
         end;
(******** end of stack operations **********)
```

Figure 3.1: Pascal Stack Implementation – Multiple Subprograms

other operation subprograms.

A further reason for the necessity of the global declaration is that local data in Pascal subprograms exists only for the duration of the invocation during which it is established: local data items do not survive between calls, in other words. This means that a locally declared data structure would have to be passed, in its entirety, via parameters with each call to any of the operation subprograms — a distinctly cumbersome arrangement with a relatively high interface commitment and thus high level of coupling.

The dangers inherent in the implementation may perhaps be illuminated by imagining a slightly unreal scenario, but one with its roots quite firmly embedded in reality. The reader is invited to imagine that he or she is a member of a programming team and has been asked to provide a stack module for incorporation into the system under development. The project leader, a man given to dramatic gestures, has asked that an absolute guarantee (signed in blood) is given that the stack will work correctly — after all, it's a simple enough bit of code isn't it?

The reader has produced the obvious implementation, not unlike the version shown in Figure 3.1. But of course the reader would be extremely foolish to give any guarantee about the working of the stack, because he or she *simply does not have enough control over the way that it is used.*

We are not here talking about errors in using the defined interface, such as popping an empty stack, that are part of the behaviour of a stack. What cannot be prevented is the circumvention of the means that the implementation provides for the manipulation of the stack — the operation subprograms. The global declaration of the data structure means that direct assignments may be made to it from any point in the program. So that, for example, the TOS could be decremented directly, rather than as the result of pop operations. This would destroy the discipline of the structure: the next item popped would not then be the item that had remained within the stack for the least duration.

The moral of the story is that the designer of a module should allow him or herself to be committed to its correct working only to the extent that users are made to use the module via the intended interface. Furthermore, the obvious Pascal implementation does not so constrain users of the stack, because of its tight global coupling .

3.2.4   A Single Subprogram Implementation

If we attempt to find a solution within the Pascal context it is clear that we need to isolate, or *encapsulate* to introduce a resonant term, the declaration of the data structure so that it is protected from the rest of the program. In other words, to restrict the scope of the declaration so that attempts to include assignments to the data structure in other parts of the program will be rejected by the compiler.

The only way that Pascal provides for this is to make the declaration local to a single subprogram. Now as we have seen this raises the problem of the ephemeral nature of local data; for the purposes of this discussion, however, we will assume the use of a Pascal variant, such as VAX Pascal, which provides a *static* qualifier for local declarations. The effect of this is to make the contents of any variable so qualified survive the exit of control from the subprogram to which the declaration is local. This feature is somewhat far from the spirit of Pascal but it will allow the implementation of the stack as a single procedure. The implementation, in the form of a procedure called stack, is shown in Figure 3.2.

The incorporation of all the operations within the single procedure means that the implementation is obliged to provide a *control parameter*, called s_func in the Figure, in order to select from the five operations that characterise the stack. As we have seen already in Chapter 2, the use of control coupling tends to produce both an unclean interface, with the requirement for dummy actual parameters, and an over-complicated internal structure. These characteristics are quite in evidence even in something as simple as the stack.

The messy interface is illustrated by a selection of calls to it shown in Figure 3.3, along with the corresponding calls of the earlier implementation. The directness and simplicity of the original implementation of the operations as individual subprograms, each displaying a high level of cohesion, is lost.

3.2.5   Pascal's Deficiencies

It can be seen then that the possibilities provided by Pascal for the implementation of the stack, as represented by the two candidates shown, both possess unfortunate characteristics that make them less than ideal from the point of view of modular design. The multiple subprogram version possesses a clean interface, but which can be circumvented because of the tight cou-

```
program stack_user(input,output);
type    item    = (* the type of the items to be stacked *)

        procedure stack(s_func: integer; in_val : item;
        var out_val : item; var ok : boolean);
          (******* stack data structure *******)
        const   stack_size      = (* some suitable number *)

        type    stack_range     = 1 .. stack_size;
                TOS_range       = 0 .. stack_size;(* allow for
                                                empty stack *)
        var     stack           : [static] array [stack_range]
                                                of item;
                TOS             : [static] TOS_range;

        begin (*** stack ***)
                case s_func of
                  0 : (* initialise stack *)
                            TOS   := 0
                  1 : (* push *)
                          begin
                                TOS         := TOS + 1;
                                stack[TOS] := in_val
                          end;
                  2 : (* pop *)
                          begin
                                out_val := stack[TOS];
                                TOS     := TOS - 1
                          end;
                  3 : (* stack empty? *)
                            ok:= TOS <> 0
                  4 : (* stack full? *)
                            ok:= TOS < stack_size
                end
        end; (* of stack *)
```

Figure 3.2: Pascal Stack Implementation — Multi-function Subprogram

```
if token in op
then
      if not stack_full
      then push(token)
      else
          begin
              writeln ('stack overflow');
            .  .  .  .


if token in op
then
      begin
          stack(4,dummy,dummy,not_full);
          if not_full
          then
              stack(1,token,dummy,dont_care)
          else
              begin
                  writeln('stack overflow');
                .  .  .  .
```

Figure 3.3: Comparison of the Two Implementations

pling resulting from the global data structure that it requires. The single subprogram, multiple-function implementation necessitates control coupling with its inevitably ugly interface and is, in any case, dependent on a nonstandard Pascal feature. We are left with the conclusion that, in this respect at least, Pascal is deficient. What is perhaps of more interest is to consider how the language might be extended so as to support the concepts of modular design that we have discussed.

3.2.6 Encapsulation — a Syntactic Wall

If we return to the point of the discussion that led to the investigation of the single procedure implementation we recall that the requirement was to restrict, or encapsulate, the scope of the declaration of the data structure on which the implementation depends. Pascal provides only two scope-defining structures: program blocks and subprograms. The first is clearly too large for this purpose; the second too small, because the several operations that need to have access to the data structure are each implemented as subprograms. What is needed is a scope-defining structure smaller than a program block but bigger than a subprogram — a *syntactic wall* that can be placed around the data structure *and* the subprograms that implement its associated operations. This syntactic wall would need to provide encapsulation in such a way that the data structure is visible only to the operation subprograms, whilst the subprograms themselves remain callable from the rest of the program. This idea is that the *signatures* of the subprograms — their names and parameter lists, the information necessary to allow them to be called — 'shine through' the encapsulating wall while the code of the subprograms and the data structure that they share is hidden. Given this arrangement the only external access provided to the data structure would be *via the operation subprograms* — and so the designer of the structure could control completely the way in which external users use the structure because of this indirection.

The qualification implied by the word *syntactic* means that the encapsulation is a source program feature, enforced by the compiler, which will simply refuse to compile inappropriate accesses to the data structure. There are no 'walls' visible in the object program.

3.3   The Data Abstraction

This notion — an encapsulated data structure that can be accessed only by means of associated operations — is known as the *data abstraction*, and it forms the basis of many advances in software engineering techniques over the last fifteen years or so.

It should be pointed out that there is a fair amount of variation in the use of the term. Quite often it is used as a verb phrase, as though derived from the verb 'to data abstract', denoting a process or activity *of* data abstraction. Abstraction in general, as we have seen, means the removal of inessential detail. In the context of (the) data abstraction this inessential detail is that concerned with the actual implementation of the underlying data structure and we may regard the term as denoting either the result of this abstracting away, or the process itself, with little danger of ambiguity. In this book the term is used generally in its noun-phrase version, following the definition in Liskov and Zilles [1], and so appears in the form of its introduction above as *the* data abstraction.

3.3.1   Informational Strength

The introduction of the data abstraction permits us finally to tie up the ends that were left loose in the last Chapter in relation to *Informational strength*. The reader may recall that Informational strength, according to Myers' definition, is possessed by a module that contains a data structure shared by a number of 'entry points', each corresponding to a Functional strength module.

At the time that this concept was introduced it was remarked that the term 'entry point' is something of an anachronism. We can now see that the operation subprograms of a data abstraction act as its entry points, and that, with suitable implementations, they will possess Functional strength and the data abstraction as a whole will possess Informational strength. Furthermore, the encapsulating qualities of the data abstraction mean that the data structure that is accessed by the entry points, i.e. the operation subprograms, is isolated from direct access by external modules and so avoids the tight coupling that a global data structure normally implies.

3.3.2 Kinds of Operation

The data abstraction has been defined as an encapsulated data structure that may be accessed only via the operations associated with it. As we have seen, this arrangement enables the designer of such a structure to control the way in which its external users are permitted to access it. There is a corresponding responsibility placed on the designer to ensure that the interface supported by a data abstraction — the collection of operations that are externally accessible — is adequate to enable the users to realise its complete functionality. To return to our example: a stack data abstraction that omitted the `is_empty` operation would be functionally incomplete, and therefore useless, because a user would be unable to detect the empty condition and so would not know whether a subsequent `pop` operation would be valid or not.

The design of data abstraction interfaces is a comparatively new activity and is one that has received surprisingly little attention in the literature. The objective is a fairly clear one: to present the user with an adequate and convenient language of operations that is complete and consistent but which allows no more access than is necessary. There are, as we shall see, different styles of interface design, but there are also some basic principles and categorizations that it will be useful to introduce at this point.

Constructors and Observers

Returning, yet again, to the stack, we can see that there is an obvious difference between on the one hand the characteristic `push` and `pop` operations, which actually change the encapsulated data structure, and on the other hand operations like `is_empty`, which simply report on some state of the data structure without actually changing it. Following Liskov and Zilles, we will adopt the terms *constructors* to apply to the former kind of operation, and *observers* to the latter. Obviously constructors require special care on the part of the designer (and user), but also, as the example of the `is_empty` operation shows, observers are equally important from the point of view of completeness.

A very significant, and general, constructor, which tends to be overlooked by programmers used to more conventional techniques is the *initialise* operation. Data abstractions invariably require the ability to reset, or return to an empty state, the underlying data structure to provide a well-defined 'baseline' in the sequence of operations.

Selector Operations

A common, if somewhat unexciting, data abstraction, is a simple repository of data, consisting essentially of a record structure containing a number of fields, normally of different types (the reader may recall the File Header Block structure referred to in Chapter 2). The interface to such a data abstraction will consist of a collection of pairs of operations, one constructor and one observer per pair, with basically one pair per field.

The constructor item of each pair enables the setting of the related field to a particular value, and hence is often named a *set* operation; the corresponding observer operation allows the current value of the field to be read. An observer operation that is associated with a particular field or component of the data structure in this way is known as a *selector* operation and often given a name including *get*. Typically, set operations are implemented as procedures, with a read-only parameter containing the new value for the field, while get operations are implemented as functions, returning the current field value. A naming convention that associates each set/get pair with its related field, e.g. `set_start_block`, `get_start_block`, can provide useful self documentation in user modules.

As a slight diversion, the reader may be wondering quite what the point of such a data abstraction is. Its significance is that it provides the answer to the question posed in Chapter 2 in relation to data structure parameters: how is it possible to communicate grouped data, of the kind of which the File Header Block is a typical example, without using such parameters? This answer is — by encapsulating the structure into a data abstraction and making its various fields accessible as the result of operations. The indirect access to the underlying data structure means that, for example, the `set` operations may include checks on the values submitted, both in terms of their individual values and also their consistency with other values. Such checks would, of course, be impossible to associate *with the data structure* in the case of a conventional global record.

Again, although ultimately set operations must be provided for every field, applications that require read access only to some or all of the fields can be accommodated by providing them with a second data abstraction that 'encloses' the first, whilst making available only those set operations that are required.

Finally, the underlying structure may be changed, but the external interface maintained, by modifying the internally hidden details of the set and get operations.

It might also be remarked that a database is essentially a data abstraction of this type, albeit normally with a somewhat more elaborate external interface.

Operations for Repetitive Structures

The use of constructor/selector, or set/get, pairs is natural for a data structure of the record or **struct** kind, with a relatively small fixed number of fields. It is not so appropriate for data structures with a potentially variable number of fields, of which examples abound in software — trees, lists, sequences, strings, and so on.

A typical component found in a File Header Block structure is a character string containing the alphanumeric filename. Character strings provide a miniature paradigm of the applications of the data abstraction. Conventional imperative languages, certainly including Pascal, invariably have trouble with character strings. The problem is the essentially indefinite length of a character string — "how long is a piece of (character) string?" — which is difficult to map onto the fixed-size character array: the obvious data structure available for realising character strings in such languages. There are inevitable problems with different conventions for representing the length of a string, for example by some terminator character, or by a length value stored in a record structure with the array containing the string sequence.

The existence of a 'difficult' data structure, with what are really coupling problems because of the requirement for users to know about format details, suggests an appropriate application for the data abstraction. The question then arises as to the nature of the interface, the set of subprogram signatures visible through the encapsulation, that is to be provided. Obvious candidates for inclusion are, inevitably, **initialise** and also **length_of_string** — an observer that returns the length of the string.

Perhaps less obvious is, or are, the constructors. The constructor operations perform the insertion of the sequence of characters that forms the content of the string into the data abstraction. One possibility would be to adopt a numerical index approach. In other words, to provide a **set_character_at** operation that takes two parameters:

1. the character to be inserted

2. the position in the string at which the character is to be inserted

This is certainly a workable solution, indeed it is used in a slightly developed form in a very well-known case-study in techniques of data abstraction (see Chapter 6). The only quibble with it is that it provides an *over-specified* abstraction, with too powerful a functionality. The point is that character strings are sequences that derive their meaning from the predecessor — successor relationships between successive characters. The index mechanism provides effectively a random access to the string structure: there is nothing for example to prevent a succession of operations like:

```
set_character_at(4,'X');
set_character_at(5,'Y');
set_character_at(4,'A');
```

where the string is being used essentially as an array. There is nothing particularly harmful with this, except that it involves an additional complication, the index parameter, which might well be used in a 'tricky' way that is difficult to understand and which is really unnecessary. Also, the index mechanism inevitably suggests an array-based implementation, which may or may not reflect the real underlying structure.

If we consider a typical use of a string data abstraction provided with an indexed interface, we can imagine that characters will be transferred into it by a piece of code something like the following:

```
    pos := 1;
(* get first character in next_ch *)
    set_character_at(pos, next_ch);
    pos := pos + 1;
    while (* some characters left *)
    do
        begin
          (* get next character in next_ch  *)
            set_character_at(pos, next_ch);
            pos := pos + 1
        end;
```

The variable pos, which is used to index the characters, is simply incremented for each character, so that the sequence of the input is maintained. It is, in fact, just being used to indicate 'the next character position' — a function that does not require the generality of an integer variable and which could be accommodated perfectly easily within the data abstraction itself.

Auto-Incrementing

What is required is largely covered by a constructor that automatically incre-
ments the character position every time it is called, say set_next_char_to.
The qualification 'largely' is necessary because of the need to initialise the
process, i.e. to indicate that the next character should be placed in the
first position. This could be done either by a standard initialise operation, or by a more specific constructor that is used for the first character
only — say set_first_character_to. This is a matter of taste, as is the
decision to provide an explicit termination operation, or to leave open the
possibility of extending a string at some future point simply by more calls to
set_next_character_to. The latter choice has a slightly unsatisfactory air
about it and so we might decide on the following set of constructors, showing
only their signatures as, of course, their implementation is irrelevant:

```
procedure set_first_character_to(C: char);
procedure set_next_character_to(C: char);
procedure terminate; (* calls to set_next_character_to
will be ignored until after next set_first_character_to *)
```

The revised piece of code would then look like the following:

```
(* get first character in next_ch *)
set_first_character_to(next_ch);
while (* some characters left *)
do
      begin
   (* get next character in next_ch  *)
              set_next_character_to(next_ch)
      end;
terminate;
```

This is clearer than the earlier version and illustrates the idea that complexity can be reduced by providing an appropriate set of operations that can
considerably improve the self-documentation of the program.

Iterators

Turning to the observer operations that enable the extraction of a string, we
can see that a straightforward reversal of the constructors will provide an ap-

propriate interface. The main observer will return the value of the 'next character' in the sequence of the string, a function called get_next_character or perhaps next_character. (The reader may find this agonising over names rather trivial, but the use of well-chosen names can illuminate the interface of a data abstraction in a very significant way.)

The next_character operation, like its constructor counterpart, requires complementary operations both to start the read-out at the beginning of the string, say get_first_character or first_character, and also to allow the user to terminate the process. Again, there is a range of possibilities — the data abstraction may provide a length_of_string function that returns the number of characters in the string. The user is then obliged to set up a count in the loop that performs the extraction — the counterpart of the pos variable in the first example above. In view of the 'next character' approach adopted for the main observer this seems slightly inappropriate. A more consistent design would support a boolean operation that allows the user to test for the exhaustion of the string, say string_exhausted or no_more_characters_left. The complete observer interface might be, therefore:

```
function first_character  : char;
function next_character   : char;
function string_exhausted : boolean;
```

A set of observer operations like this, which is designed to allow for the systematic read-out of the items in the encapsulated data structure of a data abstraction, is known as an *iterator*. The general structure of the application of an iterator is shown below:

```
    next_ch := first_character;
(* do something with next_ch *)
    while not string_exhausted do
    begin
        next_ch := next_character;
      (* do something with next_ch *)
    end;
```

```
procedure set_first_character_to(C: char);
procedure set_next_character_to(C: char);
procedure terminate; (* calls to set_next_char_to will be
                ignored until after next set_first_char_to *)

function first_character : char;
function next_character  : char;
function string_exhausted : boolean;

function length_of_string : integer;
```

Figure 3.4: Interface for a Character String Data Abstraction

The significant point about an iterator such as this is that the internal format of the string is hidden — abstracted away to an interface that allows the user to deal with strings in their simplest form: a sequence of characters with a beginning, an end, and a successor relation. All strings must possess these characteristics and so no modifications to the underlying implementation can affect them. It should also be noted that all parameters are read-only and either characters or boolean.

It might also be remarked that a **length_of** operation, although stylistically undesirable as an iterator component, provides a very convenient functionality, for example in applications where the string is to be read into an array that requires dimensioning. There is no problem in providing this functionality, even though it overlaps with the iterator, other than the requirement placed on the implementor to ensure that consistency between the operations is maintained. (That is to say that the **string_exhausted** operation returns **true** after **length_of** characters have been extracted and **false** before.)

The complete interface for the string data abstraction is shown in Figure 3.4.

This is obviously a very basic string data abstraction. The knowledgeable reader may query the lack of features such as substring handling, and also the way in which limit problems, both empty strings and over-sized strings, have been ignored. The addition of these sophistications does not require alteration to the basic pattern shown, and has been avoided at this stage to retain the clarity of the main concepts.

The last caveat to mention is that, of course, the data abstraction is not supported by Pascal in its standard version(s), and so, again, we must end the Chapter in a somewhat indeterminate state. We will look at some languages that do provide support for the data abstraction in the next Chapter.

3.4 Summary

In this Chapter we have investigated the extent to which the precepts of good modular design are supported by a conventional language such as Pascal. The investigation has revealed serious shortcomimgs, but also led to the suggestion of a new program structure, the data abstraction, which, if it was actually available would contribute powerfully to the ability of the software designer to achieve the ideals of modular programming.

The data abstraction has been defined as an encapsulated data structure accessible only via operations associated with it, which form its externally visible interface. The syntactic information necessary to allow for the use of this interface may be given by the signatures of the operations: their names and parameter lists. The roles of these operations — the nature of the access that they afford to the encapsulated data structure — can be usefully categorised in terms of constructors and observers, the latter with sub-categories of selectors and iterators.

Chapter 4

Languages and Data Abstraction - 1

4.1 Introduction

In this and the next chapter we consider developments in the design of programming languages that have been introduced to support data abstraction.

We have seen already that Pascal provides little in the way of support for data abstraction. It is rather unfair to expect that it would provide such support in view of the fact that the design of Pascal, at least in its first version, predated the widespread recognition of the power and usefulness of the data abstraction, although at least one language of the sixties (SIMULA 67) had incorporated it in a modified form.

The developing interest in the data abstraction in the early to mid seventies coincided with a major growth in the popularity of Pascal, particularly in the United States, where UCSD Pascal became the standard language for 8-bit microprocessor software. It is no surprise, therefore, to find that many Pascal extensions produced in this period, including UCSD Pascal itself, provided support for the data abstraction; Concurrent Pascal and Pascal Plus are notable examples.

In this and the next Chapter we discuss two Pascal extensions , representing two points in a roughly linear progression from the parent language — the first representing a comparatively minor, though significant advance, the second a much more radical one, to such an extent that the phrase 'Pascal extension' is probably hardly appropriate. These two points are identified respectively with the languages MODULA-2 and Ada. This Chapter is devoted to the relevant aspects of MODULA-2, Chapter 5 to those of Ada.

4.2   MODULA-2

The first Pascal extension that we shall consider is one devised by the original designer of Pascal, Nicklaus Wirth. This is in fact his second essay in this area and is accordingly named MODULA-2.

MODULA-2 has become perhaps the best-established of all the Pascal extensions, with a significant and growing usage outside its original academic environment and, recently, the imprimatur of the British Standards Institute. The question of standardisation is a slightly thorny one, as MODULA-2 has become sufficiently popular to cause the spawning of a fair number of implementations, both commercial and academic, with little control over what constitutes the 'real' language. As the involvement of the BSI suggests, this situation is improving, and in any case the lack of standardisation has not been anywhere near sufficient to impact on the aspects of the language that are relevant to this discussion.

MODULA-2 differs from Pascal in two major aspects that are immediately relevant to this book; these are both additional features, with no corresponding Pascal equivalents, and are:

- support for the separate compilation of modules

- support for the data abstraction

As can be seen, these additional features compensate for precisely those weaknesses in Pascal, in the context of modular design, that were identified in the last Chapter.

4.3   Modules

The construct that provides the basis for both these features is called, appropriately enough, the *module*. Syntactically, the module possesses much the same structure as the Pascal scope-defining units: program, procedure and function blocks. It consists of a *statement part*, enclosed by the reserved

```
MODULE  identifier_1;

    (* declarations *)

BEGIN

    (* statements *)

END  identifier_1.
```

Figure 4.1: Basic Form of a Module

words BEGIN and END, which is preceded by a *declarative part* in which constants, types, variables and program units may be declared. Like the Pascal blocks, a module is headed by by a distinguishing reserved word, in fact MODULE, which is followed by an identifier that serves to name the whole construct. One rather pleasing improvement in MODULA-2 is the requirement for the name of a module, and indeed of a subprogram, to follow the final END, thus providing an often much-needed documentary strengthening of the conventional text indentation.

The basic form of a module is shown in Figure 4.1.

The module construct provides the equivalent of the *program* block in Pascal. Or, to put it rather more precisely: there is no *program* construct in MODULA-2 because the language is intended to be used for writing software components that will be assembled to form program systems. In this context there is no requirement for an enclosing 'envelope' construct within which various subordinate units are collected, which is the Pascal program block model. The 'collecting', or assembling, of software components is a function of the dedicated linker, which is effectively a secondary part of the compilation process, taking semi-compiled units from a library and integrating them into the operational system. So, for any particular program system there will be a 'master' or *program* module, which is essentially distinguished by the fact that it is used by no other program unit. The relationship of the program module to the other program units in the system is, however, that of a user, a 'first amongst equals', rather than a higher-level 'super unit'.

This distinction between the MODULA-2 module and the Pascal program block can be seen also in the fact that a module may itself contain modules, in line with the fact that modules do not necessarily act as the 'outermost' enclosing structure of a program system. It is the case, however, that compilation units — the text items expected by the MODULA-2 compiler — are modules.

4.3.1   Local Modules

As noted above, a module may be nested within another. Such a module is known as a *local* module, in much the same way that variables and procedures are referred to as being local in Pascal when they are declared within an enclosing procedure. There is a major difference between modules and procedures, however, which is that modules are not *called* as such.

The question then arises as to the role of the statement part in a local module — when is it executed? The answer is: at the start of execution of the program, in fact *before* the start of execution of the module in which it is declared. If modules are nested to a depth of several levels, which is perfectly in accordance with the grammar of the language, the statement parts will be executed "from the innermost out" until the statement part of the outermost, or program module — *the* program in conventional terms — is executed. The nature of this arrangement effectively dictates that the statement parts of local modules are brief, and invariably devoted to initialising the values of variables; for this reason they are known as *initialisation sections.* The existence of initialisation sections both compensates for a notable deficiency in Pascal, at least in its later versions, and they also, in their 'once per program run' mode of execution, point to another important difference between modules and procedures — the variables declared local to a module exist for the duration of the whole program. Modules are not called and not exited from, and so their variables enjoy the same permanence as those of a main program.

As described so far, local modules would appear to have a rather minimal usefulness, limited to enclosing some declarations and a, possibly null, initialisation section. Their full significance can be seen only in the light of the regions of scope that they introduce into program structures.

Scopes and Local Modules

In the schematic program layout in Figure 4.2, the local module `Inner` contains the declaration of an integer variable `IntVar`. (MODULA-2's improve-

```
MODULE Outer

(* some outer declarations *)

        MODULE Inner;

        VAR     IntVar : INTEGER;

        BEGIN

              (* statements *)

        END Inner;

    BEGIN (* Outer statement part *)

       (* statements *)

         IntVar := 0;

    END Outer;
```

Figure 4.2: Nested Modules — IntVar in an Illegal Assignment

ments over Pascal do not extend as far as dispensing with the 'words' CONST
and VAR to introduce, respectively, constant and variable declarations. The
schematic also exhibits perhaps the least lovable of MODULA-2's characteristics — its case sensitivity, and the rule that reserved words are always
upper case.)

The scope rules of MODULA-2 follow closely those of Pascal, or indeed any
other statically block-structured language, and dictate that the scope of a
variable like IntVar in Figure 4.2 extends as far as the END of the structure
that most closely encloses its declaration. In this case, the scope of IntVar
extends to the END of Inner, which in accordance with the commendable
rule is labelled 'Inner'. This, of course, means that the assignment to IntVar
contained in the initialisation section of module Outer is outside the scope
of IntVar and will therefore give rise to a compiler error (assuming that the
declarative part of Outer does not contain a declaration of an IntVar also).

```
MODULE Outer
           MODULE Inner;
                 EXPORT IntVar;
           VAR     IntVar : INTEGER;
           BEGIN
                 (* statements *)
           END Inner;
BEGIN (* Outer statement part *)
      (* statements *)
        IntVar := 0;
END Outer;
```

Figure 4.3: Nested Modules with an EXPORT CLause

EXPORT Clauses

Clearly, the usefulness of a scope region that is entirely isolated from its environment is, again, limited, particularly as the 'uncalled' nature of modules precludes any parameter passing, which might have provided a basis for external communication. In the next schematic, shown in Figure 4.3, we include a new feature immediately following the heading line of module Inner. This is the addition of what is called an *EXPORT clause*, and it has the effect of extending the scope of any identifier included in it to the END of the next outer enclosing module: in this case Outer. The incorporation of the EXPORT clause in the above has the effect, therefore, of making the assignment to IntVar syntactically correct. The general use of the export mechanism is to provide a means of *selectively* making available the items declared in a local module to enclosing modules.

The effect of an EXPORT clause in a local module is restricted to one level of nesting, so that the introduction of an intermediate level, as shown in the schematic in Figure 4.4, will have the effect of constraining IntVar's scope to the END of the new module middle, and yet again render the assignment illegal. Once again an export clause can be used to pierce the encapsulation of an enclosing unit, this time in the middle module, as shown in Figure 4.5. Figure 4.5 illustrates the fact that an EXPORT clause may include an identifier that is not declared at the same lexical level — all that is required is that the scope of the identifier, which may have been extended by another EXPORT clause, includes the EXPORT clause. We may also note the fact

```
MODULE Outer

     (* some outer declarations *)

        MODULE Middle;

            MODULE Inner;

                    EXPORT IntVar;

                VAR     IntVar : INTEGER;

                BEGIN

                      (* statements *)

                END Inner;
          BEGIN
          END Middle;
  BEGIN (* Outer statement part *)

        (* statements *)

         IntVar := 0;

  END Outer;
```

Figure 4.4: An Intermediate Level of Nesting

```
MODULE Outer
   (* some outer declarations *)
   MODULE Middle;
        EXPORT IntVar, Proc;

        MODULE Inner;

            EXPORT IntVar, Proc;

        VAR     IntVar : INTEGER;
                PROCEDURE Proc;
                (* declarations *)
                BEGIN
                    (* statements *)
                END Proc;

        BEGIN

            (* statements *)

        END Inner;
   BEGIN
   END Middle;
BEGIN (* Outer statement part *)

        (* statements *)

    IntVar := 0;
        Proc;

END Outer;
```

Figure 4.5: Exporting through Two Levels of Nesting

```
       MODULE Outer

VAR    IntVar  :  INTEGER;

       MODULE Inner;          (*            / \            *)
                              (*             |             *)
       BEGIN                  (* hole in IntVar's scope *)
              IntVar := 0; (*             |             *)
       END Inner;             (*            \ /            *)
       BEGIN


       END Outer;
```

Figure 4.6: Fragmented Scope of the Global Variable IntVar

that in MODULA-2, unlike Pascal, the scope of a declaration extends over
the whole of the most closely enclosing declarative part, including the region
before the declaration. If this was not the case, EXPORT clauses would not
work because they are always placed just after the module heading line and
thus before any declarations — including the declarations of the EXPORTed
identifiers.

We also take the opportunity, by including the schematic declaration of
procedure `Proc` in module `Inner`, to emphasise that subprogram identifiers
are subject to precisely the same rules as those of variables. This means that
the call to `Proc` in the statement part of module `Outer` requires the pair of
export clauses to make it legal.

IMPORT Clauses

So far we have considered the expanding of scopes from local modules over
enclosing modules, but the rules of MODULA-2 require also that scopes
be explicitly 'filled in' where they extend from enclosing modules over local
modules. In the schematic program shown in Figure 4.6, the scope of the
variable `IntVar` *does not* extend over module `Inner`. There is in fact a 'hole'
in the scopes of any identifiers declared in the declarative region of `Outer`
corresponding to the extent of `Inner`, and once again the assignment to
`IntVar` is incorrect.

```
    MODULE Outer

VAR     IntVar  :  INTEGER;

        MODULE Inner;

            IMPORT IntVar;

        BEGIN
                IntVar  := 0;

        END Inner;
    BEGIN


    END Outer;
```

Figure 4.7: IntVar's Scope Extended by an IMPORT Clause

This can be corrected by the inclusion of an *IMPORT Clause* in Module
Inner, which has the effect of extending the scopes of identifiers mentioned
by it from the enclosing module over the whole of the module in which
it occurs. Like the EXPORT clause, an IMPORT clause is placed at the
beginning of a module, immediately after the heading line. Where both
IMPORT and EXPORT clauses occur in the same module the IMPORT is
placed first. The corrected version of the schematic is shown in Figure 4.7.

4.3.2   Modules and the Data Abstraction

The reader may well have recognised, in the above references to 'extending
scopes' and 'piercing encapsulation', more than a hint of the flavour of the
Data Abstraction, and indeed the simple structure of the module and the
associated mechanism of the export clause is quite sufficient to support the
concept. The encapsulation required by the data structure underlying a data
abstraction is provided, by default, by enclosing it in a local module. The
visibility of the applicable operations of the data abstraction is provided by
including their identifiers in an export clause.

Without more ado, we may now return to our old friend the stack and show

how the model that was sketched in the last Chapter may be achieved using MODULA-2. In so doing it is perhaps appropriate to say a little more about the sub-module structure of MODULA-2:

- **Procedures** differ very little from their Pascal counterparts.

- **Functions** in MODULA-2 are referred to as 'FUNCTION PROCE-DURES' and are distinguished syntactically from procedures only by the return type, which terminates the heading line, prefixed by a colon, and the use of RETURN statements to cause both the evaluation of the returned expression and the actual exit from the function. The declaration of a FUNCTION PROCEDURE without parameters must still include the (empty) parentheses that contain the empty formal parameter list.

- **Subrange** type definitions rather than array type definitions are associated with square brackets; this means that, once a subrange type has been declared, its name may be used in an array type declaration without the adornment of square brackets.

The MODULA-2 realisation of the Stack Data Abstraction is shown in Figure 4.8.

4.4 Library Modules

The features of MODULA-2 that have been discussed above, specifically local modules and export clauses, provide a comprehensive support for the Data Abstraction but are incapable of standing alone — they must be textually incorporated within another program module. In order to be of *practical* use in the creation of modules with low coupling and high cohesion these features, or some similar, must be combined with the facility of independent compilation, in such a way that their attributes are not lost.

4.4.1 Separate Compilation

MODULA-2 does this by providing for *separate compilation* , which includes all the facilities of independent compilation — the ability to compose a software system from a collection of compiled components held in one or more *component libraries* — but with the additional feature that strong typing

```
MODULE Stack;

EXPORT Init, Push, Pop, IsEmpty, IsFull;

(*** beginning of encapsulated structure ***)

CONST
        StackSize    =    100;
TYPE
        StackRange    =    [1..StackSize];
        TOSRange      =    [0..StackSize];
VAR
        StackArray    : ARRAY StackRange OF INTEGER;
        TOS           : TOSRange;

(***** end of encapsulated structure ******)

PROCEDURE Init;
BEGIN
        TOS    := 0
END Init;

PROCEDURE Push (IntVal : INTEGER);
BEGIN
        TOS    := TOS + 1;
        StackArray[TOS] := IntVal
END Push;

PROCEDURE Pop () : INTEGER;
BEGIN
        TOS    := TOS - 1;
        RETURN StackArray[TOS + 1]
END Pop;

PROCEDURE IsEmpty () : BOOLEAN;
BEGIN
        RETURN TOS = 0
END IsEmpty;

PROCEDURE IsFull () : BOOLEAN;
BEGIN
        RETURN TOS = StackSize
END IsFull;
END Stack;
```

Figure 4.8: MODULA-2 Realisation of the Stack Data Abstraction

and encapsulation are maintained over the separately compiled components. This additional feature has considerable implications for the properties of the libraries and the linker. In conventional, independent compilation systems, e.g. such as the standard Unix library system, type information and 'syntactic walls' disappear after the compilation phase — they are simply not present in the library-resident versions of the components and so the compiler is quite incapable of checking, say, parameter type matching against a library procedure.

The ability to check these attributes over separately compiled units, therefore, requires a library format capable of storing relevant type and other syntactic information. This will be specific to the language involved, and so the library will be dedicated, in this case to units compiled from MODULA-2. The advantages of separate compilation, then, carry the penalty of losing the flexibility and generality of independent compilation. Additionally, the linker is required to be driven by information contained within source modules rather than the conventional language-independent parameters, and so it also must be a language-specific tool. The upshot is that a language like MODULA-2, a *secure* language in the current terminology, requires more than a compiler in order to be practically useful. The term *language processor* has been coined to denote the necessary combination of compiler, dedicated library (with library maintenance tools) and linker.

4.4.2 External and Internal Views

The MODULA-2 program unit corresponding with a library component is the module: in a different form, however, from the *program* and *local* modules that we have met so far and called, logically enough, *Library* modules . This version possesses a form that reflects the two views of a module, particularly one that realizes a data abstraction:

- the **user's view** — defining the interface presented to an external user — *what the module does*

- the **implementor's view** — *how it does it*

A library module is syntactically split into two components that correspond to these two views called, respectively, the DEFINITION MODULE and the IMPLEMENTATION MODULE. The definition and implementation modules of a library module are distinct as source language entities only. When compiled into the library they form a single unified component.

Of the two the definition module is the most important from the point of view of programming in the large — it provides the external users with the interface details that enable the use of the module, and its design determines the quality of the interaction with other modules in terms of functionality and level of coupling. Syntactically, definition modules contain only declarations, which may be any of the usual range of constants, types, variables and procedures. Procedure declarations in definition modules have a special form, however, which defines the interface presented by the procedure: its name and parameter list, and result type if a function procedure, and nothing else. Effectively, procedure declarations are given as the 'heading line' of a conventional procedure: the signature, to use the term introduced in the last Chapter. The declarations local to the procedure and its statement part are not shown because these are implementation details that are, or should be, of no concern to a user and are accordingly hidden within the implementation module.

The definition module contains all the entities that the underlying module needs to export to permit its use by an external module. For this reason, definition modules, in later versions of MODULA-2 at any rate, do not contain export clauses: there is no reason for including an item within a definition module if it is not to be exported and so an implicit export clause may be considered to include every item. (Earlier versions of the languge did require export clauses in definition modules, an illogicality that has been removed.)

The definition module for a library module providing a stack data abstraction is shown in Figure 4.9.

Implementation modules possess the same format as the program and local modules that have been described previously, with the difference that the heading line is introduced by the reserved words IMPLEMENTATION MODULE. An implementation module must include full declarations for any items that are incompletely declared in the corresponding DEFINITION MODULE — all the procedures declared there, for example.

4.4.3   Importing Library Modules

How does one module avail itself of an existing library module? The answer is by including the name of the library module in an *Import Clause*, which appears immediately after the Module heading line. The effect of the import clause is analagous to that of an import clause in a local module — it extends

```
DEFINITION MODULE Stack;

    PROCEDURE Init;

    PROCEDURE Push (IntVal : INTEGER);

    PROCEDURE Pop () : INTEGER;

    PROCEDURE IsEmpty () : BOOLEAN;

    PROCEDURE IsFull () : BOOLEAN;
END Stack;
```

Figure 4.9: Definition Module for a Stack Data Abstraction

the scopes of the identifiers that it includes, over the module that contains it. This means that the types, procedures and any other imported objects whose identifiers appear in the import clause may be utilised in the module that includes it, as though they were declared at the module's outermost lexical level.

Obviously the dedicated linker, which forms part of the language processor, uses import clauses in order to scan the libraries in the environment to find the nominated library modules and link them into the final executable image.

4.4.4 Name Space Management

An apparently banal, but nonetheless significant, problem that occurs when several programmers work together on a software system is that of avoiding name clashes— the inadvertant use of the same name for two or more distinct objects.

The hierarchical file system supported by many program development ori-entated operating systems provides, by means of the extended name (the 'path-name') that identifies each file uniquely within the system, a way of overcoming this problem. As long as each programmer keeps his or her files within a separate directory then each individual need worry about avoiding name clashes in this directory only, as every file name is prefixed automati-cally with the path of directories leading from the root of the file system to the one in which the file is held — which must be unique.

When a secure language processor for a language such as MODULA-2 is used the use of large numbers of library components provides the potential for an exacerbation of the name-clash problem. Clashes may arise in the names of the operations exported by library modules. There is obviously a strong chance of duplication (or multiplication) of names like `initialise` or `is_empty` in a number of modules realising data abstractions. Equally obviously, it would be a tedious imposition if the designer of such a module had to scan through all the other modules in the library to avoid such name clashes.

The use of the extended filename is not appropriate in this context because the names by which modules reference each other must be syntactically correct in the language being used, rather than to the operating system command interpreter. MODULA-2, for example, would not be happy with '/usr/res/progs/JSmith'. It is also the case that in many language processors the names of files containing source modules are not required to reflect the names of the modules contained within them, and in any case are not retained within the library into which they are compiled.

Instead, in line with the incorporation of library facilities actually in the language, rather than being supported by the operating system environment, MODULA-2 provides for extended names in the form of *qualified identifiers* or 'qualidents'. A qualified identifier consists of the identifier that names an object: type, variable, procedure or whatever, exported from a library module prefixed by the identifier that names the exporting module, the two identifiers being separated by a full stop. So if operations named `is_empty` are exported by two modules `Stack` and `Queue`, they may be differentiated by using their qualified identifiers, of the form `Stack.is_empty` and `Queue.is_empty`, in a module that uses both.

The existence of the qualident has led to the elaboration of the IMPORT clause to allow for variations in whether or not the full qualified identifier is used or not. If the IMPORT clause takes the form:

> `IMPORT` *module name*

then any object imported from the nominated library module must be qualified with the module name. On the other hand, the module name (and full stop) may be omitted, if an IMPORT clause of the form:

> `FROM` *module name* `IMPORT` *identifier list*

is used, from the identifiers included in the list. It is generally recommended that the shortened (i.e. unqualified) form is **not** used except in the case of very commonly used library modules. This is because the value of the self-documenting properties of the qualident far outweighs the incovenience involved and, even though the IMPORT clause will always enable the source of an identifier to be discovered, it is better to avoid the need constantly to be turning back to the beginning of the listing. This is a good example of an application of the principle that *a program is read many more times than it is written.*

4.5 Abstract Data Types

The quite extended discussion of the data abstraction and its realisation in MODULA-2 that has occupied most of this book so far has tended to identify individual data abstractions with specific instances of the construct — the module, that provides the syntactic wall e ncapsulating the underlying data structure. In other words, we have assumed one data abstraction per module.

It this were to be the general case then some practical problems would become fairly rapidly apparent. Many applications require several copies of a data abstraction — even our paradigm case, the ubiquitous stack, is needed in pairs for Dijkstra's algorithm. The character string abstraction might well be required in thousands in a text processing application. If a separate module was required for each character string then clearly requirements of memory size alone would rule out this approach.

The solution to this problem represents a step beyond the concept of the data abstraction as it has been discussed so far. The idea is to break the one-to-one relationship between module and data abstraction, replacing it by a one-to-many relationship. This is done in MODULA-2 by the means of *hidden* or *opaque* types.

4.5.1 Opaque Types

An opaque type, as its name so aptly captures, is one whose implementation is hidden from its users. It is exported from a module and may be used to declare objects such as variables, array elements and record fields, in modules that import it. But because the implementation of such a type is hidden, the only manipulations that can be carried out on these objects,

```
DEFINITION MODULE STACK;

    TYPE    Stack;   (* Opaque Type *)

    PROCEDURE Init(VAR S : Stack);

    PROCEDURE Push (VAR S : Stack; IntVal : INTEGER);

    PROCEDURE Pop (S : Stack) : INTEGER;

    PROCEDURE IsEmpty (S : Stack) : BOOLEAN;

    PROCEDURE IsFull (S :   Stack) : BOOLEAN;
END STACK;
```

Figure 4.10: Definition Module for a Stack Abstract Data Type

within an importing module, are those provided by the *applicable operations*
of the type. Applicable operations are exported from the same module as
the opaque type, and are procedures with one or more parameters of the
opaque type, via which objects of the type may be manipulated.

An opaque type is declared in a DEFINITION MODULE simply by the
appearance of its name after the TYPE heading, with the usual adornment
of a semi-colon, and commas if more than one appears, but without any
definition of how the type is implemented. The full declaration is then given
in the corresponding IMPLEMENTATION MODULE, and is therefore un-
available to an external user.

The use of an opaque type to permit the Stack module to export an indefinite number of stacks is shown in Figure 4.10. As can be seen we have
adopted the slightly dubious MODULA-2 style by distinguishing the new
module from the old one, and also from the Stack type, by making its name
all upper case. Otherwise, the important changes are the declaration of the
opaque Stack type, and the use that is then made of this type to declare the
formal parameters of the applicable operations. An external user may then
declare any number — perhaps an array or linked list, of Stacks, but these
may be used only as actual parameters in calls to the operations exported
by STACK.

The important point to note is that every externally declared object of type

Stack is as protected from its users as if it had been the single data abstraction realised by the original Stack module. The only way in which their underlying data structures can be manipulated is via the operations exported from the module, in this case STACK. In other words, every object of type Stack is a stack data abstraction.

From now on we will use the term *Abstract Data Type* to refer to types, such as may be realised by opaque in MODULA-2, that permit the declaration of external data abstractions in the way just described. This usage is a slight distortion of the normal meaning of the term: conventionally 'abstract data type' and 'data abstraction' are synonymous. Terminology in this area is far from standardised, however, so that the introduction of a useful distinction would seem to be quite justifiable.

4.5.2   Data Abstraction *versus* Abstract Data Type

This introduction of a useful but rather artificial distinction should be followed by a careful review of what actually is involved. The data abstraction has been (frequently) defined as an encapsulated data structure accessible only via its applicable operations. The definition of an abstract data type extends this concept to the generality characteristic of a type — essentially a schema or pattern for defining many objects, thus producing a higher level of abstraction. As defined, the relationship between the two is that of the particular to the general: a data abstraction may be seen as the only instance of an unnamed abstract data type. Typical applications require both unique data abstraction objects and also abstract data types that may be used to declare many replicated objects — a payroll program, for example, recognises the existence of both **a** payroll and **many** employees.

4.5.3   Implementing Abstract Data Types

The fact that the full declaration of an opaque type is given in the relevant IMPLEMENTATION MODULE, and not in the corresponding DEFINITION MODULE, raises the question of how the compiler can compile the DEFINITION MODULE separately, which is the normal way in which MODULA-2 language processors handle the compilation of library modules. The point is that the compiler is required to allocate storage for the parameters of the applicable operations that are of the opaque type, and yet it must do this in ignorance of the declaration of the opaque.

```
IMPLEMENTATION MODULE STACK;

CONST
   StackSize    =    100;
TYPE
  StackRange    =    [1..StackSize];
  TOSRange      =    [0..StackSize];
  StackArray    =    ARRAY StackRange OF INTEGER;
(*************************************************)
      Stack         =   POINTER TO StackStruct;
      StackStruct   =   RECORD
                           StackItems : StackArray;
                           TOS        : TOSRange
                        END;
(*************************************************)
```

Figure 4.11: Hidden Declaration of the Opaque Type Stack

Conventionally this problem has been overcome by requiring that all opaque types are actually pointer types, declared to provide an indirect access to the 'real' data structure. As all pointers occupy a fixed memory size — invariably one word of storage — the compiler is enabled to allocate appropriate amounts of memory for the parameters concerned. External modules that import the opaque type may also be compiled because the nature of opaque types, particularly the fact that no 'internal' manipulation can be performed on them by an external user, means that opaque type objects can be treated as one-word 'black-box' areas. In practice this would mean that the IMPLEMENTATION MODULE for Stack would begin with the declarations shown in Figure 4.11: (*Note: some necessary IMPORT items have been excluded for the sake of clarity*). MODULA-2 replaces the Pascal caret by the rather more meaningful phrase POINTER TO, and so type Stack is actually declared as a pointer type, the objects of which are pointers to, or addresses, in some sense, of objects of the RECORD type StackStruct. Each StackStruct object is, of course, the data structure necessary to record the state of a stack. The use of a RECORD type here is effectively mandatory as only RECORD types permit the declaration of heterogeneously typed components, which are typically a feature of the kind of data structures that underlie data abstractions.

```
PROCEDURE Initialise (VAR S : Stack);
BEGIN
        NEW (S);
        S^.TOS := 0
END Initialise;


PROCEDURE Push (VAR S : Stack; IntVar : INTEGER);
BEGIN
        S^.TOS := S^TOS + 1;
        S^.StackItems[S^.TOS] := IntVar
END Push;
```

Figure 4.12: Implementation of Stack Operations

When `Stack` objects are declared they are uninitialised pointers — the creation of the necessary data structures must be explicitly programmed, a fact that makes the `Initialise` procedure particularly important. `Initialise` must execute the NEW procedure (or the lower level equivalent MODULA-2 provides) to allocate memory for the new data structure. Each of the operation procedures must therefore take account of the fact that access to the data structure is via this pointer link. Code for the `Initialise` and `Push` operations is shown in Figure 4.12, revealing that the caret still retains its Pascal role as the dereferencing operator in MODULA-2. The requirement that opaque types should be pointer types would appear to be somewhat of an imposition, at least in so far as it necessitates additional complexity in the form of referencing and dereferencing. It is a fact, however, that abstract data types are very frequently implemented as pointer-connected data structures because of the representational power and flexibility that they possess. Given this it is quite natural to implement opaque types as pointer types.

4.6   Review of MODULA-2

MODULA-2 represents a considerable advance over Pascal, particularly in those areas relating to programming in the large that we are interested in. That it does so by introducing a comparatively economical set of additional features might be seen either as an indication of the fertility of the original design of Pascal, or of the ingenuity of the design of MODULA-2. Either way, a tribute to the designer of both languages is appropriate, before turning to a language that represents, in its provenance at least, a very different approach.

4.7   Summary

In this Chapter we have discussed a language, MODULA-2, that builds on Pascal by providing support for Data Abstraction and, thus, for enabling the construction of programs that satisfy the criteria for good modular design identified in earlier chapters. We have seen how MODULA-2 makes explicit the distinction between the external interface of a data abstraction and its implementation, when realised as a library module. We have also seen how the concept of the data abstraction is generalised to allow the definition of classes of objects, each possessing the characteristics of an exclusively operational external interface and hidden implementation details, rather than just single objects possessing these qualities, in the notion of the Abstract Data Type.

In the next Chapter we move on to the more complex reworking of these ideas found in the Ada programming language.

Chapter 5

Languages and Data Abstraction - 2

5.1   Ada

The Ada programming language represents perhaps the ultimate, and final, stage in the evolutionary family of strongly-typed, imperative languages that descended from Algol 60 and includes Pascal and its immediate offspring, MODULA-2. This is not the place to relate the history of Ada. Suffice it to say that it is a large and complex language that, perhaps as a result of its association with the military and its general 'establishment' aura, has attracted a rather mixed press, including some occasionally somewhat intemperate criticism.

Ada's importance in the context of this book lies in the fact that it was designed specifically to support the ideas of 'programming in the large' that have been discussed in earlier chapters. Essentially, it covers the same objectives that inspired Wirth in the design of MODULA-2, but without the latter's rather 'minimalist' approach. MODULA-2 provides sufficient extensions to Pascal to support the Data Abstraction, and component software. Many of the features of Pascal, including some of the less desirable such as the lack of facilities for variable initialisation, are still visible unchanged in MODULA-2.

By contrast Ada, although still recognisably a descendent of Pascal, represents a much more radical revision of the parent language. The fascinating aspect of Ada is its orthogonality — the way in which virtually every point in the 'space' defined by the axes of types, program and control structures is well-defined. In other words, the designers of the language did a very thorough job of thinking through the implications of the inclusion of the various features: strong-typing, data abstraction, separate compilation, concurrency and so on, and particularly in their interaction. It is precisely because of this thoroughness that the language is complex. The author cannot resist remarking that PL/1 — a language with a complexity equivalent to Ada's but without its systematic consistency — does not seem to have attracted the same level of vituperation.

In this book we will not attempt to provide anything approaching a comprehensive introduction to Ada. The aim is rather to impart an appreciation of the major features that support data abstraction and, thus, good modular design. To provide, in other words, a top-down view with the emphasis firmly on the wood rather than the trees. It should be noted that this is more than an exercise in programming language dilettantism — Ada was designed to provide a vehicle for program design and a firm grasp of its relevant characteristics is perhaps the most important requirement for successful use of the language.

5.2   Ada Program Units

Ada provides a number of program units, i.e. constructs that are self-contained in some way and define named components for the construction of program systems, as follows:

- **subprograms** — both procedure and function subprograms exist in Ada, corresponding quite closely to their Pascal equivalents.

- **tasks** — are program units designed to run concurrently, and are thus identified both with static collections of code and processes.

- **packages** — are the constructs that support data abstraction and are the basis of component software in Ada.

Like MODULA-2 (a phrase that will recur fairly frequently in this section) Ada does not have a 'Program' construct, and for the same reason: the language is intended to be used for writing secure software components for reuse in many applications, not for monolithic programs. Ada differs, however, in that the role of 'main program' is invariably assumed by a procedure. This is because the Package is purely a *passive* syntactic construct that cannot be 'executed' as such, unlike the MODULA-2 module, which supports both the roles of active and passive program components.

5.2.1 The Package

The name Package is perhaps less appropriate than module. It has over-tones of the 'subroutine package', which was (is?) a major feature of the FORTRAN programmer's world, with examples such as GINO-F and other graphics libraries, and the NAG library. This connotation certainly conveys the idea of a set of components collected together for the convenience of external users. But it fails to capture the idea of encapsulation, which is the key to data abstraction and which is in fact comprehensively supported by the Ada package.

Format

The duality of views of the data abstraction, those of the external user and the implementor, was noted in connection with the syntactically sepa-rate DEFINITION and IMPLEMENTATION modules of MODULA-2. Ada similarly splits the logically unified package into two syntactically separate constructs: the package *specification* and, perhaps rather less meaningfully, the package *body*. The contents of the package specification are very similar to those of the DEFINITION MODULE — declarations of various kinds of entity but particularly subprograms, defining the operational interface to the encapsulated data structure. The body corresponds to the IMPLEMEN-TATION MODULE and is exclusively the concern of the implementor. The body provides the syntactic wall that encapsulates the data items declared within it, and also any subprograms or packages whose specifications do not appear in the corresponding specification. Package bodies possess much the same format as IMPLEMENTATION MODULEs, including an initialisation section.

An impression of the flavour of the Ada package can be obtained from the re-alisation of the familiar stack in Figure 5.1. The structure is reasonably self explanatory. The specification of a package is distinguished by the heading **package** rather than **Package body**. As in MODULA-2 the identifier that names a unit is repeated after the final **end**; in Ada this highly desirable prac-

```
Package Stack;
--
-- a package that provides the semantics of a push-
-- down stack data abstraction with integer items
--
      Procedure Init;

      Procedure Push (Int_val : integer);

      Function Pop return  integer;

      Function Is_empty return  boolean;

      Function Is_full return  boolean;

end stack;
```

Figure 5.1: Ada Package Specification for a Stack Data Abstraction

tice is optional, however. Ada comments are introduced by contiguous pairs of dashes and terminated by line ends. The specifications of the interfaces of the subprograms — procedures and functions — are given as signatures in a manner very similar to MODULA-2. The result type of a function appears after the reserved word **return**, rather than the Pascal/MODULA-2 ':', mimicking the RETURN statement that fulfills a similar role to its MODULA-2 (or C) counterpart. Ada permits the use of the underscore character to provide identifiers with simulated 'spaces', which leads to a recognisable Ada style. The Ada Language Reference Manual (the 'LRM') , uses upper case characters for user-supplied identifiers, a curious usage that we see no particular need to follow slavishly.

Implementation

For completeness, and again to give a flavour of the language, the package body for the **stack** package is shown in Figure 5.2. Two points are worth noting:

```
package body stack is

--
--   encapsulated data structure
--
     stack_limit : constant := 100;
     subtype stack_range is integer
               range 1 .. stack_limit;
     subtype TOS_range is integer
                       range 0 .. stack_limit;
     --
     stack_array : array ( stack_range )
                           of integer;
          TOS : TOS_range;
     --
     procedure init is
     begin
          TOS := 0;
     end initialise;


     Procedure Push (Int_val : integer) is
     begin
          TOS := TOS + 1;
          stack_array(TOS) := Int_val;
     end Push;

     Function Pop return   integer is
     begin
          TOS := TOS - 1;
          return stack_array(tos + 1);
     end Pop;

     Function Is_empty return   boolean is
     begin
          return TOS = 0;
     end Is_empty;

     Function Is_full return   boolean is
     begin
          return TOS = stack_size;
     end Is_full;
 end stack;
```

Figure 5.2: Ada Implementation of the Stack

- Ada has finally done away with the unlovely non-words, CONST, etc. to introduce the various kinds of declaration. Variable, constant and type (also subtype — see below) declarations are sufficiently distinguished by key words such as `constant` and `subtype`, or their absence.

- the subtype concept is a new feature of Ada and was introduced to support some of the applications of types, without incurring the full rigour of the strong typing — which, in Ada, is *very* strong. The examples given in Figure 5.2, `stack_range` and `TOS_range`, provide the kind of properties that subrange types provide in Pascal and MODULA-2. That is, they provide well-defined ranges of equally-spaced, exact values for applications such as array indexing.

Packages and Library Units

Like modules in MODULA-2, Ada packages may be nested — declared within other program units. Unlike MODULA-2 there is not a different format as is the case for local modules: packages have only the one two-component format. The declaration of a package within the specification part of another package may include only the specification; the body must be placed within the body of the enclosing package.

There are no equivalents of EXPORT clauses in Ada. When a package is nested within another unit the scopes of any identifiers declared within the *public part* of the package specification are extended to the end of the enclosing unit. In packages, such as the `stack` example, that do not export *private types*, which will be described shortly, the public part comprises the whole of the specification. Unlike the case in MODULA-2, nested packages do not create a 'hole' in the scopes of globally declared identifiers and so there is no need for the equivalent of an IMPORT clause to make them available within the enclosing package.

Ada is designed above all for the writing of libraries of secure software components. The package is the main unit for the creation of components but, perhaps surprisingly, procedures and functions, and also *generic units* (q.v.), may be compiled into an Ada library. The requirement to allow procedures to be compiled into, and called from, libraries, apart from its conformance with the general 'subroutine library' idea, is necessary anyway. This is because any successful Ada compilation results in the creation of one or more library units. In other words, there is no way in which the 'main program unit' can exist outside a library — the only distinction from an ordinary library unit is that a main program unit, normally a procedure, is invoked by the operating system rather than another library unit.

The great majority of library units, however, can be expected to be packages. The requirements for reusability, obviously the most important attribute for a library unit, in effect dictate that data abstractions should be employed (this topic will be discussed in more detail in a later Chapter), and so the package is the natural choice.

5.2.2 Context Clauses

The way in which one Ada program unit avails itself of a library unit is by means of a *context clause*, which must be placed at the beginning of the compilation unit that contains it – presumably to help the compiler to find the dependencies as quickly as possible. The context clause consists of the reserved word **with**, followed by one or more identifiers, separated by commas if there are several, the whole clause being terminated by a semicolon. The effect of a context clause is much the same as an IMPORT clause in MODULA-2: it causes the scopes of the identifiers exported from the 'with-ed' library unit to be extended over the whole of the compilation unit that it introduces.

A procedure that wishes to use the **stack** package must therefore be submitted as a compilation unit with the first line:

```
with stack;
```

The name clash problem that was discussed in relation to MODULA-2 is confronted by Ada in a similar manner. The identifiers exported by a package are combined with the name of the package, separated by a full-stop, to form *extended names* which are the Ada equivalents of qualified identifiers. The stack-using procedure would therefore invoke the stack operations as, for example, **stack.init** or **stack.push**.

Also like MODULA-2, Ada provides a means of missing out the package name (and its attendant full-stop), the *use clause*. This has the same format as the context clause except that the reserved word **use** replaces **with**. A use clause may appear anywhere in a declarative part and has a scope like a conventional declaration. Within the scope of a use clause any package name included in the clause may be omitted from a name exported from the package. There is little doubt, however, that the use clause is a **bad thing**. The arguments for using extended names in Ada are similar to those for the corresponding use of qualified identifiers in MODULA-2, but are strengthened by the fact that the Ada context clause does not list the individual identifiers imported from the nominated library unit, only the name of the unit itself. There is, therefore, no way of telling, other than by inspecting the specifications of all the packages mentioned in the context clause, from where an identifier has been imported if its source package name has been omitted by means of a use clause. This is by no means a trivial problem — a reasonable size Ada program may contain several dozen packages and it is not uncommon to find ten in the context clause of a high-level package.

5.2.3   Private Types

We have discussed previously the additional power given to the concept of the data abstraction by the abstract data type, using the term in the rather specialised sense defined at the time. It is not surprising, therefore, to find that Ada provides very comprehensive support for abstract data types, in the form of *private* and *limited private* types.

Private types are Ada's equivalents of MODULA-2's opaque types. As usual the Ada design team do not seem to have quite possessed Wirth's flair for suggestive terminology, but the basic notion of a type whose implementation details are hidden from its users is fully supported. In the Ada context we must be rather more precise about what is meant by 'user', because the implementation details of a private type *may* be completely revealed to a *human* user. The additional features in the specification of a package that exports a private type are:

- the declaration, in the public part of the specification, of one or more private types. Each such declaration takes the form:

  type *identifier* is private

- a section following the reserved word private and terminated by the end at the end of the specification, in which the implementation details of the private type or types are declared.

A package derived from the stack package that permits the external declaration of many stacks is shown in Figure 5.3:

```
Package Stacks;
--
-- a package that exports an abstract data type
-- that provides the semantics of a  push-down
-- stack data abstraction with integer items
--
        type STACK is private;

        Procedure Init(S : in out STACK);

        Procedure Push (S : in out STACK; Int_val : integer);

        Procedure Pop (S : in out STACK);

        Function Top (S : STACK) return  integer;

        Function Is_empty (S : STACK) return  boolean;

        Function Is_full (S : STACK) return  boolean;

        private
        --
        --      definitions for type STACK
        --
                stack_limit : constant := 100;
                subtype stack_range is integer
                                        range 1 .. stack_limit;
                subtype TOS_range is integer
                                        range 0 .. stack_limit;
                --
                type STACK is
                    record
                        stack_array : array ( stack_range )
                                                of integer;
                        TOS : TOS_range;
                    end record;
    end stacks;
```

Figure 5.3: Specification of an Ada Package Exporting a Stack Abstract
Data Type

Before discussing the specific details concerned with the private type a few words of explanation are in order in respect of the changed operations. The **stack** type parameters are used to pass stack objects into the package where they are either modified, for example by the **push** operation, or simply read out in part, for example by the **is_empty** operation. In the former case read-write parameter modes are required: the Ada equivalent of the Pascal/MODULA-2 VAR mode is the considerably more readable 'in out', which appears with the type, rather than the inevitably forgotten position before the complete parameter declaration. In the latter case, read-only parameter modes are appropriate; in Ada the mode is specified, quite meaningfully as 'in'. In mode is the default for procedure parameters, and is not normally specified explicitly. More importantly, the parameter modes for functions may *only* be specified as in. In other words, Ada functions *may not modify their parameters*. This is the reason for the introduction of the additional function **top**, which returns the value held at the top of the stack, the **pop** operation being unable both to provide this value and truncate the stack.

Turning now to the private type: as can be seen, the data structure for each stack type object is defined in full, as a record type, in the private part of the specification. Ada places no restriction on the implementation of private types. The important point here, though, is that these implementation details are quite invisible to *another program unit* — i.e. a non-human 'user'. Any attempt to compile a direct assignment to one of the components, **stack_array** or TOS, of a variable declared as being of type **stack** in an external unit will cause an error. In other words, the syntactic wall that provides the encapsulating properties of the package is pushed out into the specification, up to the **private** heading. Note that not only the immediate details of the STACK type are hidden — the auxiliary subtypes **stack_range** and TOS_range are also encapsulated.

The reader may well be wondering for what purpose this visibility of the implementation of a private type is required. The answer is concerned with the need for the compiler to inform itself of these implementation details so that it can compile the specification, and also any unit that uses it. However, the (human) user of such a private type may well find the implementation details of interest, but would be quite wrong to base the design of any external unit on these details and their visibility can be seen only as a kind of temptation. More seriously, the incorporation of implementation details into a specification compromises its role as essentially an interface definition that can be defined and, often, finalised during the design phase. The implementation detail should be decided at a later stage in the project — in fact at *the latest possible stage* in line with the well-established software engineering principle of *decision deferment* — a reinterpretation of the biblical tenet "sufficient unto the day is the evil thereof".

The reader may suggest that the value of Ada as a design language need not be affected by this because there is no need to compile a design language and so the requirement to provide the implementation details of private types can simply be ignored until the actual implementation phase is reached. In fact, the ability to compile individual package specifications into a library provides the powerful checks on consistency and visibility characteristic of automatic translation and is an important support tool for Ada, one that considerably increases its viability for this application.

There is also a more practical reason for questioning this arrangement, which derives from the dependency rules of Ada.

Dependency

Part of the design aims of Ada were concerned with providing support for *configuration management* — the control of the production of a software system composed of many separate components, each of which has its own development pathway, along which its compatibility with the other components of the system will vary. As a contribution to the control of program development in this kind of environment an Ada system is required to impose an order on the sequence in which units are compiled, and recompiled. This order is determined by the *dependency* between units, the essential rule being that if unit A is dependent on unit B, then A cannot be compiled before B is compiled, and if B is recompiled then A must be recompiled. The dependency rules that are relevant to this discussion are

1. A unit that nominates a package in its context clause is dependent on the *specification* of the package, *and not its body*

2. A package body is dependent on its specification.

The significance of these rules is that a change to a package specification will necessitate the recompilation of all units that 'with' it, together with its body. In this context, a change to the declarations following the PRIVATE heading are just as visible from the point of view of recompilation as those made to the public objects in the specification.

Access Private Types

The recommended practice of compiling package specifications during the design phase, with the consequential requirement to provide implementation details for private types, would therefore seem to raise two awkward problems:

1. the need to arrive at detailed implementation decisions during the design phase

2. the need frequently to recompile the units (including other package specifications) that depend on a specification as these implementation details, inevitably, are changed.

The solution to these problems lies in the use of pointers, following closely the earlier MODULA-2 practice of requiring opaque types to be pointer types.

Ada's version of pointer types are known as *Access* types, perhaps suggesting that, as in the current context, they have uses other than in the construction of pointer-connected data structures. Access types resemble pointer types in Pascal and MODULA-2, with some relatively minor modifications intended to do away with some of the known drawbacks of the earlier version: notably the 'dangling-pointer problem'. Like Pascal pointers, values of an Ada access type are addresses of objects of one specified type — known as the *designated type*; there is no possibility of a pointer value being allowed to point to arbitrary objects.

The form of an access type declaration is:

```
type a_t_identifer is access d_t_identifer
```

Typically, for quite logical reasons, the designated type of an access type is a record type and, again typically in the construction of data structures, the record type in question is required to contain one or more fields of the access type — i.e. pointers to its own type. This recursive arrangement then allows the setting up of pointer connections between nodes of the record type. It also causes a problem because the mutually recursive definitions of the two types, access and designated (record) types, cannot be done without some form of forward reference. In Pascal and MODULA-2 this is done simply by allowing a forward reference in this one special case. In Ada, the problem is solved in a rather more elegant manner by the device of an *incomplete declaration*, which introduces the name of the designated type without giving any further details. For the moment this is all the compiler needs to know, on the understanding that the full declaration will be given at a point later in the program text.

The declaration of a typical access/designated type pair is shown below:

```
type NODE; -- incomplete declaration
type NODE_PTR is access NODE;
type NODE is  record  -- complete declaration
                 data : data_type;
                 NEXT : NODE_PTR;
              end record;
```

In the context of private types the important point is that the complete declaration need not appear in the specification of a package even though the incomplete declaration does. As long as the complete declaration appears within the package body the incomplete declaration is acceptable as a perfectly respectable declaration. In other words, the above set of interrelated declarations could be split over the specification/body boundary, as shown in Figure 5.4. The use of this technique can be employed both to hide the implementation details of a private type and, initially, to avoid the need to arrive at decisions about the implementation. It thus solves both the problems identified previously, albeit at the cost of the kind of slight increase in complexity in the implementation of the operations that we have seen already in the MODULA-2 context. The **stacks** package specification would then look as shown in Figure 5.5. The complete declaration of STACK_STRUCT would then be given in the package body as shown in Figure 5.6. It seems, then that what Ada appears to give in the way of freedom to use non-pointer types for the implementation of private types is a somewhat mixed blessing: the requirements of good software engineering practice invariably tend to militate against their use anyway. In fact Ada is now rather more restrictive in this matter than MODULA-2, as the result of the dependency rules of Ada. These permit the compilation of a complete package, specification and body, that depends on a package, only the specification of which has been compiled. The complete hiding of the implementation of a private type in

```
--
-- package specification for pack_1
    type NODE; -- incomplete declaration
    type NODE_PTR is access NODE;
end pack_1;

package body pack_1 is
    type NODE is  record  -- complete declaration
                       data : data_type;
                       NEXT : NODE_PTR;
                  end record;
--
-- remainder of body
--
```

Figure 5.4: Declarations of NODE Split Over Package Components

the package body would mean that the compiler would have no clue as to memory allocation for private type objects in the dependent package. The use of an access type allows this allocation to be performed — albeit really by pushing the problem onto the run-time kernel, which handles dynamic memory allocation.

5.2.4   Limited Private Types

The ability to declare variables normally carries with it the ability to manipulate these variables by a number of standard operations. Typically these include assignment — the operation that allows the value of one variable to be overwritten by the value of another — and also an operation to test that the values of two variables are equal. These standard operations are available for objects of any private type, and so the complete set of operations for such objects is:

1. **Applicable Operations** — subprograms exported from the same package that exports the private type with at least one parameter, or the result type if a function, of the private type.

2. **Assignment** — the operation that overwrites a variable with the value of an object.

```
Package Stacks;
--
-- a package that exports an abstract data type
-- that provides the semantics of a push-down
-- stack data abstraction with integer items
--
   type STACK is private;

   Procedure Init(S : in out STACK);

   Procedure Push (S : in out STACK; Int_val : integer);

   Procedure Pop (S : in out STACK);

   Function Top (S : STACK) return  integer;

   Function Is_empty (S : STACK) return  boolean;

   Function Is_full (S : STACK) return  boolean;

   private
         type STACK_STRUCT;
         type STACK is access STACK_STRUCT;
   end stacks;
```

Figure 5.5: Type Stack Declared as an Access Type

```
package body stacks is
--
--      definitions for type STACK_STRUCT
--
stack_limit : constant := 100;
subtype stack_range is integer range 1 .. stack_limit;
subtype TOS_range is integer range 0 .. stack_limit;
--
type STACK_STRUCT is record
                            stack_array : array ( stack_range )
                                                   of integer;
                                 TOS : TOS_range;
                  end record;
--
-- remainder of body
--
```

Figure 5.6: Implementation of the Stack Private Type

3. **Equality Test** — a boolean-valued function, which is pre-defined for all types and private types.

This latter operation seems to be a very sraightforward affair for variables with types such as integer or character. It becomes rather more complicated for more complex types, however: are two records carrying the same data in the same set of fields, but arranged in different orders, equal? These problems become more significant when abstract data types are considered, particularly when they are realised as private types implemented as access types .

The nature of the problem can be seen by imagining a (slightly unreal) requirement to test if two stacks, both declared as being of the type **stack** exported from **stacks**, are equal. In order to see what is involved it will be useful to show the implementation of the **init** operation:

```
procedure init(S : in out STACK) is
begin
        S := new STACK_STRUCT;
        S.TOS := 0;
end init;
```

As can be seen, Ada distinguishes a subprogram *body* from its specification, as given in a package specification, by the word **is** that follows the formal parameter part. Other points to note are that

- The familiar word *new* in Ada denotes an *allocator* which is more visibly like the memory allocation system calls provided in the unix-C environment. An allocator is functional in the sense of returning a value — the address of the newly created object — rather than procedural as in Pascal. The effect of the execution of an allocator is rather clearer than its Pascal equivalent, because the 'operand' of the expression is the type of the object that is actually created, rather than the pointer to it.

- There is no dereferencing operator in Ada, because an expression such as S.TOS quite obviously refers to a field of the object that S is pointing at — the value of S itself is an address and has no fields. An ambiguity can arise when the whole of a 'pointed-at' object is required, in which case the expression .all is appended to the access variable name.

The two stack variables in question, after being initialised, will denote two distinct address values obtained by two distinct executions of the allocator. Of necessity these values will be different — something would be seriously wrong if this was not the case because it would mean that dynamically created objects would overwrite each other. The important point is that any attempt to compare these values for equality will *always* produce the answer FALSE, no matter what the contents of their respective STACK_STRUCT records happen to be.

Structure-Specific Equality

What equality between two stacks actually means is presumably something along the lines that each corresponding pair of items in the two are equal. A test to determine equality would have to examine the contents of the two stack_array fields, but only in their 'used' parts, i.e. up to the elements indexed by the (common) TOS value. It is quite clear that the application of the standard equality test to the address values does nothing approaching this, and so the requirement to test for equality can be satisfied only if it is possible to disable the standard test and replace it by one specific to stacks.

This, in fact, is (one half of) the significance of *limited* private types. Objects — variables or constants — declared as being of a limited private type have available *only* the applicable operations exported from the package in which the type is declared, for their manipulation.

In particular, in the context of the preceding discussion, the standard equality test is disabled, and in the case of limited private type operands only, Ada permits the redefinition, or *overloading*, of the equality test operator : "=". This is done by declaring a function with a specification of the form:

```
function "=" (left,right :  LPT) return boolean;
```

where LPT is some limited private type. This feature allows for an operation specific to the data structure in question to be defined.

Structure-Specific Assignment

As implied above, the standard assignment operation also is disabled for limited private types. The reason for this follows that for the equality test — the assignment of one private type object, implemented as an access variable, to another will simply cause both to point to the same data structure. This can lead to unexpected, and unwelcome effects, symbolised by the following:

```
x := y;
modify(x);
```

modify is assumed to be a procedure that changes in some way its parameter. If x and y are of ordinary types, say integer, then the value of y will remain unchanged after the execution of the two statements. By contrast, if x and y are pointers, then the call to modify(x) will affect y, or at least the structure that y points at, a result that may well catch the programmer napping. What is normally required is a copying operation that produces a new structure to be denoted by the left hand side of the assignment, and once again the standard operation cannot perform this operation for generalised structures; instead, it must be disabled and replaced by a specific version. In the event that assignment is required for a limited private type, which may well be the case if a 'functional' style of interface is used, the operation must be exported as an applicable operation — a procedure, because assignment essentially modifies its left hand operand. Note that Ada does not regard := as an operator like = and it cannot be overloaded. A procedure named assign or some such must be used. The final version of the stacks package, with exported assignment and equality test operations is shown in Figure 5.7.

```
Package Stacks;
--
-- a package that exports an abstract data type
-- that provides the semantics of a
-- push-down stack data abstraction
--
    type STACK is limited private;

    Procedure Init(S : in out STACK);

    Procedure Push (S : in out STACK; Int_val : integer);

    Procedure Pop (S : in out STACK);

    Function Top (S : STACK) return  integer;

    Function Is_empty (S : STACK) return  boolean;

    Function Is_full (S : STACK) return  boolean;

    Function "=" ( left,right : STACK)
                                  return  boolean;

    Procedure assign ( left : in out STACK;
                                  right:  STACK);

private
    type STACK_STRUCT;
            type STACK is access STACK_STRUCT;
end stacks;
```

Figure 5.7: Stack Defined as a Limited Private Type

5.3   Review of Ada

Despite its size and complexity Ada has become well-established as a standard language, particularly in the field of defence applications. Much of the reason for this is precisely the standardisation imposed on the language by its design authority — the US Department of Defense. This has meant that genuinely portable programs can be written on such diverse platforms as Personal Computers, workstations, mini and mainframe computers. It is also the case that the spur of competition provided by the restriction of much of the software commissioned by the DoD to the use of Ada has encouraged the manufacturers of compilers for the language to achieve prodigious feats of performance — both at compile-time and run-time.

In the context of this book, the importance of Ada lies in the fact that its design is centred about the use of data abstraction as a constructional technique for software systems. There have been a number of languages that have exhibited a similar orientation including Alphard, Clu and, of course, MODULA-2, which we have already discussed. If the use of data abstraction was restricted to these languages, however, the technique would remain an interesting curiosity with a significant but small following, restricted largely to the academic world. The adoption of Ada by the DoD, with its huge financial muscle, has changed this picture substantially and placed data abstraction techniques in the centre stage of software production.

5.4   Summary

In this and the preceding Chapter we have looked in some detail at the support for the data abstraction provided by two languages descended from Pascal: MODULA-2 and Ada. The practical considerations of the use of the data abstraction, which have been recognised by the designers of both languages, have led to the incorporation of support for abstract data types — a generalisation of the original concept, which provides a very powerful facility at the expense of a certain increase in complexity when the practicalities of compilation and also considerations such as equality are accommodated. The discussion has remained on a fairly abstract level with the well-worn stack example as the sole basis for discussing applications. In the next Chapter this lack of practical application will be redressed by the consideration of an extended case study.

Chapter 6

Information Hiding - A Case Study

6.1   Introduction

In this chapter we consider a very well-known case study of the application of data abstraction to program design. The case study is taken from one of the most significant papers to have been written on the subject of data abstraction — significant enough to have introduced a related term into the language of computing, and indeed to have formed the basis of a new design methodology. The paper in question is by David Parnas and is entitled, with a rare clarity, "On the Criteria to be used in Decomposing Systems into Modules". As the reader will see, the title at least would appear to indicate some relevance to the subject matter of this book.

Parnas' paper was published in 1972 in the Communications of the Association for Computing Machinery. It is therefore not a new paper, although a surprising number of popularisers of program design methodologies seem oblivious to its existence. The material in this Chapter is heavily borrowed from the paper and the author would like to acknowledge both it and Parnas' general contribution to modular program design concepts.

6.2   The Problem

The case study is based on the problem of the generation of a KWIC (which stands for **K**ey **W**ord **I**n **C**ontext) index. A KWIC index is formed from a list of phrases, normally titles of books or papers such as might be found in a library catalogue. Each title contains a number of significant or *key* words that give a strong pointer to the contents of the book or paper. The title of Parnas' own paper contains the obvious key words *criteria, decomposing* and *modules* with others such as *the* that are obviously not key words. The KWIC index consists of a list of all the key words in all the titles, sorted in alphabetic order and shown, emphasised in some way, within the titles from which they are extracted — hence 'in context'. Every title will therefore appear the number of times in the index that it possesses key words.

Clearly, words like 'module' can hardly be expected to be unique in an index concerned with computing topics, and the question arises as to how repeated key words are to be ordered. The answer is that in such cases the *remainder* of the titles in question, viewed as a sequence of key words, are considered in an alphabetic comparison. So, if an index contains the titles:

On the Criteria to be used in Decomposing Systems into Modules
and
A Metric for Determining the Coupling between Modules

the ordering of the appearances of 'Modules' is determined by forming the 'circular shifts' of the titles concerned, so that the key word appears in the first position in the line:

Modules On the Criteria to be used in Decomposing Systems into
and
Modules A Metric for Determining the Coupling between

and then by determining the lexical, or alphabetic, ordering of the shifted titles, considering the key words only. In this case the first will appear before the second because its remainder *Criteria ...* is alphabetically prior to *Metric....*

The complete, if somewhat short, index generated from the two titles would be, therefore:

A Metric for Determining the **Coupling** *between Modules*

> *On the* **Criteria** *to be used in Decomposing Systems into Modules*
> *On the Criteria to be used in* **Decomposing** *Systems into Modules*
> *A* **Metric** *for Determining the Coupling between Modules*
> *On the Criteria to be used in Decomposing Systems into* **Modules**
> *A Metric for Determining the Coupling between* **Modules**

It will be seen that the problem is unlikely to require anything like a large program. It is not completely trivial, however, and is significant enough to illustrate some important principles.

6.3   The Algorithm

Parnas suggests a straightforward solution to the problem with the following algorithm:

1. Input the titles

2. Form the circular shifts for all the titles (so that every title has a set of circular shifts containing one for each key word in the initial position)

3. Sort the circular shifts alphabetically

4. Create the index by outputting, for each circular shift in the sorted order, the title from which the circular shift was generated, with the word in the initial position of the circular shift emphasised.

6.4   Design — the Conventional Approach

In considering the design of the program to generate the KWIC index Parnas first adopts what he characterises as the obvious or conventional design approach. This approach might well be derived from a Data Flow Diagram of the realisation of the algorithm, showing the data flows between the *processes*, which correspond reasonably enough with the stages of the algorithm and are therefore *input, circular shift, sort* and *output*. A typical such data flow diagram is shown in Figure 6.1.

The next obvious conventional step is to modularise the design into a partitioning suggested by the Data Flow Diagram: i.e. with a module corresponding to each process, together with a 'main' module that controls the

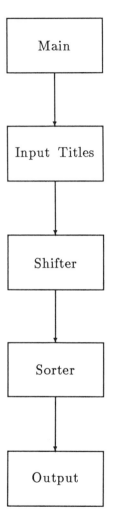

Figure 6.1: Data Flow Diagram for the Conventional Solution

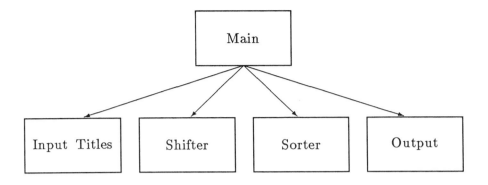

Figure 6.2: Structure Chart for the Conventional Solution

sequence in which the 'process' modules execute. Each of the process modules is called, in turn, by the main module to perform its single, discrete function, and might be thought of as a very powerful program statement or command. This approach to modular design, which emphasises the *imperative* aspect of modules, is known as *procedural abstraction*, because it allows for the creation of procedures, or commands, that are abstracted away from the machine-orientated level of the ordinary program statements. The sequence of process modules effectively forms a program, comprising a 'pipeline' that accomplishes the transformation from the input list of titles to the output index.

The 'Structure Chart' representation of the design is given in Figure 6.2 showing the simple modular structure and straightforward execution sequence, i.e. without loops. (The reader may recall that modules derived in this way possess 'procedural' strength according to the classification described in Chapter 2.) It might be noted that Parnas' view of what was 'conventional' in 1972 would be unlikely to cause many surprises to one of the practitioners of the many currently well-marketed methodologies based on Data Flow Diagrams and Structure Charts.

The next step, and the first interesting one in the context both of Parnas' paper and this book, is to evaluate the suggested design from the point of view of the criteria that have been discussed in earlier chapters.

6.5   Analysis of the Conventional Design

It takes relatively little analysis to discover that the proposed design is a
very poor one from the point of view of module coupling. If we consider the
interface between the `input` and `circular_shifter` modules we see that
it must consist of a data structure, containing the entire set of titles from
which the index is to be generated, populated by the input process. The
nature of the input module is defined by the structure diagram as the first
of a sequence of functions, which is never invoked again. This implies that
the input set of titles must be handed over 'all of a piece' via what must
inevitably be a wide and complex interface.

The nature of this interface may be parameterised, i.e. the call by the main
module to `input` may return the data structure or, more likely, a pointer to
the data structure, which may then be passed to `circular_shifter` on its
invocation. But this is a perfect example of a parameterised interface being
almost indistinguishable from a global data area because the data structure
involved is so large. Additionally, the data structure must provide for a
nested structure of titles and words within titles and then characters within
words — perhaps a list of lists of lists, or a 'ragged-edged' two-dimensional
array. Whatever data structure is chosen it will be complex and, importantly,
place a heavy commitment to it on both the communicating modules. (It
is assumed that `main` performs no processing of the data structure but simply transmits it between `input` and `circular_shifter` and so would be
relatively uncommitted.)

We can see then that the proposed design exhibits a high level of coupling
between the first two modules in the sequence, with the characteristic problems of modifications to one having profound effects on the other. If we
imagine an initial implementation based on an array structure a subsequent
change to a list-based approach would necessitate a complete rewrite of both
modules.

When we turn to the next interface, that between `circular_shifter` and
`sorter`, we see that the situation is even worse than is the case for the
first. Again a large data structure must be handed over. Not only is its
size a multiple of the first, because of the generation of several circular
shifts for each title, but, more crucially, another level of nesting and thus

complexity must be provided to represent the relationship between titles and their circular shifts.

Again, the level of coupling is very high, and it is clear that the whole 'pipeline' is inextricably committed to a large and complex interface, that will allow any modifications in an earlier module to 'ripple through' the remainder. From the point of view of achieving the benefits of modularity the design can hardly be said to be modular at all.

6.6 Improving the Design by Narrowing Interfaces

The above analysis may well have struck some resonances in the reader's mind. The essential cause of the shortcomings of the 'conventional' design is the necessity for each module to hand over, in a single action, the large data structure that the next module is to work on. On seeing the phrase *data structure*, the related concept of the data abstraction should be asserting itself in a positively Pavlovian way. Clearly a possible approach to improving the design might lie in the encapsulation of the data structures so that their implementation details are hidden, and thus cannot form part of an interface commitment. If we consider the nature of a collection of titles as a rather complicated multi-level list, with character strings at the bottom level (to hold the words), and recall the character string data abstraction introduced in Chapter 3, we may see how to elaborate the latter so as to provide the semantics of the former.

6.6.1 A Titles Data Abstraction

What then are the requirements that a data abstraction for a collection of titles must satisfy? We can see that its essential nature is that of a 'data repository' that simply allows the titles to be inserted into it and extracted from it, but over an interface that requires no commitment to its internal structure. Like its counterpart in the character string data abstraction this interface is basically one character wide, but with an additional complexity necessitated by the nested structure of the titles.

As is often the case, a good starting point for its design is to imagine a piece of (pseudo) code that actually uses the data abstraction, say as part of the input process. The code has just read a title and is about to transfer a

```
TITLES.START_NEW_TITLE;
while some_input_characters_left
loop
      read (next_character); -- from input stream
      if end_of_word
      then
            if end_of_title
            then TITLES.START_NEW_TITLE;
            end if;
            TITLES.START_NEW_WORD;
      else TITLES.SET_NEXT_CHARACTER_TO(next_character);
      end if;
end loop;
```

Figure 6.3: Inserting into the TITLES Data Abstraction

character from it into the titles data abstraction. Normally, in a manner that should be familiar from the discussion of *Iterators* in Chapter 3, the transfer will be accomplished by a SET_NEXT_CHARACTER_TO operation, but of course the transfer must reflect the structuring of the input into words and titles, and so it is necessary to provide operations corresponding to *start a new word* and *start a new title*.

The code to read the set of titles and to insert it into the data abstraction might therefore appear as shown in Figure 6.3 using an Ada-like pseudo-code and assuming that the data abstraction is implemented as a package called TITLES. The corresponding constructor operations of the TITLES package specification would be declared as follows:

```
package TITLES is
--
      procedure START_NEW_TITLE;
      procedure START_NEW_WORD;
      procedure SET_NEXT_CHARACTER_TO(CHAR : character);
--
```

(This example shows the Ada versions of the *while* and *if* statements. The former follows the Pascal model quite closely, apart from the use of the **loop .. end loop** brackets instead of a compound statement. The latter again uses a self-bracketing terminator, **end if**, in a way that is quite consistent in the language.)

The complementary set of observer operations must provide for the extraction of the complete collection of titles from the data abstraction. Clearly an iterator is required, but again we must take acount of the three-level structure and provide observer operations that allow for the detection of the end of words and the end of titles. The following Ada declarations provide a possible realisation:

```
function SOME_TITLES_LEFT return boolean;
-- returns TRUE until all titles read
--
function SOME_WORDS_LEFT return boolean;
-- returns TRUE until the current title is exhausted
--
function SOME_CHARACTERS_LEFT return boolean;
-- returns TRUE until the current word is exhausted
--
function NEXT_CHARACTER return character;
```

A piece of code to extract all the titles from the abstraction might then look something like the following:

```
-- set up data areas, counts etc.
while TITLES.SOME_TITLES_LEFT
loop
        while TITLES.SOME_WORDS_LEFT
        loop
                while TITLES.SOME_CHARACTERS_LEFT
                loop
                        NEXT_CHAR := TITLES.NEXT_CHARACTER;
                        -- transfer NEXT_CHAR to local area
                end loop;
                -- initialise next word
        end loop;
        -- initialise next title
end loop;
-- all titles extracted
```

At the risk of labouring what should be a fairly obvious point, by the introduction of the TITLES data abstraction we have narrowed the interface, over which the entire set of titles may be transmitted, to the width of one character. In the context of the design for the KWIC index program this interface may be established between the **input** and **circular_shifter** modules so as to reduce their coupling and interface commitment drastically. It can be

```
package TITLES is
--
-- constructor operations
--
    procedure START_NEW_TITLE;
    --
    procedure START_NEW_WORD;
    --
    procedure SET_NEXT_CHARACTER_TO(CHAR : character);
--
-- iterator
--
    function SOME_TITLES_LEFT return boolean;
    -- returns TRUE until all titles read
    --
    function SOME_WORDS_LEFT return boolean;
    -- returns TRUE until the current title is exhausted
    --
    function SOME_CHARACTERS_LEFT return boolean;
    -- returns TRUE until the current word is exhausted
    --
    function NEXT_CHARACTER return character;
    --
end titles;
```

Figure 6.4: Ada Realisation of a Titles Data Abstraction

seen that the operations provided by the `titles` package/data abstraction require no commitment to the underlying implementation — either an array or list based data structure could be used, and indeed changed one to another without affecting the external operations and, thus, the implementations of the two 'process' modules.

The complete package specification corresponding to the titles data abstraction is shown in Figure 6.4.

Before considering the other interfaces we will examine Parnas' own abstraction, which differs somewhat from the above.

6.7   Parnas' Solution

Parnas suggests the addition of a data abstraction (although he does not use
the term) which he calls LINE_STORAGE. Its role in the design is essentially
the same as the TITLES package but it provides an index-based interface
rather than one based on an iterator.

The constructors of the interface are an INITIALISE operation and an operation, called PUT_CHARACTER_FROM, that takes, in addition to the value of
the character that is to be inserted, parameters that give the number of the
line (i.e. title) in which the character occurs, the number of the word within
the line within which the character occurs and then the number of the character within the word. There are thus four parameters, one character and
three *natural* — i.e. positive integers or zero. The interface provided by
PUT_CHARACTER_FROM is thus slightly more complex than that of the corresponding operation in the titles package, but it still represents a very low
interface commitment — integers and ASCII characters are unlikely to be
affected by implementation changes.

The observer operations for LINE_STORAGE   consist of a main index-based
function that performs the mirror image of the PUT_CHARACTER_FROM operation, i.e. it returns the value of the character at a specified line, word and
character number. Additionally, because of course the writer of a routine
that uses the data abstraction does not know how many titles there are, how
many words there are in each title or characters in each word, natural valued
observers are provided to allow these to be extracted. An Ada realisation of
the interface to LINE_STORAGE is shown in Figure 6.5: The way in which the
operations exported by this package may be used to extract the complete
set of lines is shown in Figure 6.6. (Figure 6.6 shows the Ada version of
the for statement, in which the body of the loop, enclosed by the loop ..
end loop brackets, is executed once for every value that the control variable
takes. The control variable follows the word for and takes, successively,
each value in the range specified after in.)

The reader may recall that, in the discussion of the string data abstraction
in Chapter 3, the use of the indexed style of interface was criticised on
the grounds that it was an 'over specification' of what is conventionally
thought to be appropriate to a character string. That is to say, it provided
a functionality, particularly in supporting random access to any character
position within the string, that is over and above what might be required for
any application involving character strings. By contrast, the iterator style

```
package LINE_STORAGE is
    procedure INITIALISE;
    procedure PUT_CHARACTER_FROM(LINE_NO,WORD_NO,CHARACTER_NO:
                                                natural;
                              CHAR : character);
    function NO_OF_LINES return natural;
    function NO_OF_WORDS_IN (LINE_NO : natural) return natural;
    function NO_OF_CHARACTERS_IN(LINE_NO,WORD_NO : natural)
                                            return natural;
    function GET_CHARACTER_FOR(LINE_NO,WORD_NO,CHARACTER_NO:
                              natural) return  character;
end LINE_STORAGE;
```

Figure 6.5: An Ada Realisation of the LINE_STORAGE Module Interface

```
LINE_NO := 1;
for LINE_NO in 1 .. LINE_STORAGE.NO_OF_LINES
loop
        for WORD_NO in 1 ..
                LINE_STORAGE.NO_OF_WORDS_IN(LINE_NO)
        loop
                for CHARACTER_NO in 1   ..
            LINE_STORAGE.NO_OF_CHARACTERS_IN(LINE_NO,WORD_NO)
                loop
                    NEXT_CHAR := LINE_STORAGE.GET_CHARACTER_FOR
                                (LINE_NO,WORD_NO,
                                CHARACTER_NO);
                    -- transfer NEXT_CHAR to local area
                end loop;
        end loop;

end loop;
```

Figure 6.6: Code to Extract the Titles from LINE_STORAGE

of interface appeared to match more naturally the semantics of character strings.

As we have seen, Parnas' approach to the KWIC index program, at least as far as the `line_storage` data abstraction is concerned, is very definitely based on the indexed style, and the obvious question arises as to why he chose this type of interface. The first version that we have discussed is based on the use of an iterator, and we have seen how the entire collection of titles may be extracted via this interface. Is there any deficiency in the use of the iterator style that dictates the use of the indexed approach? In order to discuss this question in more detail we need to look at the remaining inter-modular interfaces.

6.8 The Circular Shifter Interface

The essential functionality that the `circular_shifter` must support is to enable the `sorter` to extract the collection of circular shifts generated from the titles. We have seen how the addition of a data abstraction, along the lines of either TITLES or LINE_STORAGE, can narrow the interface between input and `circular_shifter` to an acceptable level. We should also note specifically that the nature of this interface has changed from the original version in that it involves a (large) number of calls to the operations of the data abstraction. We have abandoned the 'single-shot' approach.

Should the interface between `circular_shifter` and `sorter` be similarly provided with a separate data abstraction, to perform a corresponding service? A moment's thought shows that this is unnecessary, because we can modify the interface of `circular_shifter` itself to provide the low coupling that we are trying to achieve. The interface is closely modelled on that of the `titles` or `line_storage` data abstraction but replaces *title* by *circular_shift*. An Ada realisation of this interface, utilising the Parnas indexed style, is shown in Figure 6.7.

The main difference, apart from the substitution of SHIFT for LINE, is the lack of an input or PUT operation. This is replaced by the internal operations of the `circular_shifter`, comprising calls to `line_storage` in the manner shown previously in Figure 6.6.

An immediate design decision concerns the necessity for `circular_shifter` to contain its own data structure within which the shifts are stored as they are generated, presumably in response to the `initialise` operation.

```
package CIRCULAR_SHIFTER is
    procedure INITIALISE;
    function NO_OF_SHIFTS return natural;
    function NO_OF_WORDS_IN (SHIFT_NO : natural) return natural;
    function NO_OF_CHARACTERS_IN(SHIFT_NO,WORD_NO : natural)
                                              return natural;
    function GET_CHARACTER_FOR(SHIFT_NO,WORD_NO,CHARACTER_NO:
                                   natural) return  character;
end CIRCULAR_SHIFTER;
```

Figure 6.7: An Ada Realisation of the Circular_Shifter Interface

This seems a natural approach, but a viable alternative is for the module to generate the shifts 'on the fly' — that is, as the sorter repeatedly calls GET_CHARACTER_FOR in order to construct the collection of shifts prior to sorting them, the code of circular_shifter extracts the titles from line_storage as they become needed. The difference between the two implementations is a trade-off between memory occupancy and code complexity, but the important point is, of course, that either can be used without any need for alterations in any other modules. This is, as the reader will require no reminding, the direct consequence of the decoupling effect of the narrow interface supported by the data abstraction.

6.9   The Sorter Interface

It is when we come to the interface between sorter and output that the choice of design style, namely iterator *versus* indexed, adopted for the interface to TITLES/line_manager necessitates significant differences in implementation. The basic functionality of sorter must enable output to extract the collection of circular shifts, sorted in alphabetic order *together* with sufficient information to allow, for each shift, the reconstruction of the title from which it was generated. If the indexed style of interface design has been adopted for TITLES/line_manager then the sorter interface can be simplified to one that provides an iterator for the extraction of pairs of natural numbers. The number pairs are supplied in an order determined by the alphabetic sort. One number gives the line number of the title from which the 'next' shift was derived, the other gives the position of the key word that is to be emphasised in the output (which is the same as the number of key words that the shift was rotated).

An appropriate package specification is shown below.

```
package Sorter is
--
     procedure INITIALISE;-- must be called before NEXT_SHIFT
     --
     procedure NEXT_SHIFT(LINE_NO,KEY_WORD_NO : out natural);
--
end Sorter;
```

It is at this point that the apparent over-specification of the indexed style of the interface to line_storage can be seen to be justified, because its random access capability allows output to extract lines in any sequence as dictated by sorter. Output may therefore look something like the following:

```
SORTER.NEXT_SHIFT(LINE_NO,KEY_WORD_NO);
word_count := LINE_STORAGE.NO_OF_WORDS_IN(LINE_NO);
for word_no in 1 .. word_count
loop
     emphasised := word_no = KEY_WORD_NO;
     for CHARACTER_NO in 1   ..
        LINE_STORAGE.NO_OF_CHARACTERS_IN(LINE_NO,WORD_NO)
     loop
                NEXT_CHAR := LINE_STORAGE.GET_CHARACTER_FOR
                                      (LINE_NO,WORD_NO,
                                       CHARACTER_NO);
                -- transfer NEXT_CHAR to output area
                -- if emphasised is true then emphasise
                -- the word
     end loop;
end loop;
```

Once again it may be noted that, as compared with the first version of the design, the interface presented by the sorter to output, consisting of pairs of natural integers, requires a very low level of commitment. The sorting algorithm and, importantly, the data structure on which it is carried out, are completely hidden. This is made possible both because of the encapsulation of line_storage's data structure, and also because of the relationship between the line_storage and the other modules, which involves many invocations throughout the various phases of the processing, rather than the single delivery of the complete set of titles. The modular structure no longer reflects closely the processing sequence of the program but is more determined by the significant data structures — procedural abstraction has given way to data abstraction.

6.9.1   An Iterator-based Interface

The question now arises as to whether or not the iterator style as exhibited by the specification of the TITLES package in Figure 6.4 is in fact capable of supplying a functionality adequate to support the requirements of output. The answer is that it is, but at the cost of a considerably more complex implementation of output, which is obliged to provide a reverse circular shift in order to recreate each title. This recreation is necessary because the iterator-based TITLES package is incapable of providing a random access to individual titles and so cannot be used by output to obtain the reordered sequence. Instead, the titles must be provided, each in the form of one of its circular shifts, in the correct sequence by the sorter. The interface of the iterator-based version of the sorter, shown in Figure 6.8, thus closely resembles that of the circular_shifter with an additional operation that returns, for each shift, the ordinal number of the key word in the original title (that is, the number of key words that the shift must be reversed in order to recreate the title). The additional operation is a function that may be called after the characters for the shift in question have been extracted. The word to be emphasised in the output is identified by the fact that it is the first in the shift, of course. When the two variations in interface style are compared it is fairly clear that what has been defined as Parnas' indexed style provides for a simpler sorter interface and output functionality. Indeed, in the iterator-based version it might with some justification be suggested that the output module should be supplemented by a 'reverse shifter' module to balance out the functionality.

6.9.2   A Hybrid Interface

Whilst accepting that the random access to lines supported by the indexed interface produces a better design we might still query the need for random access to words and characters. This is clearly not necessary, as the words, and the characters that form them, are always extracted in their order as input. We might finally, therefore, adopt a hybrid version for the TITLES/line_storage data abstraction that provides indexing for lines, but

```
Package sorter is
        function SOME_SHIFTS_LEFT return boolean;
        function SOME_WORDS_LEFT return boolean;
        -- returns TRUE until the current shift is exhausted
        -- at which point the following operation:-
        function KEY_WORD_POSITION return natural;
        -- returns the position of the first word in the shift
        -- in the original line
        --
        function SOME_CHARACTERS_LEFT return boolean;
        -- returns TRUE until the current word is exhausted
        --
        function NEXT_CHARACTER return character;
        --
end sorter;
```

Figure 6.8: Interface of an Iterator-based Sorter Module

an iterator for words and characters — a compromise that seems to pitch
the level of functionality appropriately over the whole interface. This hybrid
interface is shown in Figure 6.9, realised as the specification of a package
called, appropriately, TITLE_STORAGE. The iterator operates on the 'current
line', which is established by the SET_CURRENT_LINE operation.

6.10   The Circular Shifter Revisited

The designer of a data abstraction must ensure that its interface is sufficient to enable users fully to exploit its functionality. The reader may have
wondered about the interface of the circular_shifter module — is it adequate for the sorter to carry out its task? In particular, how can the sorter
identify the source line from which each circular shift is generated?

The answer is that this is possible only if the sorter makes some specific assumptions about the way that the circular_shifter works: in particular,
that the circular_shifter generates all the circular shifts from one line in
an unbroken sequence, and the shifts for line k are all generated after those
for line j, if $k > j$ in the line number sequence generated by LINE_STORAGE.
The sorter can determine how many shifts there are for each line by invoking the NO_OF_WORDS_IN function from the LINE_STORAGE package and so, by

```
package TITLE_STORAGE is
    procedure INITIALISE;
    --
    --    constructor operations
    --
        procedure START_NEW_LINE;
        procedure START_NEW_WORD;
        procedure SET_NEXT_CHARACTER_TO(CHAR : character);
    --
    --    observers
    --
        function NO_OF_LINES return natural;
        procedure SET_CURRENT_LINE_TO(LINE_NO : natural);
        --
        function SOME_WORDS_LEFT return boolean;
        -- returns TRUE until the current title is exhausted
        --
        function SOME_CHARACTERS_LEFT return boolean;
        -- returns TRUE until the current word is exhausted
        --
        function NEXT_CHARACTER return character;
        --
end TITLE_STORAGE;
```

Figure 6.9: A Hybrid Interface to TITLES/Line_Storage

monitoring the count of shifts as they are extracted, associate the set of shifts generated from each line with its number. However, this technique is based on some assumptions that although quite reasonable are assumptions nevertheless, and place a commitment to a particular implementation on the two modules involved. The coupling between the two is thus undesirably high and could cause problems in the event of a change to the implementation of the `circular_shifter`. Once again we see that interface design requires considerable thought if inadvertent commitments are not to be placed on the related implementations.

The answer to this problem is to provide an operation, exported by the `cirular_shifter`, that returns the line number corresponding to the circular shift whose number is supplied as its argument. The `sorter` is then not obliged to make any assumptions about the order in which the circular shifts are generated, with a corresponding reduction in the coupling of the modules involved.

6.11 Information Hiding

In view of the quite dramatic improvement in the design of the KWIC Index program that is obtainable by the use of a relatively straightforward data abstraction, Parnas suggests that the technique might usefully form the basis of a design methodology. Essentially, the approach is to identify the large-scale decisions, particularly those concerned with data structures, that must be made in the design of a program and to *hide*, or encapsulate them, using the kind of module structure that has been discussed in previous chapters. This approach, which Parnas (perhaps not originally) called *Information Hiding*, in effect transforms program construction into the identification and assembly of sets of data abstractions. In comparison with the conventional functional decomposition approach, information hiding emphasises the importance, to its modular design, of the data structures of a program rather than of the sequence of actions undertaken when the program is executed. As the case study shows, procedural abstraction, because it ignores the nature of the data that is manipulated by each action in the sequence, tends to lead to wide and complex interfaces with the inevitable implications for implementation and maintenance.

By contrast, information hiding views the interfaces to program modules, which implement data abstractions, as being of primary concern in the design process. The resulting programs then, provided that the necessary attention to interface design that has been illustrated in the case study is exercised, will exhibit the benefits that modular design can achieve.

6.12   Summary

In this Chapter we have considered a design case study that illustrates the potential that the data abstraction possesses for providing the basis of good modular design. The necessity for care in the design of data abstraction interfaces has been discussed, particularly in the context of the design approach termed Information Hiding.

In the next Chapter this question of design methodologies is developed considerably to provide a discussion of *Object-Oriented Design*, on which Parnas' Information Hiding may be seen as a major influence.

Chapter 7

Object-Oriented Design

In the preceding Chapters we have looked at the problems that arise in the construction of large software systems and, it is hoped, the reader will have been convinced both of the desirability of the modular approach and of the utility of the data abstraction in providing the basic architectural unit for this approach. So far, however, the subject has been treated in an analytical way: in other words we have established some criteria that enable us to evaluate the quality of a modular design and have investigated, in some depth, a programming language paradigm that, if used correctly, can ensure that good modular design is achieved.

The significant phrase here of course is 'if used correctly' — perhaps 'imaginatively' would capture the intended meaning better — because the software design process involves more than the analysis of designs: it must also depend on a synthetic, or creative, component that generates the design, which may then be analysed and found to meet the criteria or not. Again, and perhaps obviously, it is not particularly satisfactory to have these criteria and the knowledge of the data abstraction, if they are isolated from the creative component of design. This is perhaps the main criticism of Parnas' attempt to derive a design methodology from the idea of information hiding: to put it crudely, we have got too far down the design track by the time we know what information we want to hide — in other words, information hiding is essentially a desirable quality that a design may exhibit rather than a technique that may be followed from the start.

What we are looking for is a way of guiding the design process, a methodology to use the somewhat pompous terminology, so that it will result in a design that meets the criteria for good modularisation. As an initial step in this search it seems reasonable to examine the well-established conventional design methodologies in the light of this requirement.

7.1   Conventional Methodologies

to implementation domain, The great majority of established design methodologies are based on an analysis of the data flows in the application, leading to the production of a hierarchy of *data flow diagrams*. A data flow diagram, or DFD, is a directed graph in which the nodes represent *processes* that effect *transformations* on the data, linked by arcs that show the data flows between the transformations.

The hierarchy of DFDs is generally created in a top-down fashion. At the highest level the *context* DFD shows the data flows between the system and its environment. Each transformation at the context level is then elaborated, by decomposing it into sub-transformations and internal data flows, into a DFD at the next lower level. This process is continued until the transformations are sufficiently limited in their extent as to be realisable as modules.

As this description suggests, methodologies based on data flow analysis tend to identify modules with data transformations, and it is worthwhile investigating this approach from the point of view of the quality of the modularisation to which it is likely to lead. A data transformation produces one or more output data flows from one or more input data flows. A characteristic transformation is a sort as, for example, in the initial modularisation in Parnas' KWIC Index case study. Modules derived in this way are essentially procedural abstractions — they are very large-scale 'program statements' that carry out the transformations necessary to generate the output data flows from the inputs. As we have seen, such modules tend to exhibit procedural strength. Importantly, in the context of this discussion, any information hiding exhibited by such a modularisation will be either fortuitous, or imposed *after* the modular structure has been defined. Nothing in the technique of data flow analysis assists in the identification of the significant data structures on which the design will depend; such considerations are essentially secondary. The technique cannot, therefore, be expected to arrive at a modularisation in which the idea of encapsulating the data structures is a primary concern. Clearly, then, conventional, DFD-based methodologies are unlikely to satisfy the quest for a technique leading to good modular design.

It is also the case that conventional methodologies possess shortcomings other than those relevant to modular design. The nature of these derives from the longevity of the methodologies (DFD techniques were established well before the end of the 'sixties) and the character of the software design process. By a remarkable coincidence, as we shall see, the approach to avoiding these shortcomings will provide the basis for the discovery of the kind of methodology for which we are searching. The first thing to do, then, is to step back from detailed consideration of particular design techniques and to undertake a brief philosophical enquiry into the nature of the software design process.

7.2 Software Design

The characteristic problem of software engineering centres on the discontinuity, or dissimilarity, between two worlds, or *domains* as they have become known. The term domain has become rather overworked of late. It has a very precise meaning in an area of mathematics called, appropriately enough, *domain theory*, which is certainly relevant to computing but is beyond the scope of this book. In the more informal usage of the term that we are concerned with the essential concept is that a domain is a self-contained fragment of the world, or universe if you take a more cosmic view of things. The idea is used quite often in non-technical contexts. We are all used to reading phrases like 'the world of ********' where the '********' may be anything from 'small-bore rifle shooting' to 'Viennese Opera'. The implication underlying the use of such a phrase is a well-understood set of rules, conventions, terminology and so on. The term domain is roughly equivalent to 'world' as used in 'the world of ...'.

The production of software systems inevitably involves two domains: the *problem domain* and the *implementation domain*. The problem domain is populated by the 'real-world' objects that are significant to the application in question — people, aircraft, inventory items, whatever. The implementation domain is populated by the objects that can be manipulated by the computer on which the system is to run. Or, more precisely, by the objects that are available to the designers and programmers of the system. This distinction is made because it is now (fortunately) rare to find systems writ-

ten in assembler, and so normally the objects of the implementation domain
are the more abstract, less machine-oriented, constructs that can be manipulated by the programming language that is being used in writing the
system. Software design is essentially concerned with modeling the objects
of the application domain using the objects of the implementation domain,
and its characteristic difficulty arises from the dissimilarity between the two
domains noted above.

If the implementation is done using a first-generation programming language
such as FORTRAN or COBOL the gap between the two domains is often
a very large one indeed. FORTRAN, for example, provides only the array
data structure to model the colossal variety of the real world. As arrays
are intrinsically limited to holding elements of one type each, the array is
not a suitable data structure for modelling the multiple attributes that are
so characteristic of real world objects. An aircraft, for example, possesses
numerous attributes that are relevant to the kind of systems that are ever
more common in the operation of air transport. There are attributes that
are unchanging, the manufacturer and type for example, and others that are
dynamic, such as the position of the aircraft during flight. Any program
that is intended to represent, or model, aircraft must be able to associate
the collection of such attributes, which are clearly of different types, in such
a way that they remain associated with an identifiable individual aircraft.
The unfortunate FORTRAN programmer is obliged to declare an array for
each attribute of a class of objects and then to model each object as a 'cross-
section' across these arrays — an object being identified as a particular index
into all of the attribute arrays. The unity of an object modelled in this kind
of way is quite lost in the program structures.

The reader may ask why is this dissimilarity between the two domains important? The answer is that because the objects of the two domains are
often so dissimilar it is almost impossible to recognise the features in the implementation that correspond with those of the problem domain. This gives
rise to a number of characteristic problems. It is the common complaint, for
example, of the customers of software systems that 'it works alright but it
doesn't do what we wanted'. The reason for this is that, as we have seen, in
the process of translating the objects of the problem domain into the quite
different implementation domain, the details of the former became obscured.
The designers, who are experts in computing, not the application after all,
naturally tend to concentrate on the implementation details — the wood
that obscures the problem domain trees. When the discontinuity between

the two domains is great, the analysts — who are supposed to act as the custodians of the functionality of the system on behalf of the customer — often cannot understand in sufficient detail the implementation and so it takes on a life of its own: related to but often quite distinct from the intentions of the original requirements specification. For the same reason maintenance programmers, who were rarely involved in the original design process, have considerable difficulty in correcting bugs or implementing enhancements that are identified or specified in terms of the application.

The principle to be drawn from this is that considerable benefits are to be obtained from the use of program constructs that, as far as possible, reflect or resemble the 'real-world' objects of the problem domain.

The relevance of this discussion to considerations of design methodology is that the conventional methodologies approach the problem of the discontinuity between the problem and application domains by emphasising one — the implementation domain — in order to enable the modelling. One way of characterising DFD-based methodologies is that they require the designer to describe the problem domain in terms of the implementation domain, that is in terms of entities, data flows and transformations, that are easily translated into the entities of a typical first-generation language. This was, of course, quite natural when such languages were all that was available. There have, however, been developments in programming language design in the intervening years that make possible an alternative to this dominance of the implementation domain, with its typical shortcomings arising from the decomposition, and obscuring, of the objects of the problem domain.

7.3 Real World Objects

In order to present an alternative approach to design, one that does support the retention of the problem domain objects in the implementation, it will be useful to consider in more detail the characteristics of what have been up to now referred to merely as 'real-world objects'. Obviously the nature of these objects is, in their full reality, effectively infinitely variegated. The list of computer applications is lengthening daily. As each new application area is addressed a new domain of objects, with their associated concepts, attributes, and network of relationships, must be accommodated by the software. Now it is very clear that the objects of an application domain are represented only by *models* within the relevant application software. Programs cannot *really* contain cars, ships, people, molecules, and so on. Rather, a collection of information sufficient to represent the objects *for the purposes of the application* is required — a model, in other words.

So, the model of an employee adequate for the purposes of a payroll program contains such information as name, rate-of-pay, tax-code, pay-to-date etc. Characteristics of the real human being such as colour of hair, musical ability, political opinions etc., are irrelevant and are therefore excluded from this particular model. On the other hand, a model perhaps of the same person maintained by a police security system might well include these details.

The question then arises as to whether the models of real world objects have a sufficient similarity in order for generalisations to be made about them; in other words, is there a modelling technique that is generally applicable to many different problem domains?

7.3.1   Behaviour

It is clear that these models must be capable of maintaining the association within their respective collections of data over periods of time. It is also clear that a simple passive collection of data is not a very satisfactory general representation of a real-world object.

Consider a program that contains a model of an electrical circuit containing a number of components exhibiting variously resistance, capacitance and inductance. These attributes of the circuit components can certainly be represented by values held in a straightforward array data structure, but the modeling of the response of the circuit to an input waveform requires *computation* — the active evaluation of a set of program statements that must exist in addition to the data structure and access it. Thus an adequate model of the circuit must consist of both passive data and active statements, and these two are logically interdependent in the sense that neither is meaningful without the other.

This requirement for the association of computation with the data values defining the characteristics of an object arises from the fact that in nearly every significant case the objects that are modelled within an application system exhibit *behaviour*, the representation of which is essential if the software models are to be adequate for the purpose. Typical examples of behaviour exhibited by objects are:

- The accumulation week by week of pay-to-date by an employee

- The change in position of an aircraft as it continues in level flight or undertakes a manoevre.

- The change in value of a stock bond as the result of market movements

When we discuss the behaviour of objects it is a very natural to do so in terms of *stimulus* and *response* — how does the object *react* to an externally applied input? This approach is so general as to underlie much of our thought and language about the real (external) world, and the need for an active or computational component in adequate models of real-world objects, that we have discussed above, clearly reflects it. It seems very appropriate, therefore, that the program structures used to model real-world objects should do so in a way that allows them to exhibit behaviour in this kind of stimulus-response way.

In conventional programming languages the closest representation of the stimulus-response pattern is provided by the subprogram call, with its corresponding return, the procedural abstraction of the subprogram encapsulating the computation underlying the response. The basis of object behaviour modelling, therefore, is the provision of subprograms that will provide appropriate responses, in the form of returned data values, to stimuli in the form of calls, possibly with input data values. The nature of the responses of a particular object will be determined by the data associated with it, which generally will be modified as the result of the calls/stimuli made to the object, and from which the returned data will be derived.

By this time the reader is almost certainly prepared for what is about to come, bearing in mind both the title of this book and the content of the earlier chapters: *the program objects that can most appropriately model real-world objects are data abstractions*, because they provide the unified association of the subprograms, which provide behaviour modelling, with the underlying data that determines the individual nature of the object.

Having accepted the viability of this approach from the perspective of the requirements of faithful modelling, we are also guaranteed, because of the properties of the data abstraction, a sound basis for good modular design — two birds with one stone in fact. This duality of beneficial roles for the data abstraction — on the one hand as providing the architectural unit for good modular design, on the other as providing a flexible and powerful program object capable of modelling a huge variety of real-world objects — is one of those inspiring discoveries that comes somewhat rarely in any branch of applied science, and perhaps particularly in software engineering.

7.4   Object-Oriented Design

The foregoing discussion has led to the notion of a Design Methodology based on the use of the Data Abstraction to model the real-world objects of the application domain, an approach that has become known by the term *Object-Oriented Design*. Object-Oriented design presents two beneficial aspects corresponding to the analytic/synthetic split that was referred to at the beginning of this chapter.

- **Analytic** — the end product of the technique is the specification of a collection of data abstractions defined *by their external interfaces*. As we have seen in previous Chapters, this is a prescription for good modular design *provided that the data abstractions are appropriately chosen.*

  This last proviso may strike the reader as the inevitable let-out clause, but of course it is possible to arrive at a collection of data abstractions that include members that are too large — and so whose internal complexity causes design problems within the modular structure. The complementary problem — data abstractions that are too trivial — at the level of a straightforward program variable say, is unlikely to be serious in itself but to be indicative of an unbalanced design that includes over-complex members as well. Clearly the role of an Object-Oriented design methodology is to arrive at a well-balanced, compatible set of data abstractions.

- **Synthetic** — the combination of data and operations that the data abstraction supports provides a far more natural modelling unit than the more traditional methodologies, which fail to support the association between computation and data that is characteristic of faithful models of real-world objects, and thus fail to allow the carrying through of the objects of the problem domain into the implementation domain.

There appear to be clear advantages, therefore, both to the design process and to the resulting program structure, in using Object-Oriented design: a design methodology based on the data abstraction as its main architectural building block.

7.5 The Methodology

In arriving at this conclusion we have hinted fairly strongly at the starting point and the destination of the Object-Oriented methodology.

We start with the problem domain and finally arrive at the specifications of a number of data abstractions. If we are using a language such as Ada the end-product of the design process will be a list of package specifications, some of which will almost certainly declare private or limited private types, so that replicated objects may be modelled. There are a number of stages in this process:

- Identify the Objects of the Problem Domain

- Define the Behaviour of the Objects in terms of Operations associated with them

- Establish the Dependency Relationships between these objects

- Design the Interfaces that the Objects present

The first question that needs to be answered is: how are the objects of the problem domain to be identified so that they may be satisfactorily modelled by an interdependent collection of data abstractions? When the methodology was first introduced this question exercised the Object-Oriented community to a level that might be described as obsessive. Before going on to discuss it in detail the point might be made that the proponents of more conventional design methodologies, typically based on the use of data flow diagrams, never in the experience of the author explain from where the 'processes' and 'data-flows' are derived. They are presumably so obvious as to require no extraction from the requirements specification, but spring fully defined from the brow of the designer. This thought might be kept in mind in the folllowing discussion.

7.5.1 Booch/Abbott

The term 'Object-Oriented Design' is understood, in some communities, to denote quite specifically a methodology devised and popularised by Grady Booch, with at least an initial input from Russell Abbott. Booch's methodology has been presented specifically in the context of the Ada language, although there is no reason why it cannot be applied, with suitable and fairly minor modifications, to other language contexts, certainly including MODULA-2.

The novelty, which relates specifically to the identification of the objects and the elaboration of their behaviour, of Booch's approach is actually revealed by the title of an article written by Abbott in which it was first discussed: *'Program Design by Informal English Descriptions'*, which was published in the Communications of the ACM in 1983. Abbott's article describes a technique whereby the objects of the problem domain, their behaviour and thus the operations associated with them can, it is suggested, be derived from a grammatical analysis of a statement of the *informal strategy* devised to provide the solution of the problem.

The essential nature of the grammatical analysis rests on the idea that *nouns* — 'naming words' — can be used to identify objects. More specifically, common nouns identify types, which may well be Abstract Data Types as we have come to know them. Proper nouns identify single, individual objects, or data abstractions. Verbs and adverbial expressions identify operations.

A more detailed exposition of the methodology is as follows:

- Develop an informal strategy for a solution of the problem. This, according to Abbott, should be 'at the same conceptual level as the problem itself' — in other words it should not attempt to describe an implementation of a program solution, but should be written, in English, using the terms of the problem domain .

- Formalise the strategy by:

  - Identifying the data types — by finding the common nouns in the informal strategy.

  - Identifying the Objects — by finding the proper nouns and direct references.

  - Identifying the operations to be associated with the objects (Booch uses the phrase 'suffered by the objects', which may strike the reader as a more illuminating terminology) — by finding the verbs, adverbs and descriptive expressions.

The descriptions of this analysis included in both Abbott's article and the first edition of Booch's book *Software Engineering with Ada* include examples of its application to several 'informal strategies' which show the nouns and verbs etc. actually underlined in the text. The phrase 'underlining the nouns' seems to have become indissolubly associated with the technique, usually mentioned in a rather disparaging way by its detractors.

It is perhaps the case that both the original article by Abbott and the first edition of Booch's book did something to damage the appealing simplicity of the basic idea by introducing some very fine distinctions into the analysis in order, the suspicion cannot be avoided, to obtain the right answer. In particular, the somewhat metaphysical distinction between *direct references* and *descriptive expressions* is found to possess a very considerable significance when it comes to the resulting program structures. Something of the flavour of the distinction may be gained from the following extract:

> 'If a term refers to something that is already known to exist, and the term is simply a way to refer to that known thing, then it is considered a direct reference and is associated with an object.
>
> If the term describes a possible object whose identity (and possibly even whose existence) must be determined by some computation — no matter how simple the computation — then the term is a descriptive expression and is associated with the operator that performs that operation.'

Apart from this rather unconvincing stretching of the basic idea the original version of Object-Oriented design seems limited to 'problems' whose solutions are individual algorithms. The examples given: the determination of the number of days between two given dates, even the KWIC index problem, are typically single algorithm problems. The technique has been criticised therefore, for example in Nielson and Shumate [2], as being unsuitable for the design of large systems in which there are many algorithms and where the technique would simply be too time-consuming and unwieldy if applied to the complete 'informal strategy', or design specification, of the system.

The critics of Object-Oriented Design have mainly, by accident or (possibly) by design, failed to notice that Booch has considerably modified the technique both in the second edition of his first book, and also the more recent *Software Components with Ada*. In the latter particularly, the intricate grammatical analysis has been abandoned in favour of a straightforward 'examination of the problem domain', with whatever assistance might come to hand, including the identification of nouns and verbs in the specification, but also conventional data-flow diagrams of the system. In fact, the important feature of Object-Oriented design, *a la* Booch, is not the 'underlining the nouns' technique but the subsequent treatment of the problem space objects, no matter how they are identified.

With the benefit of hindsight we can perhaps see that the 'underlining the nouns' technique was something of a red herring that has tended to obscure the quite real advantages of the Object-Oriented design methodology. The technique was invoked to solve the problem of 'finding the objects' — a problem that is certainly not trivial but which is mainly susceptible to an intelligent and flexible insight on the part of the designer.

At this stage the author would like to introduce an alternative to the Abbott/Booch technique for identifying, and characterising, the objects of the problem domain. Little originality is claimed for the technique: it is closely related to the grammatical analysis technique but requires neither a deep knowledge of English grammar nor any of the rather unconvincing subtleties that this technique appears to require.

7.6   Object Discovery by Prototyping

Essentially the technique is based on a crude, and incomplete, form of prototyping. As we know the aim of Object-Oriented design is to arrive at the specification of a collection of data abstractions that will, when provided with a relatively small amount of 'glue' in the form of a 'main program', work together to form the complete software system.

The concepts of information hiding and so forth that are now so familiar must mean that the main program will consist of calls to the operations of the data abstractions of the system embedded within some appropriate control structure. This, we might reasonably expect, will be composed from the 'classical' control structures of *structured programming*, so as to obtain the quite real advantages of clarity that flow from this discipline.

By its nature, if the design process has been successful, the main program should be both brief and self-documenting: this will not be so if the interfaces are ill-designed either individually or in their interdependencies. The technique, then, is simply to sketch, using either the intended language or an appropriate pseudo-code, the main program *before all the data abstractions have been specified*. The suggestion in the last sentence (*all the data ..*) derives from the almost invariable fact that there will be some very obvious objects, with their corresponding data abstractions. There are, for example, very few systems that do not support both a user interface and some form of permanent data storage. Both of these entities are prime candidates for establishing as objects of the design, to be implemented as data abstractions.

It may be noticed that these 'obvious' objects are not, directly, models of application objects. The desirable characteristic of Object-Oriented design, that it provides for the carrying through of the application objects into the,implementation domain does not require that *all* the implementation domain objects are models of application domain objects. The `line_storage` module in Parnas' solution to the KWIC Index problem does not obviously model anything in the problem domain . The important thing is that the significant application objects should be visible within the implementation; additional non-implementation objects may well be required: our exemplary stacks and queues being common examples. One criticism of the Booch/Abbott approach is that it tends to ignore the existence of these kinds of objects.

Other 'obvious objects' are very much more application dependent, but require little effort to identify them. It is in the discovery of the best of several alternative object sets, and particularly in the design of the individual interfaces, that the technique is useful.

Before going on to consider examples of its application it may be of interest to compare it with the Abbott/Booch technique. Instead of using an 'informal English' description of the solution to the problem, the prototyping technique works from a semi-formal solution — the formality being derived from the use of the features, control-structures, subprogram call and so on, of the implementation language. There is no requirement to identify the 'operations suffered by the objects' because, of course, the program sketch is largely written in terms of them. What *is* required is the association of particular operations with a particular data abstraction. This, however, tends to be strongly suggested by the logical structure of the program. We are essentially doing the same thing as in the Abbott/Booch method but in a way that is more direct and, it is believed, more natural to the typical programmer. The 'informal strategy' is still used, but in order to produce the semi-formal program sketch. It is also the case that some other form of initial description, system flow-charts say, may be used. Rather than identifying the objects and their operations directly from the informal description, their required external behaviour can be deduced from the program unit in which it is apparent. The process of working from the nouns and verbs

is transmuted into one informed by the program structures derived from a
specification.

Booch gives as an example the problem of counting the leaves of a binary
tree. The informal strategy is given as follows:

> Keep a pile of the parts of the tree that have not yet been
> counted. Initially, get a tree and put it on the empty pile; the
> count of the leaves is initially set to zero. As long as the pile is
> not empty, repeatedly take a tree off the pile and examine it. If
> the tree consists of a single leaf, then increment the leaf counter
> and throw away that tree. If the tree is not a single leaf but
> instead consists of two subtrees, split the tree into its left and
> right subtrees and put them back on the pile. Once the pile is
> empty, display the count of the leaves.

The basic form of the algorithm suggested by this description is a simple
loop. The number of iterations of the loop is determined by the (initially
unknown) number of subtrees, and so a condition-controlled, rather than
a count-controlled, loop is appropriate. The 'program' may be sketched as
follows:

```
add_to_pile(get_tree_from_somewhere);
leaf_counter := 0;
while   not_empty(pile)
loop
    current_tree := next_tree_from_pile;
    if is_a_leaf(current_tree)
    then  leaf_counter := leaf_counter + 1;
    else
        add_to_pile(left_subtree_of(current_tree));
        add_to_pile(right_subtree_of(current_tree));
    end if;
end loop;
display(leaf_counter);
```

The reader may well object that this is hardly distinguishable from the initial
stage of a process of design by functional decomposition, simply rendering
into pseudo-code a straightforward algorithm. In fact this is the case — the
difference being at the next stage. In functional decomposition the next stage
would be to take the various 'high-level' operations such as add_to_pile and

decompose them into more implementation-oriented lower-level operations. In Object-Oriented design, the objects/data abstractions are defined by examining the required operations. If we list the operations:

- **get_tree_from_environment**

  – the informal description is very vague on this point — we simply assume a function that returns a tree (object), as a rather specialised *initialise* operation.

- **add_to_pile**

  – inserts a tree object into the pile

- **next_tree_from_pile**

  – returns a tree. The implication is that the read-out must be destructive — not simply a copy, so that once removed a tree cannot be re-read. It is the equivalent of a stack 'pop' operation but provided for the pile. Note that the requirement to 'throw away' trees is satisfied by this property of a `pile` operation, rather than an operation suffered by `tree`.

- **is_empty_pile**

  – a boolean operation on the pile.

- **is_leaf**

  – a boolean operation on a tree

- **left_subtree, right_subtree**

  – operations respectively returning the left and right subtree of a tree argument.

- **display**

  – an operation exported by the user interface object. As the values to be displayed will be positive integers there is little further analysis required.

It takes very little analysis to identify two major objects: `pile` and `tree`. The two are entirely distinct. `pile` is a single, unique object that is essentially a 'store and yield' object, with its only slightly unusual feature being the 'destructive' nature of the 'yield' or 'pop' operation.

`tree` on the other hand is indefinitely replicated. Also the fact that the operations on each tree are subject to a condition test by the main program means that a tree object must exist, in the sense of the value of a declared variable, in the main program — so that it can be tested and then, if it is not a leaf, split. These requirements dictate that `tree` must be an abstract data type in the slightly specialised sense that we have found it convenient to employ — i.e. a limited private type in the Ada context.

Staying with Ada, we can now define, or formalise to use Booch's terminology, the interfaces of these objects. First it is necessary to determine the dependency relationship between them, in other words, to decide on the visibility of one from the other. This is an issue that can become tricky — to the level of pathologically circular dependencies, However, in this case it is fairly clear that the `pile` object must be dependent on the `tree` abstract data type: the operations associated with the `pile`, such as `add_to_pile`, have parameters that must be of type `tree`, which is obviously exported from a package 'withed' by the package that realises the `pile` data abstraction. The package specifications are shown in Figure 7.1. In realistically large systems the relationships between the objects will often be too deep to permit the establishing of all their interfaces simply by considering the 'main program'. Invariably, not all objects are actually visible in the main program. The technique can still be employed, however, by considering the subprograms that implement the operations of a 'high-level' object, or abstract data type, by using the operations of 'lower-level' objects, as 'main programs' for the purpose of defining the lower-level interfaces. The process is analogous to top-down refinement, but will typically involve far fewer levels.

7.6.1   Objects as Agents of Behaviour

The prototyping approach described in the last section may be seen as an example of a general approach to Object-Oriented design, which reverses the order 'identify the objects' then 'identify the operations associated with the objects'. Instead, operations, in the sense of behaviour to be exhibited by the system, are identified by consideration of the application and then objects are identified as the agents performing the behaviour — 'suffering the operations'. The two approaches are by no means mutually exclusive and may be used together, in accordance with the general recommendation to flexibility on the part of the designer.

```
package trees is
----
-- A package exporting an abstract data type that provides the
-- semantics of the binary tree for objects of the type.
--
        type TREE is limited private;
        function GET_TREE_FROM_ENVIRONMENT return TREE;
        --
        procedure ADD_ITEM_TO(T : in out TREE; E: ELEMENT);
        --
        function IS_LEAF(T : TREE) return BOOLEAN;
        --
        function LEFT_SUBTREE_OF(T: TREE) return TREE;
        function RIGHT_SUBTREE_OF(T : TREE) return TREE;
private
        type TREE_STRUCTURE;
        type TREE is access TREE_STRUCTURE;
end trees;

package pile is
--
        procedure INITIALISE_PILE;
        --
        procedure ADD_TREE_TO PILE(T : TREE);
        function NEXT_TREE_FROM_PILE return TREE;
        function PILE_IS_EMPTY return BOOLEAN;
end pile;
```

Figure 7.1: Package Specifications Defining Objects for the Leaf-counting
Problem

7.7   A Final View

The foregoing discussion of the specific problem of finding the objects on which to base an object-oriented design has perhaps obscured the fundamental principles of the methodology. The essential idea of Object-Oriented design is to produce a program structure in which the objects of the implementation domain are modelled by data abstractions. The methodology that is intended to achieve this objective can be broadly defined as follows:

1. **Define the Problem Domain** — this may well be done by an informal or semi-formal requirement specification.

2. **Identify the Objects of the Problem Domain** — by using a combination of techniques, which may include:

   - defining 'obvious' objects such as the user (interface) and persistent data structures (such as `line_storage` in Parnas' KWIC Index program)

   - inspection of the requirements specification, either simply based on an intelligent perception of the application or an approach, to some level, of the Booch type of grammatical analysis.

   - determining the 'Agents' of the behaviour to be exhibited by the system, again as defined by the requirements specification. Using this approach, Step 3 precedes step 2.

3. **Identify the Operations Associated with the Objects** — by familiarity with the application and the intended behaviour of the system, by prototyping or by grammatical analysis.

4. **Determine the Visibility between the Objects** — so that the dependency relationships between them, as defined by context or import clauses, can be established.

5. **Formalise the Interfaces of the Objects** — by determining whether they possess a unique status within the application, or are replicated. Then by specifying the interfaces using an appropriate language such as Ada or MODULA-2.

6. **Design the Implementations of the Objects** — no particular technique is recommended, because of the generally subordinate importance, from the design point-of-view, of the implementation details.

The essential aim of Object-Oriented design is to produce software system designs that simultaneously:

- Meet the criteria for good modular design — low coupling and high cohesion.

- Provide well-defined, easily-identifiable models of the objects of the application domain, as objects of the implementation domain.

Both these characteristics have beneficial effects on the subsequent stages of the software life cycle, particularly on maintenance.

7.8 Inheritance

In this discussion we have referred a number of times to relationships between objects or abstract data types. It is clear that in many application domains the objects will exhibit 'family resemblances'. The valves controlling the flow of chemicals in a plant, for example, may well have a common set of operations including `open`, `close`, `report_position` etc. Some will possess more specialised characteristics, such as `set_to_default`, `set_percent_open` etc., and it seems natural to reflect this kind of general/special relationship in the corresponding design.

So compelling is the naturalness of this approach, in fact, that many exponents of Object-Oriented design regard the recognition of this kind of relationship between objects, generally called *inheritance*, as being fundamental to the whole Object-Oriented philosophy. From the point of view of inheritance, any object in an application domain is seen as a specialisation of some higher-level, more abstract object. The only exception to this rule is the most abstract level possible, an abstract data type often called 'object', which provides the most general characteristics shared by all objects. (The proponents of inheritance point to the ubiquitous nature of *classification* in human thought, citing, for example, the taxonomies of botany and zoology, as the basis of the power of the technique. It should be pointed out that this view is not universally held. It is not clear, to the author at least, and using a somewhat extreme example, to see how an auto-pilot system may be characterised as a specialisation of some more general system.)

When inheritance is included in the Object-Oriented design picture, the process of identifying objects and their characteristics becomes subtly changed.

The process becomes not so much one of *identification* but of *recognition* — to find characteristics that are largely exhibited by an existing object, and then to define the specialisation necessary to characterise the object in question.

To give an example: let us consider a system concerned with cars: perhaps a car-hire management system. The 'family resemblance ' of cars — their common attributes and operations — include items such as maker's name, engine size, accumulated mileage and so on. If we assume that an abstract data type exporting this set of operations is already in existence, then the creation of more specialised cars — limousines, estate cars, sports cars — can be seen as a matter of adding alternative sets of additional characteristics in the form of operations to the general, parent car type. A tree-structure of relationships growing from a general root to specialised leaves can easily be envisaged.

When we go back up the tree, again it is not difficult to move from the generalised car to vehicle, to artefact and, eventually, to the ultimate, abstract object.

7.8.1   Inheritance in MODULA-2 and Ada

In view of the apparent power and generality of the use of inheritance in Object-Oriented design it is natural to consider the extent to which the languages that have been highlighted because of their support for data abstraction — MODULA-2 and Ada — can accommodate the technique.

When we translate the concept of inheritance into, say, MODULA-2, then continuing with the example of cars, the pattern would require a high-level, 'parent' library module that exports an opaque type `Car`, together with a collection of more specialised modules exporting types for `EstateCar` and so on.

The parent and a specialised 'child' module might appear as shown in Figure 7.2. The way in which inheritance should work is that all the operations that are provided for the parent, `Car` in this case, are also available to a child, such as `EstateCar`, in addition to its specialised operations. So that a variable representing an estate car, declared as being of type `EstateCar` could be supplied as the actual parameter for a procedure exported from module `Cars`, of type `Car`.

This kind of arrangement would allow for the following:

```
DEFINITION MODULE Cars

   TYPE Car;


   PROCEDURE SetMaker(VAR C : Car; Name : ARRAY OF CHAR);
             (* Specify Maker's name *)

   PROCEDURE SetEngineSize(VAR C : Car; size: CARDINAL);
             (* Specify Engine Size *)

             (*       *        *         *)

   PROCEDURE AddMileage(VAR C: Car; miles : CARDINAL);
              (* Increment recorded mileage for car *)

   PROCEDURE Mileage(C : Car) : CARDINAL;
              (* Return current recorded mileage *)
END Cars.


DEFINITION MODULE EstateCars;

   FROM Cars IMPORT SetMaker, SetEngineSize, AddMileage,
             (* etc. *)

   TYPE EstateCar;

   PROCEDURE Create(VAR E : EstateCar);
   (* Create a new estate car object *)

   PROCEDURE SetLuggageSpace(VAR E : EstateCar;
                             Space : CARDINAL);
      (* Specify luggage space in cu. feet *)

                 *        *        *        *

   PROCEDURE IsDiesel(E : EstateCar) : BOOLEAN;
        (* returns TRUE if diesel powered *)
END EstateCars.
```

Figure 7.2: Module Definitions for Attempted Inheritance

```
VAR NewCar : EstateCar;
BEGIN
        Create(NewCar);
        SetMaker(NewCar,'Mercedes');
    *       *       *       *
```

Unfortunately the rules of MODULA-2 would not permit this fragment to compile, because `SetMaker` can be used only with variables of type `Car`, and thus not with `EstateCar`. The importation of the operations for `Car` does not extend their applicability to `EstateCar`, and there is no mechanism in MODULA-2 for this kind of extension. This is a direct consequence of the combination of MODULA-2's strong typing , and the encapsulation imposed by the MODULE structure. The former dictates that a subprogram parameter may possess one type only; the latter that the implementation of an applicable operation for an opaque type must be entirely contained within one IMPLEMENTATION MODULE. There is thus no possibility of extending the operations for a type in another module.

We are left with the inescapable conclusion that inheritance cannot be supported directly by MODULA-2. The same is true for Ada, for essentially the same reasons. This conclusion is enough to persuade a large segment of the Object-Oriented community, for whom inheritance is a *sine qua non*, that neither of these languages can be considered to be an Object-Oriented language, despite their strong support for data abstraction. Nevertheless, inheritance may still be used as a design aid in conjunction with MODULA-2 or Ada written systems, particularly in the investigation of the problem space. Languages that directly support inheritance will be considered in Chapters 10 and 11.

7.9   Summary

In this Chapter we have discovered the relevance of the Data Abstraction to the synthetic component of software design, and discussed the methodology that recognises this relevance — Object-Oriented design. A particular approach to this methodology, that associated with Abbott and Booch, has been investigated and placed in the larger context of a less-specific technique. Finally, we have introduced the concept of inheritance and noted the limitations with which our established language exemplars, MODULA-2 and Ada, can deal with this concept.

Chapter 8

Reusability

8.1   Introduction

At a conference on software engineering some years ago, one of the wittier participants delivered himself of the following:

> "In software engineering we should stand on the shoulders of those who have gone before us. In fact we stand on their feet"

This sums up rather well the very general and regrettable tendency for the wheel to be reinvented constantly in software engineering. Rare indeed is the software product that is not written 'from the ground up', with virtually every module actually designed and written by the project team, from the high, application-specific level to the low, general routine level, which contains much that is common to many applications. Normally, little attempt is made to exploit existing software 'off the shelf'.

This is perhaps a slightly black picture. Every user of a high-level language unavoidably reuses software in the form of the input/output facilities, which may be built into the language or provided as separate,standard libraries as in C or Ada. (The author is tempted to add 'separate non-standard libraries as in MODULA-2', but this situation is improving.) On a more significant level from considerations of functionality, a few areas have developed a strong dependence on reusable software. The notable example of this is in computer graphics, where libraries such as GINO-F and the various language 'bindings' of the Graphical Kernel System have achieved wide penetration — within a relatively small volume of actual use, however. Even here though the reused software is normally essentially peripheral in nature, excluded from the central core of the application, and this seems typical of reuse in general.

8.1.1   Component Software

In the context of this kind of discussion software engineering is often compared unfavourably with electronic systems engineering. The electronic system designer charged with the design of, say, a radar transmitter does not either begin or end the process by designing the resistors or even transistors that form the 'atomic' components of the design. Instead, the design is expressed in terms of components that are 'one level down' in complexity from the transmitter itself: amplifiers, modulators and so on. Typically these components are not only not designed by our designer but they are, in many cases, not produced by the manufacturer for which he or she works. These components are supplied with well-defined interfaces and functionality, catalogued in sufficient completeness to allow their incorporation in a design still at the 'paper' stage.

Design, in this environment, is therefore largely a matter of devising the best collection of components, from those available, to satisfy constraints such as price and performance. As such, in being concentrated at one level of abstraction, it is intrinsically simpler than the 'deep structure' characteristic of software products, with a correspondingly higher chance of being successfully carried out.

This is, of course, a picture seen through the rose-tinted spectacles of the software engineer. In practice electronic components frequently react in unpredictable and awkward ways when connected into assemblies, and much of the time of the designer is occupied in solving the resulting problems. The picture does contain a good deal of truth, however, certainly sufficient to provide a model or ideal towards which software engineering might well aspire. The question then arises as to whether software can be 'componentised' so as to achieve, or at least approach, this ideal. Clearly there are some stringent criteria involved, and it is to the consideration of these that we now turn.

8.2 Criteria for Reusability

The component software idea is obviously dependent on a basic level of compatibility. The traditional absence of reuse in software engineering stemmed not from any absence of motivation, but from an absence of the minimal technological support required. The multiplicity of machine architectures, operating systems, language dialects, character codes and so on, made the transfer of any significant piece of software between different platforms, to use the current jargon, a difficult business. This picture has changed radically as a result of the ever-widening use of portable operating systems, of which Unix provides the most important example, based on a 32-bit architecture. The introduction of languages with very strongly enforced standardisation, such as Ada, has also tended to enable the transferability of software.

Given that the minimal technological support for component software is now widely available, what characteristics should software items possess to make them likely candidates for reuse?

8.2.1 Negative Criteria

The first criteria that must be met are negative in the sense that the absence of the qualities to which they relate guarantees *non* reusability. These are *correctness* and *efficiency*. Clearly no item of software will be even considered as a candidate for reuse either if it is full of bugs, or if it is too large, too slow or both.

Mention of correctness immediately raises the question of specification, for the assertion of the correctness of a software item is meaningless in the absence of its specification. This is an area of considerable importance in the context of reusable software, to which we shall return shortly.

8.2.2 Functionality

Turning to criteria related to qualities that positively support reuse, the most obviously important concerns functionality. A software item is more likely to be reused the more it exhibits a functionality that is applicable in many contexts, performing some useful and significant task common to many applications.

There are the makings of a contradiction here: *useful* and *significant* are highly subjective terms, but it is clear that in each application they will be relative *to the purposes of the specific application.* This would seem to conflict with the next criterion.

8.2.3   Independence

A software item will be reusable only if it is sufficiently free of any bias towards a particular application. 'Sufficiently' in this context is relatively easy to define: the reuse of a software item should not require the distortion of its new environment so that it simulates the characteristics of the environment in which the item was first developed.

Reusable items are therefore required to be significant contributors to every application within which they are employed, while remaining independent of each of them — a difficult balancing feat.

8.2.4   Robustness

A further important requirement is that the item should be *robust* — i.e. that it should be capable of being transplanted to many different environments without compromise to its correct and efficient operation. The designer of such an item must be able to control completely the way in which external units interact with it. Robustness is the syntactic complement to the semantic criterion of independence and must be present to underpin the latter.

8.2.5   Fail Safety

The 'Contract Model' is often invoked in the context of reusable software. The idea is of a (normally unwritten) contract between the users of a software item and its implementor, with the implication that both parties incur responsibility for its successful use. (Use here means incorporation into a system.) The users agree to abide by the requirements of the public interface, in return for which the implementor guarantees the correct operation of the software.

This agreeable analogy is rarely extended to the inclusion of penalty clauses: what can the user expect if the requirements of the interface are not complied with? The usual answer is probably chaos, but this is hardly satisfactory.

The user of a reusable item should be protected from the results of his or her folly as far as possible, with a policy of damage limitation constantly observed by the designer.

A *Fail Safe* design in software terms means something rather different from that employed in other areas of technology. The major requirement is that the user must never be left in ignorance of the fact that something has gone wrong. A 'helpful' software component that tries to compensate for its misuse is highly dangerous: if misuse does occur then the (mis)user must be informed, preferably in a way that cannot be ignored.

8.3 Data Abstraction: the Basis for Reusability

The list of criteria given above point inexorably towards a particular kind of software construct as being the most suitable vehicle for reuse. The requirement for significant functionality suggests that subprograms are unlikely to be adequate in the general case, because of their inability, in most languages, to maintain an internal state over several invocations. Robustness can be guaranteed only by encapsulation — which can be provided only by subprograms or, it can finally be revealed, the data abstraction. The separation of interface from implementation detail, and the hiding of the latter, makes the data abstraction the natural form for reusable software components. This is not to say, of course, that all the criteria mentioned will be satisfied by adopting this approach — the conflict between application-specific significance and independence mentioned above is still a major problem, for example.

8.4 Genericity

A major contribution towards the solution of this problem arises from the possibility of *parameterising* some of the types involved in the interface of a software component. This possibility comes about where the characteristics of the types concerned are either irrelevant, or need be recognised to only a very limited extent. An example of the first kind is provided by our old friend the stack. The type of the items pushed into a stack is quite irrelevant to the operations of the stack, which require only the ability to assign the items to and from the internal data structure. The items are treated as black boxes, with no operational interface whatsoever.

A more interesting example, of the second possibility, is provided by a sort routine. Again the items to be sorted are treated as black boxes with no discernible features, other than sufficient individuality to permit an *ordering relation* to be determined between them. In other words, the possibility of sorting is dependent on the possibility of deciding that one item is, in some sense, less than another. Apart from this, no sorting algorithm requires any further access to the internal details of the items that it is to sort.

The natural implication of this is that it should be possible to take advantage of the irrelevance of the types of the items involved in these two examples by constructing, for example, a *generic* stack abstract data type capable of accepting any item type. (The term generic means 'applicable to a whole class or group'.) This possibility would have obvious benefits for reusability in freeing a component from inessential detail deriving from a specific application, and can be recognised as another way of raising the level of abstraction.

8.4.1   Problems of Strong Typing

In a strongly-typed language like Pascal, however, this kind of 'type blindness' cannot be permitted — every subprogram parameter must possess a type, and the types of the parameters of a subprogram are part of its declaration: change a parameter type and a different subprogram is defined.

This has the unfortunate result that routines must be replicated if they are to accommodate different types, even if these are completely irrelevant to the operations involved. It also prejudices the reusability of the software components concerned because of the complete lack of flexibility involved. An application that required the use of a stack holding, say, pointers, would not be able to use a stack declared for unsigned integer items, despite the probable similarity of the sets of values involved.

It would appear then that what is required is the ability to declare parameters as having no type at all, or 'don't care'. This approach can be adopted by a user of MODULA-2, which provides a type **WORD** that, when used to declare a formal parameter, allows substitution for it by an actual parameter with any type that occupies one word of memory. The specific size of a word is not defined in the language but is dependent on the implementation. Typically, a word will be of a 16 or 32-bit extent and capable of holding INTEGERs, CARDINALs and, again depending on the implementation, BOOLEANs.

The applicability of this feature is greatly extended by using type WORD in conjunction with the MODULA-2 *open array* type constructor, which permits the declaration of one-dimensional array formal parameters with unspecified index ranges — itself a form of genericity.

Such a parameter may be declared, for example, as being of type ARRAY OF INTEGER. This means that any one-dimensional array with INTEGER components may be substituted for it. The procedure to which the formal parameter belongs is able to determine the last, or highest, index value by the inquiry routine HIGH; the lowest index value of an open array is always 0.

An open array with components of WORD is obviously more non-specific still, and this generality is increased by the fact that a parameter declared to be ARRAY OF WORD is not even constrained to be substituted by an array, and so actual parameters of any type may be used. ARRAY OF WORD, therefore, fits more or less exactly the idea of a 'don't care' type.

It must be pointed out, however, that this feature of MODULA-2 is *not* provided to allow the recognition of the irrelevance of the types of some of the parameters to certain software components. It is provided to allow the language to be used as a systems programming language, for example in writing operating systems, where the constraints of strong typing are sometimes inconvenient. The feature is specifically included to provide a well-defined breach in the iron-clad defences of strong-typing, to be used only in the direst circumstances and with the responsibility for any ensuing disaster placed firmly on the head of the foolhardy programmer concerned. As can be seen, this is certainly not an appropriate basis for constructing highly reliable software components whose use in any hands can be safely guaranteed. The sort of abuse that might be perpetrated can be illustrated as follows, given a definition module for a queue:

```
DEFINITION MODULE QUEUE;

    TYPE Queue;

    PROCEDURE Initialise (VAR Q : Queue);

    PROCEDURE EnQueue (Q : Queue; Item : ARRAY OF WORD);

    PROCEDURE DeQueue (Q : Queue; VAR Item : ARRAY OF WORD);
```

```
        PROCEDURE IsEmpty (Q : Queue) : BOOLEAN;

    END QUEUE.
```

Then the following program fragment would incur no protest from the compiler:

```
        VAR     Rec : RECORD
                        IntVal : INTEGER;
                        FloVal : REAL
                     END;
                INTVAL : INTEGER;
                RecsQ  : Queue;
        BEGIN
                Rec.IntVal := 10;
                Rec.FloVal := 1.0;
                Initialise(RecsQ);
                EnQueue(RecsQ,Rec);

                *       *       *

                DeQueue(RecsQ,INTVAL);
```

with probable catastrophic results at run time caused by the overwriting of the memory area following that allocated to INTVAL by the additional extent of Rec.

Clearly, then, simply permitting 'don't care' types is not adequate — the compiler needs to 'care' enough to prevent the kind of situation sketched above. The minimal requirement would seem the ability to check that *the same* type is involved in logically related cases such as EnQueue and DeQueue, even though other characteristics may be ignored. Such an ability is provided by the Ada *Generic* facility.

8.4.2   Generics in Ada

As part of its design aim to support component software, Ada provides the means for writing certain program units, specifically subprograms and packages, as *Templates* with parameters which are normally types. These templates may not be compiled into executable code but must be *instantiated*, with actual parameters 'plugged into' them in order to produce normal program units. To give a (the!) simple example, a generic routine to swap over

```
generic
type ANY_TYPE is private;
procedure GEN_SWAP ( LEFT,RIGHT : in out ANY_TYPE );
procedure GEN_SWAP ( LEFT,RIGHT : in out ANY_TYPE ) is
TEMP : ANY_TYPE;
begin
        TEMP := LEFT;
        LEFT := RIGHT;
        RIGHT:= TEMP;
end GEN_SWAP;
```

Figure 8.1: A Generic Swap Procedure

its two parameters looks as shown in Figure 8.1. The body of the generic
procedure is preceded by the reserved word **generic**, the generic formal parameter type **ANY_TYPE** and its *specification*, which has the same form as in
a package specification and consists of its name and parameter list, terminated by a semi-colon. There is no need for the body to follow immediately
the *generic specification*: it may appear anywhere in a declarative region
within the scope of the specification and indeed in some circumstances it
is necessary for the two to be separated, hence the need for the apparent
duplication.

This generic template could then be instantiated with, say, integer and character, to produce procedures for swapping parameters of the nominated type;
indeed, it could be instantiated with *generic actual* parameters of *any* type:
this is the implication of the *generic formal* declaration **private**. Note the
plurality of the word procedures in the last sentence — one ordinary unit is
produced for every instantiation of a generic; it is *not* like the MODULA-2
pattern where one unit can handle any kind of parameter type.

Although any type may be substituted for **ANY_TYPE**, the fact that it defines
the type of both of the parameters of the procedure, and of the type of
the local variable **temp**, means that the compiler can check that *the same*
'any type' is used in each particular case. The use of generics involves no
breach in strong typing, therefore, and so the facility can be used to provide
software components with all the protection that strong typing affords.

The swap generic might be instantiated as follows:

```
procedure INT_SWAP is new GEN_SWAP(integer);
```

```
procedure CHAR_SWAP is new GEN_SWAP(character);
```

with the generic actual parameter in parentheses after the name of the
generic. The instantiations appear in a declarative region and have the
same significance as an ordinary procedure specification and can be used to
swap, respectively, integer and character variables.

The generic facility is essentially a *compile-time* mechanism — generic program units must be instantiated with the actual parameters required before
they can be compiled into run-time units. There are thus, typically, two sets
of parameters associated with a generic unit such as GEN_SWAP:

- **The Generic Parameters** that are substituted at compile time to
  produce a normal unit.

- **The Run-time Parameters** that are substituted when the instantiated unit is invoked at run-time, in exactly the same way as for an
  ordinary unit.

The instantiations of a generic unit are indistinguishable from an ordinary
unit as far as the final stage of compilation is concerned. The generic facility
is, therefore, essentially a text substitution mechanism confined completely
to the source program.

The generic mechanism can be used to define a template for a package also;
the Ada equivalent of the QUEUES module is shown in Figure 8.2. The
corresponding package body is written in the same way as for a normal, non-
generic package, using the generic formal parameter **Item** where appropriate.

Exceptions

The declaration of QUEUE_UNDERFLOW as apparently a variable of type
exception is, in fact, an illustration of Ada's *exception mechanism*, which
provides for the kind of fail-safety mentioned earlier. The exception mechanism is not restricted to generic program units, but a brief description seems
appropriate at this point.

An exception is associated with an error condition that is detected either by
the run-time system, such as overflow or exhaustion of memory, or by tests
written into the program. When such an error condition occurs an exception
is *raised*, automatically in the case of a system-detected condition, or explicitly by a **raise** statement in the case of a program-detected condition. Once

```
generic
      type Item is private;
package Queues is
--
      type Queue is limited private;
--
      procedure initialise(Q : in out queue);
      procedure enqueue(I : Item; Q : queue);
      procedure dequeue(I : out Item; Q : queue);
      function is_empty(Q : queue) return boolean;
--
      QUEUE_UNDERFLOW : exception;
private
      type queue_struct;
      type queue is access queue_struct;
end Queues;
```

Figure 8.2: A Generic Queues Package Specification

an exception is raised the normal execution of the program is disrupted —
thus providing the means whereby the user of a component may be 'not left
in ignorance' that an error has occurred.

The exception mechanism provides a means whereby an exception may be
trapped, or *handled*, allowing the execution of the program to continue,
presumably after some corrective action has been taken. But the writer
of a component can ensure that this error handling must be provided by
the external user simply by failing to incorporate it within the component.
Exceptions declared in the specification of a package, like QUEUE_OVERFLOW,
which is raised on an attempt to dequeue an item from an empty queue, will
invariably be intended for this purpose. Such an exception is intended to be
exported to external units and is not, therefore, handled internally.

Constrained Genericity

In the Queues example there is no problem in allowing for any type of parameter to be substituted. In some contexts, though, such freedom could
lead to incompatibilities that the compiler could not accept. A good example is a generic formal parameter that is to be the index type of an array.

Ada permits only discrete types to be used for indexing arrays, in common
with all structured languages. It would not, therefore, be appropriate for the
declaration for such a generic formal parameter to specify `private`, meaning
'any type'. Instead Ada provides the means for constraining generic parameters so that the range of possible actual parameters falls within a particular
class. The declaration of a generic formal parameter that may be substituted
only by a discrete type takes the form of the following example:

```
type INDEX_TYPE is (<>);
```

Such a parameter could then be used as part of the declaration of an array
formal generic parameter, as follows:

```
         type INDEX_TYPE is (<>);
         type ELEMENT is private;
type GEN_VECTOR is array(INDEX_TYPE) of ELEMENT;
```

GEN_VECTOR is thereby declared as a generic formal that may be substituted
by any one-dimensional array type with any component type and indexed
by any discrete type — the most abstract form of such an array.

8.4.3   Operation Parameters

In the previous discussion that led up to the idea of genericity the example
of a sort routine was mentioned. It was suggested that a sort needs rather
more than the ability to distinguish the identity of different objects — in
particular it needs to be able to *order* objects of the type that it manipulates:
to determine for each pair of objects in the set submitted to it which is the
largest, in some sense. In the case of a generic sort procedure there is an
obvious problem — if the objects that it is to sort are of a parameterised
type that has the formal declaration `private`, meaning 'any type', how can
it determine an ordering over them, in ignorance of the type that is used
as the actual parameter in each instantiation ? It is not even possible to
determine whether such an ordering is defined.

In order to overcome this problem Ada allows for the specification of generic
parameters that are *operations* — subprograms, in Ada terminology — to
permit such attributes as an ordering relationship to be parameterised. In
other words, a generic parameter may be supplied with its own version of
the "<" operator: defined with itself as the operand type. Ada allows an

```
generic
   type ELEMENT is private;
   type INDEX is (<>);
   type GEN_VECTOR is array(INDEX) of ELEMENT;
   with function "<" (LEFT,RIGHT : ELEMENT) return boolean;
procedure GEN_SORT(VECTOR : in out GEN_VECTOR);
```

Figure 8.3: Generic Specification for a Sort Routine

operator such as "<" to be *overloaded*, that is given an additional meaning
in terms of its operand types. (Virtually all languages provide overloading
for some operators. For example, Pascal overloads the "<" operator in that
it may be used to compare both integer and real operands — despite the
fact that the underlying operations are quite different. Ada's overloading
feature extends this idea by allowing *user-defined* overloadings of the arithmetic and logical operators.) Such an overloading is achieved by specifying
a function with a name of the form "<", which is then used in its conventional infix form, i.e. placed between its operands, rather than in the prefix
form conventional for functions. The complete generic specification for a
sort routine, capable of being instantiated to sort any one-dimensional array
with elements of any type, might look as shown in Figure 8.3, therefore.

An operation parameter is given as a subprogram specification preceded by
the reserved word **with**, so that the compiler does not assume that it is the
start of the generic unit.

Someone wishing to use GEN_SORT would have to provide an appropriate
overloading of "<" for the particular actual parameter type corresponding
to ELEMENT. For example, assuming that a user wishes to sort an array of
records, with the following type:

```
type CAR is record
             FLEET_NUMBER : positive;
             MANUFACTERER : string(1..20);
             MODEL        : string(1..10);
             REGISTRATION : string(1..7);
             ENGINE_SIZE  : positive;
             PURCHASE_YEAR: YEAR_RANGE:
             MILES_TO_DATE: positive;
           end record;
```

a particular application might require a listing of cars in order of their recorded mileage, and so an appropriate overloading would be:

```
function "<" ( L,R : CAR) return boolean is
begin
        return L.MILES_TO_DATE < R.MILES_TO_DATE;
end "<";
```

defining "<" for type CAR in terms of the corresponding operation for positive,
which is defined as a standard operation.

8.4.4   Genericity — Summary

Genericity as supported by Ada provides a powerful means of escaping from
the 'not specific enough to be useful — too specific to be widely reused'
dilemma that was discussed earlier. The generic facility supports the ability to produce templates with a level of abstraction appropriate for reused
components — application-specific features can be abstracted away, leaving
the essential functionality that can be tailored to many different application
contexts by a suitable choice of generic parameters. If such abstracting away
is impossible without compromising the functionality of the component in
question then almost certainly it is inadequate as a candidate for reuse.

Polymorphism

Both genericity and overloading are examples of a more general concept: that
of *Polymorphism*. As classical scholars will immediately recognise, the term
means 'possessing many forms'. In the context of computer programming
it has come to mean strictly 'capable of possessing more than one type',
although it is generally applied to operations — routines or subprograms —
in relation to which it means 'able to be applied to parameters of different
types'. Parametric polymorphism, of which the Ada generic mechanism is an
example, requires the specification of each of the types that a polymorphic
unit is to deal with by means of type parameters, as its name suggests.
Parametric polymorphism is particularly relevant to reuse; another kind of
polymorphism, of which the Ada version of overloading is a rather restricted
example, is a powerful aid to abstraction. This aspect will be examined in
more detail in a later Chapter.

8.5 Design and Reuse

Booch has suggested a basic portfolio of reusable components in [3], which includes the standard data structures such as linked lists, stacks, queues, trees and directed graphs, all defined as abstract data types with generic parameters defining the elements/nodes of the structures. It is worthwhile considering briefly the effect on the software design process that the general adoption of this and similar portfolios might have.

The discussion of Object-Oriented design in Chapter 7 characterised the output from the design process as a set of Abstract Data Type interface specifications — package specifications, in the Ada context. It seems obvious that this picture requires some modification, or at least clarification, when the existence of reusable software is taken into account. The existence of the possibility of software reuse would appear to necessitate the recognition of two reasonably distinct design activities:

- *The Design of Reusable Components*

- *Design for the Reuse of Components*

The first of these has been discussed briefly in the earlier sections. Suffice it to add that the requirements for quality assurance of reusable components must be stringent enough to give prospective reusers the necessary confidence in their integrity.

The second activity reflects a shift in the way in which design is carried out towards the idealised view of electronic systems design mentioned earlier. The objective of the design process becomes the generation not of a collection of module specifications but a 'pick-list' of reusable components forming the basis of the design, possibly with some 'glue' in the form of a few specially-written modules to make the whole thing work. To a certain extent this process must involve the imposition of the structures exhibited by the available reusable components onto the structure of the problem domain, or at least the *recognition* of these structures in the problem domain. For this to be done without undue distortion of a specific application obviously places considerable demands on the generality of the reusable components, as we have seen.

As important is the requirement for a change in the attitudes and methods of the software designer, who must perhaps lose some of the attributes of the 'master architect', carrying through the design from its broad outlines to the mass of implementation detail, becoming instead more like a medical practitioner: recognising a set of symptoms and applying the appropriate 'cure' in the form of a reusable component. The idea of 'ego-less' programming is not a new one, nor was it deployed in the context of software component reuse, but it does convey the idea of the need to take some of the individuality, and perhaps creativity, out of software design that reuse implies.

8.6   Extensibility

As we have seen, the possibility of reusing software components is greatly enhanced by the ability to tailor them to the specific requirements of a new application context. The generic facility provides considerable support for this idea, but the range of possibilities of tailoring a particular component to different contexts is circumscribed by the limits of the abstraction concerned — they will all have the 'family likeness', which is, of course, implied by the word 'generic'.

A more developed version of this idea is generally referred to as *Extensibility*, which implies not just the kind of syntactic tailoring that genericity of the Ada model provides, but adding functionality to what exists already — actually modifying the semantics of the abstraction. There is a considerable grey area between the two — the functionality of an Ada generic unit can be modified very considerably by the choice of an operation parameter, after all, but extensibility carries the suggestion of a change to the intrinsic functionality.

Once again we risk being impaled on the horns of a dilemma: the kind of modification that will qualify as being characteristic of extensibility seems incompatible with the strict encapsulation that has been identified as a hallmark of data abstraction. There are cases where this penetration of encapsulation is not required — where the functionality of one abstraction can be constructed on top of the external interface of a lower level one, with no need for any additional access to the data structure. As an example, the Queues package might well be built on top of a linked list package, with the specification shown in Figure 8.4.

The package provides operations for an abstract data type that is an abstraction of the conventional linked list — a linear structure of cells or nodes related by their positions in the sequence, i.e. by the 'next' relationship. The interface is based on the idea of an imaginary pointer that identifies

```
generic
      type element is private;
package gen_lists is
--
        type list is limited private;
        procedure initialise(L : in out list);
--
-- navigation operations for 'current element'

        procedure set_current_first(L : list);
        procedure set_current_last(L : list);
        procedure set_current_right(L : list);
        procedure set_current_left(L : list);
        function current_is_first(L: list) return Boolean;
        function current_is_last(L: list) return Boolean;
        --
-- insert/delete operations
        --
        procedure insert_right_of_current(E : element;
                                L : list);
        -- leaves current element as newly inserted one
        -- 'current' is imaginary in the empty list
        --
        procedure delete_current(L : list);
        -- leaves current element as one to left, unless the
        -- first one is deleted, when it's the one to the right
        --
-- access operation : read out the current element
        --
        function the_current_from(L : list) return element;
        --
        LIST_EXHAUSTED : exception; -- fallen off either end
        --
private
        type list_structure;
        type list is access list_structure;
end gen_lists;
```

Figure 8.4: A Generic Linked-List Package

the 'current' element for purposes of insertion into the next place, deletion
or read access. The current element pointer may be moved up and down
the list by the 'navigation' operations, with the complementary predicates
(boolean functions) allowing for the detection of the current element being
the first or last in the list.

The functionality of the `gen_lists` package is rather sparse — too sparse
for a 'real' component: it lacks any support for indexing, for example. It
does provide sufficient to support the `Queues` package, however, as we shall
demonstrate. The first question concerns the underlying data structure of
a Queue. Obviously this must be derived in some way from the `List` type
exported by `Gen_lists`, which must therefore be instantiated in the body of
`Queues`. The generic formal parameter of `Queues` is used as the actual for
`Gen_lists`:

```
with Gen_lists;
package body Queues is
    --
    --   instantiate Gen_lists to provide queue data structure
    --
        package Q_list is new Gen_lists(item);
```

The `list` type exported by the instantiation`Q_list` may now be used to
create a data structure for a queue, supplying the implementation for the
incomplete declaration `queue_struct`. In addition to incorporating a list it
includes a `natural` variable to maintain a count of the number of elements.
A record structure is therefore appropriate.

```
type Queue_struct is record
                    items : Q_list.list;
                    count : natural;
                end record;
```

The `Initialise` operation may now be implemented, using the corresponding `gen_lists` operation.

```
procedure initialise(Q :in out Queue) is
begin
        Q := new Queue_struct; -- Q points to the new
                            -- queue_struct object
        Q_list.initialise(Q.items);-- gen_lists operation
        Q.count := 0; -- no items in a new queue
end initialise;
```

```
      procedure enqueue(I: item; Q : queue) is
      begin
              Q_list.set_current_last(Q.items);
              Q_list.insert_right_of_current(I,Q.items);
              Q.count := Q.count + 1;
      end enqueue;

      procedure dequeue(I : out item; Q : queue) is
      begin
              if Q.count = 0 -- empty queue?
              then raise QUEUE_UNDERFLOW;
              end if;
              Q_list.set_current_first(Q.items);
              I := Q_list.the_current_from(Q.items);
              Q_list.delete_current(Q.items);
              Q.count := Q.count - 1;
      end dequeue;

      function is_empty(Q : queue) return boolean is
      begin
              return Q.count = 0;
      end is_empty;
   end gen_queues;
```

Figure 8.5: Queue Operations Implemented Using List Operations

The remainder of the operations may now be constructed straightforwardly using the operations exported by **Gen_lists** as shown in Figure 8.5 It must be admitted that this is a somewhat special case, and that functionality cannot often be extended in this, encapsulation respecting, way. The conflict between extensibility and encapsulation must remain unresolved as far as Ada is concerned, with the advantage firmly on the side of encapsulation. The notion of extensibility is naturally associated with that of inheritance, which made a brief appearance in the last chapter with, again, the recognition of its cold-shouldering by Ada. We must wait until Chapter 10, and a new kind of programming language, before these concepts can come into their own.

8.7   Summary

In this chapter we have discussed some of the concepts of software component reuse, and noted the significant place amongst these occupied by data abstraction. The fundamental problem of significance versus application independence has been described together with an exploration of genericity, particularly as exemplified by its Ada version, which goes a considerable way towards providing a solution. Both the brief exploration of the limitations of Ada's support for extensibility, and the introduction of the concept of polymorphism, are precursors of a more extended discussion of related matters in a later Chapter.

Chapter 9

Formal Specification of ADTs

9.1 Introduction

One of the significant phases in the Object-Oriented design technique is *formalise the interfaces of the objects*. In practice this means defining the operations that are available for manipulating the data abstractions, or abstract data types (ADTs), within a syntactical structure such as a Definition Module in MODULA-2 or an Ada package specification. Importantly, the 'formalisation' involved is purely a syntactical one: each operation is defined by its name and parameters, with their types and modes, but there is no corresponding formalisation for the definition of the *semantics* of the operations — what they actually 'mean', or 'do'.

In many cases there is a well-understood conventional semantics — the stack and the queue, for example, have functionalities that are generally known and require little interpretation. But when less well-known (and hackneyed) examples are considered the definition of their semantics cannot be left to the intuition of potential users. In the case study contained in Chapter 5, the `Pile` data abstraction exported the operation `next_tree_from_pile`, which was distinguished from a conventional read operation by the fact that it was 'destructive': more like a 'pop' operation. Nothing in the syntactic definition of the operation suggests this, and so the additional semantic information must be conveyed separately. One possibility would be simply to allow the user to inspect the code that implements the data abstraction.

153

But this would run strongly counter to the whole idea of data abstraction and is not an acceptable technique. The most common approach is to supply the additional information in the form of comments within the interface specification, aided by the use of suggestive operation names.

9.1.1 The Need for Formal Specification

In comparison with the syntactic specification of abstract data types, the semantic specification by the use of comments is, often highly, informal. As such, it frequently demonstrates all too clearly the propensity of natural language to encourage vagueness or ambiguity or both. This is not a trivial matter because, as has been remarked a number of times, the important feature of an abstract data type, from the point of view of those who are to use it, is its external interface. So the nature of this interface, in the sense of 'what it does', must be clearly understood by its users, otherwise the whole exercise of designing the abstract data type, implementing it and making it available for use, is futile.

There is, therefore, a correspondingly strong motivation to ensure that the semantic specifications of abstract data types are clear and unambiguous. In this field, as in others, the surest way of achieving this objective is by the use of mathematical techniques, because of the intrinsic economy and precision of mathematical notation. This Chapter presents an introduction to the particular mathematical or *formal* specification technique that has become associated with abstract data types, which is commonly known as *Algebraic* specification.

9.2 A Familiar Example

Initially, we will approach this formal technique in a somewhat informal way, showing the construction of an algebraic specification of our old friend the stack.

The first part of such a specification consists of an abstract version of the kind of structure with which we have become reasonably familiar — the interface definition of an abstract data type, as realised by a definition module or package specification. Consider first an appropriate Ada package specification as shown in Figure 9.1. The only unusual feature of this specification lies in the exclusive use of functions to provide the operations associated

```
generic
     type element is private;
package stacks is

     type stack is private;

     function initialise return stack;

     function push (S : stack; E : element) return stack;

     function pop (S : stack) return stack;

     function top (S : stack) return element;

     function is_empty (S : stack) return boolean;

private

     type stack_struct;

     type stack is access stack_struct;

end stacks;
```

Figure 9.1: Ada Generic Specification for a Stack ADT

with the abstract data type. The reasons for this will be explored later. For the moment the main points to notice are that the functional style requires a slight change to the 'normal' stack interface, in that the `pop` operation does not remove the top element from the stack *and* return the value of the top element: it simply returns the truncated stack. The additional `top` operation is required to provide the value of the top element. It should be noted that this is not the only way in which the operations can be defined — this way is shown because it is the closest to the 'normal' version.

Before considering the mathematical equivalent of this specification it will be useful to remind ourselves of the nature of the information that it conveys. The first point to make is that this information is really very limited, as can perhaps be more easily seen if the conventional operation names are replaced by ones that are less suggestive of the stack (see Figure 9.2).

It seems clear that a program fragment such as:

```
if not splurge(stk1)
        then e2 := tosh(stk1)
```

is considerably less meaningful than:

```
if not is_empty(stk1)
        then e2 := top(stk1)
```

but the relative clarity of the latter derives completely from the familiarity of the operation names — nothing is added to or taken from the intrinsic meaning of the specification, which is restricted to defining the names of the operations and the types of their arguments and results, by a systematic renaming of the kind shown in Figure 9.2. The implication of this is that the identifiers that appear in such a specification, both operation and type names, have a completely *symbolic* significance — they are 'place-holders' showing only where the various types associated with the operations are the same or not. For example, the **slush** (**push**) and **slop** (**pop**) operations both return values of the same type. (The one exception to the purely symbolic names in the specification is **boolean**, which has a well-defined meaning deriving from outside this specification.)

The arrangement of the 'place-holders' defines a pattern that many implementations might be devised to fit. For example, the operation named **top** or **tosh** in some versions might always return the value of type **element** that was the second argument of the first invocation of the **push** or **slush** operation. This would not be consistent with the behaviour of a stack, but

```
generic
    type element is private;
package splodges is

    type splodge is private;

    function splodgise return splodge;

    function slush (S : splodge; E : element) return splodge;

    function slop (S : splodge) return splodge;

    function tosh (S : splodge) return element;

    function splurge (S : splodge) return boolean;

private

    type splodge_struct;

    type splodge is access splodge_struct;

end splodges;
```

Figure 9.2: The Stack Specification with Systematic Renaming

an implementation that does provide a conventional stack behaviour is only
one of many possibilities — further emphasising the need for semantic, or
behavioural, specification.

The corresponding algebraic structure possesses a similarly symbolic relationship with a number of possible mathematical 'implementations', or *interpretations*, as they are more properly known. Unlike in the Ada specification
the operation names denote, or are 'place-holders' for, actual mathematical
functions, rather than subprograms that are in some sense 'functional'. The
features of an algebraic specification that correspond to the symbolic types
of an Ada specification are symbols for the sets of values from which the arguments and results of the functions are drawn. These symbolic set names
are known as *Sorts*, and it is conventional to list the sorts involved in an
algebraic specification at its head.

The sorts involved in the algebraic version of the stack obviously include
stack and *element*, but also required is a mathematical model for `boolean`,
as there is no equivalent of 'pre-defined types' in an algebraic specification.
For the purposes of the algebraic specification of a stack abstract data type
this model requires nothing more than a set containing two distinguished
values that can be thought of as representing *true* and *false*, and named as
such. This set is denoted by the sort *Bool*. The sorts of the specification,
which are conventionally preceded by the heading *SORTS*, would appear as
follows:

$$SORTS \qquad element\ stack\ bool$$

The remaining differences between a package specification and the corresponding section of an algebraic specification are simple matters of notation.
If we look at the package specification we can see that the essential information is the set of operation names and the types of the parameters of the
functions, and their result types. Parameter names, although useful for documentary purposes, are not really required for the *specification* of the stack,
and the reserved words `function` and `result` are just 'syntactic sugar' that
can be dispensed with, provided that the operations are restricted to functions. All that is required is some kind of punctuation that allows for the
distinguishing of operation names, argument and result sorts. A common
convention separates the operation name from the argument sorts by a colon,

$$
\begin{array}{rll}
SORTS & \quad element\ stack\ bool \\
OPERATIONS & \\
initialise & : & \to stack \\
push & : & stack\ element \to stack \\
pop & : & stack \to stack \\
top & : & stack \to element \\
is\_empty & : & stack \to bool \\
\end{array}
$$

Figure 9.3: Algebraic Signature for a Stack ADT

and the argument sorts from the result sort by an arrow. The specification of the *Push* operation, adopting this format, would look as follows:

$$push \quad : \quad stack\ element \to stack$$

The collection of operation specifications are headed by $OPERATIONS$. The algebraic equivalent of the stack package specification is shown in Figure 9.3.

This kind of structure is called a *signature* and it might be thought of as a language-independent, 'pared down' version of an interface definition, and we must always bear in mind its symbolic nature as defining a pattern with many possible interpretations. The signature shown in Figure 9.3, which involves several sorts, is classified as *many sorted*.

9.2.1 Semantic Specification

So far the algebraic specification technique has provided nothing more than an economical notation for conveying the same kind of information — syntactical information — as a definition module or a package specification. As we have seen, this information is inadequate to distinguish between the many different interpretations that can match a particular signature, most of which do not provide the desired semantics. The next step, which reveals the power of algebraic specification in comparison with its programming language equivalents, is to extend the technique so as to be able to specify the semantics of abstract data types in a formal way. The additional features that the algebraic technique requires to support semantic specification are perhaps surprisingly simple, they are:

- *functional composition*

- *equations*

Functional Composition

We have seen previously that the use of algebraic specification requires the operations associated with an abstract data type to be defined as functions. A function is a mathematical object that resembles quite closely its namesake in programming languages. A function defines a mapping from a number of argument values ('input values') to a single ('output') value, with the constraint that each unique combination of argument values maps to only one result. The set(s) of values from which the argument(s) of a function are drawn are known as the *domain* set(s) of the function; the set of values from which its result is drawn is known as its *range* set.

The *application* of a function is the operation of mapping its argument value(s) to a result. The conventional notation for function application shows the argument value(s) in parentheses prefixed by the name of the function, the whole expression denoting the result value. So if we have a function *square* that maps integer values to their squares, the function application of *square* to the integer value 4 is written as *square*(4), an expression that denotes the value 16. Instead of using an integer value we may use a variable, say i, and show an application as *square*(i). To take this process a step further, the value to which a function may be applied may itself be obtained as the result of another function application, provided that it is the correct type of value. For example: *square*(*square*(4)) denotes the application of *square* to 4, producing the result 16, and then the application of *square* to 16, producing the final result 256. There is, of course, no restriction on the nature of functions combined in this way, other than that noted above that requires the range set of the preceding application to be the same as (or a subset of) the domain of the successor. Nor is there any restriction on the number of functions involved.

This technique is called *functional composition* and it is utilised in algebraic specifications in expressing *axioms*. It is this usage of functional composition that necessitates the restriction of the operations included in an algebraic specification to functions. Procedures, the other kind of operation often used in implementations of abstract data types, do not possess a close mathematical analogue, unlike functions.

9.2.2 Axioms

The idea of an axiom is that it is an unquestionable, within obvious requirements of internal consistency, and unprovable assertion that is simply accepted. The axioms of an algebraic specification provide the means of specifying the meanings, or semantics, of the abstract data type that it defines. They may be seen as constraints on the operations defined syntactically by the signature. If we consider the stack example, there are several characteristics that are inseparable from the idea of *stackness*, as follows:

- if a top operation immediately follows a push operation, then the value returned by the top operation is the value of the element pushed onto the stack.

- if a pop operation immediately follows a push operation, then the stack returned by the pop operation is identical to the stack that was an argument to the push operation.

These characteristics cannot be *proved* to be uniquely associated with stacks: they simply *are* part of what the word means.

If we utilise some variables, s and e, to stand respectively for 'any stack' and 'any element', we can express these characteristics as follows:

$$top(push(s, e)) = e$$

Functional composition is used to express mathematically the idea contained in the phrase 'immediately follows', and the equality relation, symbolised by '=', is used to express the equivalence of the left and right hand sides. The equation captures formally the idea contained in an informal statement like: "The top value obtained from a stack formed by pushing an arbitrary element e onto an arbitrary stack s is e".

Similarly:

$$pop(push(s, e)) = s$$

"The value of the stack returned by a pop operation on a stack formed by pushing an arbitrary element e onto an arbitrary stack s is s".

In each case the form of the expression that defines the stack characteristic is an *equation*: it consists of a *left-hand side*, a *right-hand side* and an equals sign separating the two. The expressions are known accordingly as *equational axioms* in the context of algebraic specifications.

The relationships between the other operations provided by the stack may be similarly expressed equationally: the *is_empty* operation will obviously return the value *true* immediately after the *initialise* operation, which returns an empty stack; it will return *false* immediately after any *push* operation. These two characteristics can be expressed as follows:

$$is\_empty(initialise) \quad = \quad true$$
$$is\_empty(push(s, e)) \quad = \quad false$$

Errors

The mention of the possibility of an empty stack brings with it the corresponding possibility of applying various operations to an empty stack. Clearly there is no problem with *push*. *Pop* is more problematic — what is the effect of popping an empty stack? The usual answer is to return an empty stack, although this sounds rather like damage limitation: leaving the rather uneasy thought that it *shouldn't* have happened. But there can be no doubt that the *top* operation on an empty stack is an error — there is simply no top value to return. The immediately obvious 'solution' to this problem is to invent a special value, called *error*, that is returned by the *pop* operation on an empty stack. This will necessitate a change to the range set of the *top* operation, which must be constructed from *element* and the value *error* using set union: $element \bigcup \{error\}$. We can then add an axiom to this effect:

$$top(initialise) \quad = \quad error$$

and it is certainly the case that a number of writers on algebraic specification (Guttag for instance [4]) have been quite happy with this. But, as pointed out by Goguen [5] and others, this appears to lead to some fairly uncomfortable results. For example, what are we to make of the following:

$$push(s, (top(initialise)))$$

The value denoted by the overall expression is from sort *stack* — the result sort of the *push* operation — but the top value of the stack presumably has the value *error*, because this is the value returned by the *top* operation forming the second operand, of sort *element* ∪ {*error*}. We may imagine further *push* operations being carried out on the stack, with non-erroneous arguments, and then we would be left with a stack with a hidden *error* somewhere in its depths — obviously not an acceptable arrangement.

A more natural approach would be to regard any stack with *error* pushed into it as totally erroneous, perhaps as signified by a special error value of sort stack. In turn, we must then consider what the effect of *is_empty* on an *error_stack* would be — obviously neither true nor false is appropriate and so an additional error value must be included in *bool*, and so on. The result is a considerable proliferation both of error values, whose symbolic status is rather unclear, and of error axioms. The appealing elegance of the algebraic technique is rapidly obscured.

A number of techniques have been suggested to confront the problem of error handling in algebraic specifications. A common approach is to permit the specification of some of the operations as denoting *partial* functions — that is, functions defined over only a subset of their domain values. In the context of the stack this would allow the *top* and *pop* operations to be defined only for stacks that are not empty, the corresponding undefinedness of these operations on empty stacks implicitly defining erroneous applications.

Goguen introduces the idea of *subsorts* to support this approach, being symbolic subset names. In the case of the stack a subsort *ne_stack* might be declared to symbolise the subset of *Stacks* whose members are non-empty, permitting the appropriate specification of the *top* and *pop* operations, as shown in the complete specification in Figure 9.4. As can be seen, the subsort is declared under a separate heading and is shown in relation to its 'super-sort': in this case *stack*. This approach has the advantage of avoiding the somewhat dubious association of error values with sorts, which are purely symbolic entities after all.

9.3   An Alternative Semantics

We can illustrate the power of the use of equational axioms to specify semantics by providing an alternative set for the same signature that was used in the *stack* specification, so as to define a First In First Out list, or Queue,

STACK
SORTS

        element stack bool

SUBSORTS

        ne_stack < stack

OPERATIONS

initialise	:	$\rightarrow stack$
push	:	*stack element* $\rightarrow$ *ne_stack*
pop	:	*ne_stack* $\rightarrow$ *stack*
top	:	*ne_stack* $\rightarrow$ *element*
is_empty	:	*stack* $\rightarrow$ *bool*

VARIABLES

        s : stack e : element

EQUATIONS

$top(push(s, e))$	=	e
$pop(push(s, e))$	=	s
$is\_empty(initialise)$	=	*true*
$is\_empty(push(s, e))$	=	*false*

Figure 9.4: An Algebraic Specification for the Stack ADT

rather than a Last In First Out list, or Stack.

Informally, the axioms that capture the essential qualities of the queue are as follows:

- the insertion, or pushing, of an element into a queue affects the front, or top, of the queue only if it was empty to start with.

- the composition of a queue following a push and a pop operation is unaffected by the order in which the operations are applied, except when the queue is initially empty.

Clearly, this affects both the queue equivalents of the **pop** and **top** operations, perhaps more conventionally called **De_queue** and **Front**. In both cases, the expression of an equivalence requires the evaluation of a condition — specifically that the queue in question is empty, and in order to capture this in a notationally convenient manner the language of algebraic specifications is conventionally extended to include *Conditional Expressions*, usually adopting the **if** .. **then** .. **else** format.

Within the context of algebraic specifications, the **if** .. **then** .. **else** construct defines a family of functions with three arguments, the sort of the first of which is *bool*, that of the second and third determined by the application. The semantics of the construct can be concisely expressed using equations:

$$if\ true\ then\ a\ else\ b\ =\ a$$
$$if\ false\ then\ a\ else\ b\ =\ b$$

Armed with this additional expressivity we may now define the characteristic semantics of the queue:

$$top(push(e, q))\ =\ if\ is\_empty(q)$$
$$then\ e$$
$$else\ top(q)$$

and:

$$pop(push(e, q))\ =\ if\ is\_empty(q)$$
$$then\ initialise$$
$$else\ push(e, pop(q))$$

$QUEUE$

$SORTS$ *element queue bool*

$SUBSORTS$ $ne\_queue < queue$

$OPERATIONS$

$$
\begin{aligned}
initialise \;\; &: \;\; \rightarrow queue \\
push \;\; &: \;\; queue\; element \rightarrow ne\_queue \\
pop \;\; &: \;\; ne\_queue \rightarrow queue \\
top \;\; &: \;\; ne\_queue \rightarrow element \\
is\_empty \;\; &: \;\; queue \rightarrow bool
\end{aligned}
$$

$VARIABLES$ $s : queue\; e : element$

$EQUATIONS$

$$
\begin{aligned}
is\_empty(push(e,s)) \;&=\; false \\
is\_empty(initialise) \;&=\; true \\
top(push(e,q)) \;&=\; if\; is\_empty(q) \\
&\quad\;\; then\; e \\
&\quad\;\; else\; top(q) \\
pop(push(e,q)) \;&=\; if\; is\_empty(q) \\
&\quad\;\; then\; initialise \\
&\quad\;\; else\; push(e, pop(q))
\end{aligned}
$$

Figure 9.5: Algebraic Specification of a Queue ADT

These may be incorporated into the complete specification with, as promised, the same signature as the specification for *stack*, but with the sort changed to *queue* for the sake of avoiding confusion, as shown in Figure 9.5.

The reader may be experiencing some feelings of doubt at this point — these equations seem somewhat slight to express everything that is characteristic of queues. What about, for example, the requirement that, given a queue containing two elements, the one that was inserted first should be revealed first by the **top** operation? This does not seem immediately obvious from the equations that we have defined and obviously, if the specification does not support this interpretation, this will call into question the usefulness of the technique. The question arises as to whether it is possible to 'test' a specification to see whether appropriate implications can be drawn from it. In this case we wish to assure ourselves that, given two element values, distinguished say as $e1$ and $e2$, then the sequence of operations represented by:

$$top(push(e2, push(e1, initialise)))$$

whereby $e1$ is pushed into the queue before $e2$, will produce the result $e1$.

9.3.1   Term Rewriting

Fortunately such a technique does exist, in the form of *Term Re-writing*. Each equation is interpreted as a *Re-write Rule*, that specifies how its left-hand side may be rewritten as its right-hand side. If we examine the expression above we see that it has the form of the following axiom:

$$top(push(e, q)) = \quad if\ is\_empty(q)$$
$$then\ e$$
$$else\ top(q)$$

with q replaced by $push(e1, initialise)$. The appropriate axiom tells us that

$$is\_empty(push(e1, initialise)) = \quad false$$

and so the expression may be replaced by, or rewritten as, the **else** alternative value:

$$top(push(e1, initialise))$$

This reduced expression also has the form of the same axiom, but now the queue to which the *push* is applied *is* empty and so the **then** alternative is used, giving the expression $e1$, and so the 'correctness' of the specification is confirmed.

A more complex test is shown below, involving a *pop* operation in addition to the two *push*es. In each stage of the proof the sub-expression that is to be rewritten is shown underlined, and the appropriate axiom, or rewrite rule, is shown on the right.

To show that:

$$top(pop(push(e2, push(e1, initialise))))) = e2$$

$$top(\underline{pop(push(e2, push(e1, initialise))))}$$
$$= top(push(e2, \underline{pop(push(e1, initialise))))}$$
$$= top(push(e2, initialise))$$
$$= e2$$

9.4   A Line Editor

In this section a more significant example is used to illustrate the application of the algebraic technique, that of a simple line editor. As a precursor, it will be necessary to develop a subsidiary specification for a character string abstract data type, because clearly the operations of a line editor are intimately concerned with string operations.

The essential operations on strings include those to append one string to another, and to add a character to a string. With half an eye to the application of these operations to the line editor the ability to add a character to either end of a string may well be advantageous. An immediate question concerns the nature of the characters from which the strings are to be composed. Conventionally, or informally, they would be regarded as constants drawn from a particular set — specifically a character set, such as the ASCII character set. The language of algebraic specifications, however, is restricted to functions and variables, with a small amount of punctuation in the form of parentheses and so on. Significantly, there is no way of declaring constant values as such for inclusion in the equational axioms. Instead, constantsare considered to be functions without arguments, of *arity zero* to use the mathematical term. In the case of the constants of an appropriate character set, each must be modelled by a function with a range set which is the character set itself. As it is rather tedious, and not particularly illuminating, to write out one hundred or so function signatures of the form *letter_A* $:\to alphanum$ assuming that *alphanum* is the sort of the readable portion of the ASCII character set, a much abbreviated set of functions will be shown.

A function of arity zero that does have considerable significance is the *empty list*, that is the list with no characters in it at all, which is often written as λ. The reason for this is analogous to the significance of zero in integer arithmetic, as can be seen from a consideration of the fundamental constructors. These are *append*, which forms a single string by joining together a left and a right string, and *make*, which converts a character into a string of length 1. The existence of the empty string allows for the construction of a string of any length to be done by repeated applications of the *append* operation, each application taking as arguments a single-character string, returned by *make*, and the string produced by the *last append*. The empty string is used in the *first* application of *append*, to 'get the whole thing started'. In the signature presented below the function of zero arity that returns the empty string will be denoted by *empty*, rather than λ, to preserve a more conventional 'program-like' graphology.

In specifying the string abstract data type we shall consider the constructors only, with a view of the use to which the specification is to be put: i.e. part of the specification of a line-editor. We are interested in the way in which lines may be manipulated as things in themselves — which we assume to be simply visible, as though displayed on a (one-line) screen.

The signature of the set of operations, preceded by the list of the sorts involved, is therefore as follows:

$$
\begin{array}{rcl}
SORTS & & string\ alphanum \\
OPERATIONS & & \\
empty & : & \rightarrow string \\
make & : & alphanum \rightarrow string \\
append & : & string\ string \rightarrow string \\
make\_A & : & \rightarrow alphanum \\
etc. & &
\end{array}
$$

The axioms for append capture the ideas, respectively, that appending the empty string to a string leaves it unchanged, and that append is *associative* — i.e. when a string is constructed by two append operations the end result is the same if the third substring is appended to the result of appending the second to the first, or if the result of appending the third to the second is appended to the first. (The last sentence is a convincing demonstration of the superiority of a mathematical notation for expressing these concepts.)

$$
\begin{array}{rcl}
VARIABLES & & s, s1, s2, s3 : string\ a : alphanum \\
EQUATIONS & & \\
append(s, empty) & = & s \\
append(empty, s) & = & s \\
append(s1, append(s2, s3)) & = & append(append(s1, s2), s3)
\end{array}
$$

Again with an eye to the application, we define two versions of an operation that adds a character to a string, the two versions allowing the operation to be defined for both ends of the string:

$$rightadd \quad : \quad string\, alphanum \rightarrow string$$
$$leftadd \quad : \quad alphanum\, string \rightarrow string$$

The axioms for these operations simply define them in terms of the more fundamental constructors:

$$rightadd(s, a) \quad = \quad append(s, make(a))$$
$$leftadd(a, s) \quad = \quad append(make(a), s)$$

Armed with this 'component' specification, we may now turn to the specification of the line-editor itself.

9.4.1   Editor Operations

The arrangement of the line-editor is a conventional one in which a moveable cursor defines a position within the line at which characters may be inserted, changed or deleted. The structure of the line, therefore, consists of the two strings comprising respectively the left and right parts of the line, either of which may be the empty string, separated by the cursor, which conceptually occupies a position between characters.

The *make_line* operator generates this structure, utilising the append operation of the *String* ADT. The basic constructor operations provide for the creation of an empty line, with the cursor placed before the leftmost character position, and an insert operation that adds the specified character to the right-hand end of the left-hand string, effectively stepping on the cursor by one character position. The specification, which shows its dependency on the string specification by the expresion in the heading line, which may be regarded as a kind of 'import clause', commences as follows:

$$Line - editor \quad + String$$
$$SORTS \quad line, alphanum$$
$$OPERATIONS$$
$$make\_line \quad : \quad string\, string \rightarrow line$$

$$create \quad : \quad \rightarrow line$$
$$insert \quad : \quad alphanum\,line \rightarrow line$$

The change and delete operations generally affect the character to the right of the cursor, and have signatures as follows:

$$change \quad : \quad alphanum\,line \rightarrow line$$
$$delete \quad : \quad line \rightarrow line$$

Additionally, two 'navigation' operations provide for the movement of the cursor:

$$right \quad : \quad line \rightarrow line$$
$$left \quad : \quad line \rightarrow line$$

Now, with an appropriate set of variables:

$$a : alphanum; s1, s2 : string; l : line$$

the axioms may be defined.

First *create* is defined as constructing a line consisting of two empty strings:

$$create \quad = \quad make\_line(empty, empty)$$

Then *insert* is defined in terms of its effect on a line consisting of the strings $s1$ and $s2$:

$$insert(a, make\_line(s1, s2)) \quad = \quad make\_line(add\_right(s1, a), s2)$$

showing the stepping on of the cursor position, as it retains its position at the right-hand end of the left-hand string.

The *delete* operation requires case analysis to define its semantics where the right-hand string is respectively empty and not empty. As an alternative to the use of conditional expressions we may adopt *pattern matching* to define the normal case where the right-hand string is non-empty and the operation causes the removal of its left-most character:

$$delete(make\_line(s1, addleft(a, s2))) \quad = \quad make\_line(s1, s2)$$

The constraint that the right-hand string is the result of an *addleft* operation automatically ensures that it is non-empty. The case in which the right-hand string is empty can similarly be distinguished by pattern matching. There is then a choice of semantics — the operation may simply have no effect or, in the sub-case of a non-empty left-hand string, the right-most character of the left-hand string may be removed. As the latter is more interesting, as well as being closer to the semantics of real editors, we shall adopt it. The necessary axioms are as follows:

$$delete(make\_line(addright(l, a), empty) \quad = \quad make\_line(l, empty)$$
$$delete(make\_line(empty, empty) \quad = \quad make\_line(empty, empty)$$

Change can be defined purely in terms of delete and insert:

$$change(a, l) \quad = \quad insert(a, delete(l))$$

The cursor navigation operations *left* and *right* are straightforward enough, provided the cases where the cursor is at, respectively the left and right extremes of the line, are catered for:

$$left(make\_line(empty, r)) \quad = \quad make\_line(empty, r)$$
$$left(make\_line(addright(l, a), r)) \quad = \quad make\_line(l, addleft(a, r))$$
$$right(make\_line(l, empty)) \quad = \quad make\_line(l, empty)$$
$$right(make\_line(l, addleft(a, r))) \quad = \quad make\_line(addright(l, a), r)$$

The complete specification of the editor is shown in Figure 9.6

9.5   Implementation Bias

The significant point about this type of specification is that the semantics of the operations are always shown by the interaction of two or more of them: they are never defined in isolation. Moreover, the semantics is defined without the use of any other set of entities, but purely in terms of the set of operations associated with the Abstract Data Type. In this the algebraic

$$
\begin{array}{rcl}
Line-editor & + String & \\
SORTS & & line, alphanum \\
OPERATIONS & & \\
make\_line & : & string\ string \rightarrow line \\
create & : & \rightarrow line \\
insert & : & alphanum\ line \rightarrow line \\
change & : & alphanum\ line \rightarrow line \\
delete & : & line \rightarrow line \\
right & : & line \rightarrow line \\
left & : & line \rightarrow line \\
VARIABLES & & \\
\end{array}
$$

$a : alphanum; s1, s2 : string; l : line$

$$
\begin{array}{rcl}
EQUATIONS & & \\
create & = & make\_line(empty, empty) \\
insert(a, make\_line(s1, s2)) & = & make\_line(add\_right(s1, a), s2) \\
delete(make\_line(s1, addleft(a, s2))) & = & make\_line(s1, s2) \\
delete(make\_line(addright(l, a), empty)) & = & make\_line(l, empty) \\
delete(make\_line(empty, empty)) & = & make\_line(empty, empty) \\
change(a, l) & = & insert(a, delete(l)) \\
left(make\_line(empty, r)) & = & make\_line(empty, r) \\
left(make\_line(addright(l, a), r)) & = & make\_line(l, addleft(a, r)) \\
right(make\_line(l, empty)) & = & make\_line(l, empty) \\
right(make\_line(l, addleft(a, r))) & = & make\_line(addright(l, a), r) \\
\end{array}
$$

Figure 9.6: Algebraic Specification of a Line Editor

specification technique differs from the two other well-established techniques: *operational semantics* and *denotational semantics.* In operational semantics the meanings of operations are defined in terms of their effect on an idealised machine. In denotational semantics, they are defined in terms of their effects on mathematical entities such as sets, which are considered to be the denotations of program data structures.

In both cases, operations are defined in terms of 'something else' — something that is intrinsically better defined and understood than any particular program structure, which thereby obtains 'well-definedness' by association with this underlying reality.

In the context of abstract data types there is an obvious parallel between the underlying data structure that provides the basis of the 'real', or implementation, view, and the underlying machine or mathematical structure that provides the 'real' semantics of the applicable operations. But, of course, the encapsulation characteristic of the abstract data type is intended to *hide* the 'reality' of the implementation, and there is therefore something unsatisfactory about formally specifying an abstract data type by defining its semantics in terms of some underlying implementation, no matter how abstract.

By contrast, algebraic specifications do not define semantics by recourse to some better defined, different domain, but each is defined in terms *of itself* — a feature that often tends to inspire vague feelings of disquiet in newcomers to the technique, but which provides precisely that analogy with information hiding that the other two techniques mentioned cannot provide.

In fact there *is* an underlying object associated with an algebraic specification, which is the *initial algebra* of the specification. A brief introduction to the concept of initial algebras is given below, but we may summarise their significance by noting that such an algebra contains nothing more than what the corresponding specification requires. There is no sense in which it might be thought to be better-defined or 'more real' than the associated specification — it is simply different in a way analogous to the way that, say, an implementation module is different from its associated definition module. The initial algebra for a specification might be thought of, therefore, as capturing its essence in a way that, to employ a well-known slogan, introduces "no junk and no confusion".

In this algebraic specification contrasts with denotational and operational semantics, both of which provide a general set of operations: the 'instructions' of the ideal machine on the one hand, the standard set-theoretic operations on the other. There is therefore the risk, in using either of these techniques, of the incorporation of influences deriving from those of their operations that are not specifically concerned with the specification in question — a tendency known as *implementation bias*. Implementation bias may be thought of as the analogue of an imperfectly encapsulated abstract data type, in which the nature of the underlying data structure is allowed to determine its use in addition to the defined operational interface.

9.6 Algebras and Specifications

The non-mathematical reader, and indeed the mathematical reader with a conventional mathematical background, may find the plural 'Algebras' in the last sub-heading puzzling. Surely there is just *algebra*, a branch of mathematics in which letters are used to stand for quantities? This is certainly the view of algebra imparted by high-school mathematics courses, but in fact the term has a more specialised meaning in the context of a comparatively recently developed branch of mathematics, derived from set-theory.

As might be anticipated from this derivation, the central concept involved in algebras is that of the *set* — the essentially simple idea of a collection of unique individuals with some kind of common characteristic, which may be simply that they are members of the same set. The set is a peculiarly appropriate mathematical object for modelling the world, viewed as being inhabited, in the widest possible sense, by many unique individual objects, even if this uniqueness is a matter only of position in space and time.

As a result of the simplicity of the concept, there are many, in fact an infinite number of, sets that can be defined. A few crop up very frequently, however, particularly in the context of formal specification, including the set of all integer (whole) numbers, often called $\mathbf{I}$ or $\mathbf{Z}$, the set containing all the positive integers and 0, called $\mathbf{N}$ or *Nat*, and the set containing the two truth values **true** and **false**, called *Bool*.

An important result that follows from the common characteristics of all the members of a particular set is the fact that *operations*, in the form of functions, may be defined that can act on any, or all, of them. (The mathematical phrase is that such operations are defined *over* the set in question.)

In fact, with the rather small number of concepts that we have introduced so far, we have enough to define what an algebra is — it is a mathematical structure that allows one or more sets, known as the *carrier*, to be associated with a collection of operations defined over them, together with a number of members of the set(s) called *distinguished values*. An example of an algebra comprises:

- N the set of natural numbers (the positive integers plus 0)

- the successor operation, which maps every natural number to its successor in the ordered sequence

- the value 0

The algebra might be represented as a list:

$$< N, +1, 0 >$$

An algebraic specification is a symbolic structure containing symbols representing the salient features of a family of algebras — symbols for sets and operations, and for terms constructed from the operation symbols. Distinguished values, or constants, are represented by symbolic operations with zero arity (i.e. no argument types). The symbolic sets of a specification, known as sorts, are employed in the signature part of the specification, to characterise the domains and ranges of the symbolic operations. As such the signature defines a pattern that must be respected by any algebra that *satisfies* or *is a model of* the specification — such an algebra must possess a set for each sort of the signature, an operation for each operation symbol, with domain and range sets matching the pattern defined by the signature. The algebra described above is clearly a model for the following signature:

$$SORTS \qquad Nat_0$$
$$OPS$$
$$succ \quad : \quad Nat_0 \rightarrow Nat_0$$
$$zero \quad : \quad \rightarrow Nat_0$$

with an *interpretation* that assigns denotations to each of the symbols, as follows:

$$Nat_0 \quad \rightarrow \quad N, \text{ \textit{the set of positive integers}} + 0$$
$$succ \quad \rightarrow \quad \textit{the successor function for integers} \text{ ' } + 1'$$
$$zero \quad \rightarrow \quad \textit{integer zero}$$

Clearly, the constraints imposed by this signature are very general, and many alternative models may be found for it.

The members of the carrier, with the exception of 0, may be denoted by terms consisting of compositions of the *succ* function applied to *zero*. For example, under the above interpretation the integer value 3 is denoted by $succ(succ(succ(zero)))$. Although not a practical notation it can be seen that every member of N can be denoted in this way, and that every member is denoted by a unique term. This latter property is lost if we introduce another operation like *plus*, a binary addition function. The signature might then become:

$$SORTS \quad Nat_0$$
$$OPS$$
$$succ \ : \ Nat_0 \rightarrow Nat_0$$
$$plus \ : \ Nat_0 \, Nat_0 \rightarrow Nat_0$$
$$zero \ : \ \rightarrow Nat_0$$

The algebra extended by this additional operation permits the terms 0 and $plus(0,0)$, amongst others, to denote the same member of the carrier. To give a slightly more significant example, using m and n to stand for arbitrary values of the carrier, the following terms:

$$plus(m, succ(n))$$
$$succ(plus(n, m))$$

also denote the same member of the carrier. These equivalences define the behaviour, or semantics, of these operations and may be incorporated as *equations* into the specification to provide constraints on any (other) algebras that satisfy it. The addition of the equations section extends the format of the specification to its characteristic two-component structure as shown below:

$$SORTS \quad Nat_0$$
$$OPS$$
$$succ \ : \ Nat_0 \rightarrow Nat_0$$
$$zero \ : \ \rightarrow Nat_0$$
$$plus \ : \ Nat_0 \, Nat_0 \rightarrow Nat_0$$

$$VARIABLES \qquad m, n : Nat_0$$
$$EQUATIONS$$
$$plus(n, 0) \;=\; n$$
$$plus(n, succ(m)) \;=\; succ(plus(n, m))$$

Models

Algebraic specifications like the ones shown above might be thought of as *schemas*, or templates, for families of algebras, each member of the family satisfying the specification. This idea is sometimes a little hard to grasp because the characteristic examples used to motivate the concepts, such as the Nat_0 examples above, are so obviously identified with the conventional system of natural number arithmetic — in other words, the *interpretation* defined above and with *plus* modelled by the ordinary integer addition operator conventionally written as '+'. This is so natural as to be apparently hardly worth writing down, but the important point is that it *is* only one interpretation and that there are others that are equally valid, although less natural. One valid alternative model is one in which *succ* is +2 in conventional notation, and the sort $Nat0$ denotes the set of all positive *even* integers.

Initiality

The fact that an algebraic specification may be modelled by a whole family of algebras gives rise to a number of questions: what is the resemblance between the members of such a family; is there one member that in some way captures the essential qualities of the whole family?

Structural similarity between algebras exists when a so-called *structure-preserving* mapping can be shown to exist between them. Such a mapping is defined as follows. Given two algebras that model a specification, a mapping between them, from the *source* to the *target*, is actually a collection of functions from the source carrier to the target carrier which contains what might be termed a *conversion function* for each sort in the specification. This function converts the set denoted by the sort in the source algebra to the corresponding set denoted by the sort in the target algebra

The idea implied by the phrase 'structure-preserving' is that each pair of source/target functions denoted by an operation of the specification can be made interchangeable by the application of the appropriate conversions. In other words, the members of the carrier sets of the target algebra can be generated either by converting the result values of the source algebra functions, or by applying the target algebra functions to converted values from the source carrier. Such a structure-preserving mapping is called a *homomorphism*.

The formal expression of this idea is rather complicated in its full generality, but the principle can be illustrated reasonably straightforwardly with reference to a single-sorted specification, where only one conversion, or mapping, function is involved. Given, then, two algebras S and T (source and target) that are models for such a specification, with carriers S_c and T_c, a homomorphism from S to T will comprise a function, say f, with domain S_c and range T_c such that, for each operation σ of the specification, with arguments $a_1..a_n$:

$$f(\sigma_s(a_1..a_n)) \;\;=\;\; \sigma_t(f(a_1),..,f(a_n))$$

where σ_s and σ_t are the denotations of σ in respectively S and T.

Homomorphisms come in various classifications that determine a measure of the similarity between the algebras in question. The highest degree of similarity that may be determined is where an *isomorphism* exists, which means that every value in the target carrier is mapped to, and that there is a one-to-one relationship between the members of the two carriers — this means that the relationship is a symmetrical one, i.e. inverted functions will map the two carriers the other way. Isomorphism may be seen as defining equivalence to a level that 'fails' only in being unable to discriminate between algebras with sets that differ only in their names.

The family resemblance between the algebras that model a particular specification involves a number of special members of the family, known as the *initial algebras* for the specification. The special feature of an initial algebra is that a *unique homomorphism* exists between it and *each* member of the family. It is also the case that all the initial algebras for a specification are isomorphic to each other, and so are 'identical' within the slightly blurred perspective mentioned above. This means that 'the'initial algebra provides the answer to the first of the questions posed above, in that the notion of family resemblance can be defined in terms of derivability, by a family of mappings, from 'the' initial algebra.

Initiality, then, is a property of models, not specifications, and specifically of the 'best' models for a particular specification, in the sense of capturing its essential qualities: providing the answer to the second question in fact. This quality may be illustrated by considering again the specification:

$$
\begin{array}{rcl}
SORTS & & Nat0 \\
OPS & & \\
succ & : & Nat0 \rightarrow Nat0 \\
0 & : & \rightarrow Nat0 \\
plus & : & Nat0\ Nat0 \rightarrow Nat0 \\
VARIABLES & & m, n : Nat0 \\
EQUATIONS & & \\
plus(n, 0) & = & n \\
plus(n, succ(m)) & = & succ(plus(n, m))
\end{array}
$$

Consider an interpretation of the signature of this specification that assigns the set of integers Z to $Nat0$, whilst retaining all the other 'standard' assignments. This model would certainly satisfy the equations of the specification, but it suffers from the fact that one half of the members of the carrier — the values from -1 to minus infinity — cannot be denoted by terms that can be constructed from the operations: the anchoring of the specification to 'zero', and the additive nature of the operations of the model make this so. The term 'junk' has become adopted to refer to undenotable members of carriers, and obviously a model containing junk can hardly be said to be capturing the essence of the specification of which it is an interpretation.

Another possible deficiency of models is *confusion*. If we take the standard interpretation of the specification above and change the assignment of the *succ* operation to '+0' then, again, the resulting model satisfies the equations quite satisfactorily. But it also has the unfortunate property of making the denotations of quite dissimilar terms such as $succ(succ(succ(0)))$ and 0 indistinguishable, even though there is nothing in the specification to suggest that they are equal. Like junk, the presence of confusion in a model disqualifies it from being considered a faithful interpretation of its associated specification.

It is the fact that initial models contain, in Burstall's phrase, 'no junk and no confusion' and thus capture the essential qualities, of their specifications, that makes *initiality*, or the properties of initial algebras, so significant to algebraic specification.

It should also be noted that an alternative approach to algebraic specification exists, notably as popularised by Guttag, which deals with the so-called *final* or *loose* semantics, defined by considering the whole class or family of algebras defined by a specification. This is not the place to discuss the pros and cons of these two approaches.

Canonical Term Algebras

Whilst the foregoing discussion may have exposed the particular, and relevant, properties of initial algebras, the question as to how a useful initial algebra for a particular specification is derived has not been explored. A basis for this derivation is the *word algebra* of the specification. The word algebra is an interpretation in which the operations denote character string generating functions — 'production rules'. For example the *succ* operation is interpreted as a function that takes a character string argument and returns a longer character string obtained by prefixing the argument with '*succ(*' and suffixing it with ')'. The argument must, of course, be 'of the right type', which means that it must be a character string generated by a function denoted by an operation with the correct range sort, i.e. *succ*, *plus* or, ultimately, *zero*. As usual, it is more correct to talk of the word algebras of a specification, because, of course, systematic changes may be introduced — changing case for example — which produce different but isomorphically equivalent algebras.

The terms of a word algebra will frequently be equivalent to other terms, where 'equivalent to' is defined by the equations of the algebraic specification. For example, given a typical specification for *stack*, the denotation of the term:

$$pop(push(e1, pop(push(e2, initialise))))$$

is equivalent to that of *initialise*. The set of all terms equivalent to, for example, *initialise* forms what is known as an *equivalence class*, and if we imagine an algebra formed from the word algebra by factoring out all the equivalent terms in this way, in other words an algebra of equivalence classes, known as a *quotient algebra*, of the word algebra, then this algebra is initial.

The process of generating all the terms of the word algebra and then factoring out all its equivalence classes, whilst being conceptually comprehensible, does not appear to provide a practical method. For this we must turn to the idea of *canonical terms*, which are terms each of which is a member of a different equivalence class. It is not difficult to see that an algebra of canonical terms will be isomorphic to the quotient algebra and is therefore initial. The importance of canonical terms lies in the fact that their canonical property can often be shown, straightforwardly, to derive from their being generated in a systematic way using a subset of the operations. For example, each canonical term of the Nat_0 specification has the form:

$$succ^n(zero)$$

where

$$
\begin{aligned}
succ^1(zero) &= succ(zero) \\
succ^2(zero) &= succ(succ(zero)) \\
etc.
\end{aligned}
$$

An algebra of terms generated in this way is an initial model for the specification.

9.7   Algebraic Specification and Implementation

Algebraic specification, with its high level of abstraction, appears to possess clear advantages for the specification of Abstract Data Types. The question is frequently raised as to whether the technique is *too* abstract, particularly when used in conjunction with a conventional imperative language for the corresponding implementation. An obvious problem is the restriction of the operations of the abstract data type to functions.

There are a number of responses to this type of criticism. The first concerns the nature of specification. It is important to bear in mind the objective underlying the use of semi-formal and formal specification techniques: this is to clarify to both the implementor and the user of an abstract data type its syntax and semantics, with the main requirement being firmly concerned with the latter. As we have seen, the alternative is to use informal techniques, normally involving a natural language, with the consequent risk of imprecision that this invariably brings.

The mistake is often made that, because a formal language in some ways resembles programming languages, a specification written in a formal language in some ways provides a basis for, or is a high-level version of, the implementation. Algebraic specification, with its avoidance of implementation bias, is particularly uncommitted in this respect, and the lack of resemblance of specifications written using this style to implementations written in, say, C or FORTRAN, is neither surprising nor undesirable. The immediate purpose of producing such a specification is to communicate concepts to its human readers.

It is also the case, however, that some imperative languages, including the two that have received considerable exposure in this text, may be used to write program units that do bear a considerable resemblance to algebraic specifications, particularly if a 'functional style' is adhered to. Earlier in this chapter we moved from an Ada package specification to a related algebraic specification. The reverse process, a much more significant one in practical terms, is also possible (see Priestley [6]).

Specifications are also fundamentally important to the process of proving the correctness of an implementation — for, of course, a correct implementation is one that meets, or *satisfies*, the specification from which it was derived. The precision of algebraic specifications, and their exclusive concentration on the externally visible behaviour of the abstract data types to which they relate, provide strong support for informal and semi-formal verification of correctness of implementation: either by testing or by appeal to the details of the implementation code. Naturally, this support is reinforced by the use of a language, such as Ada or MODULA-2, that permits the writing of implementations that are closely related to algebraic specifications, at least in respect of their signatures.

A problem *does* arise, however, when the correctness of an implementation is to be demonstrated completely formally. As was described in the last section, such a demonstration must prove that the implementation is an initial model for the specification and, as such, must depend on the characterisation of the implementation as an algebra.

The problem, referred to above, is concerned with the availabilities of these *implementation algebras* , to use Goguen's term. In general, algebraic specifications of standard programming languages or machine architectures are not available 'off the shelf', and their production would be a large scale undertaking, far overshadowing the effort involved in the specification and implementation of even a complex abstract data type.

These last remarks perhaps present on overly pessimistic view, based on what is really a rather extreme view of formal correctness proof. It is certainly the case that other approaches rarely, if ever, attempt to carry their proofs right down to the level of the hardware or, indeed, rely on a *detailed* formal specification of the implementation language. It is the case, however, that formal specifications of some languages, notably including MODULA-2, are in existence although, regrettably from the point of view of this discussion, not in the algebraic form. This is an area that provides a fruitful field of research, in which many eminent workers are currently to be found.

9.8   Summary

In this chapter we have discussed the importance of formal specification in the context of data abstraction and explored in some detail one particular approach: algebraic specification. The algebraic specifications of a number of the abstract data types that have appeared in earlier chapters have been presented, together with a more practical example.

Algebraic specifications have been shown to provide a peculiarly appropriate technique for the specification of abstract data types, particularly in view of their ability to reflect the separation of specification from implementation detail that is characteristic of data abstraction. The theoretical basis for proving the correctness of implementations has been briefly introduced, together with an indication of the difficulties that may arise when a completely formal approach is attempted.

Chapter 10

The Object-Oriented Paradigm

10.1 Introduction

In previous chapters we have examined the contribution that Data Abstraction may make to the general area of good modular design and its logical extension — reusable software. We have also seen that the support of Data Abstraction is a feature of a number of programming languages, with the notable examples of MODULA-2 and Ada having been particularly emphasised in this discussion.

Although both these languages provide quite extensive support for the cluster of ideas surrounding Data Abstraction, including information hiding, encapsulation and so on, neither of them actually *imposes* the use of Data Abstraction on the programmer. Thus, it would be quite possible for an Ada programmer to use the language in complete ignorance of these concepts, as a kind of super-Pascal. Quite clearly he or she would be only half-using the language, but the fact that both Ada and MODULA-2 are to a lesser and greater extent supersets of Pascal means that the 'Pascal subset' built into each is effectively usable on its own. And, as was demonstrated fairly early on in this book, Pascal's support for Data Abstraction is not extensive.

In this and the next Chapter we will discuss a family of languages in which concepts related to data abstraction are so central that there is no possibility of their being bypassed, a family generally known as *Object-Oriented* languages. Data abstraction, however, is not the only defining characteristic of Object-Oriented languages, although it is fundamental to the other major characteristic: *Information Sharing*. The combination of these characteristics is sufficiently powerful as to establish a recognisably different style or pattern of programming, the existence of which is captured by the phrase 'Object-Oriented Paradigm'.

The term information sharing may cause surprise, after the heavy emphasis that has been placed, throughout much of this book, on *Information Hiding*, and an explanation is called for. We recall that Information Hiding denotes the separation of *Interface Specification* from *Implementation* — a separation underlying the notion of the Abstract Data Type. This separation forms the basis of, and is enforced by, Information Sharing: the 'sharing' involved is fundamentally concerned with the interfaces of Abstract Data Types. This does not preclude the possibility of the sharing of implementation information, but such sharing is always effected in a highly-structured, controlled manner, mediated via a separate, 'Information Hiding' interface.

Thus the principle of Information Hiding is respected by Information Sharing, the 'abstraction boundary' remains unbreached, but information relating to either side of the boundary may be shared between *different* Abstract Data Types. By this means, an essential feature of Object-Oriented languages is supported — that of the recognition of, and exploitation of, *resemblances* between Abstract Data Types. In other words, the enabling of the definition of one Abstract Data Type by specifying how it differs from one or more other Abstract Data Types, with an assumed commonality where differences are not specified. This idea adds a new dimension to the concept of Data Abstraction, whereby structures of interrelated Abstract Data Types may be created, with significant results for both reuse and abstraction.

In the following sections, these two defining characteristics — Data Abstraction and Information Sharing — are elaborated within the specific context of Object-Oriented languages, or OOPls, to use the vogue acronym.

10.2   Objects and Classes

The deployment of the concepts of Data Abstraction and Abstract Data Types in most OOPls involves a terminology based on 'Object' and 'Class'. The entities that are processed or manipulated by a program written in an Object-Oriented language are invariably referred to as *objects*. Perhaps surprisingly, there is little unanimity on an exact definition of the term *ob-*

ject, although 'behaviour-exhibiting entities with internal state' might perhaps gain reluctant acquiescence from a significant proportion of the Object-Oriented community. The idea of behaviour, as a pattern of stimulus (from the environment to the object) and response (from the object to the environment), together with that of behaviour modification as the result of history, recorded by some form of internal state, has been explored in Chapter 5. In that discussion it was concluded that the Data Abstraction provides a very powerful and generally-applicable program entity for modelling real-world, or application, objects. It is perhaps not surprising, therefore, to find that, in the terminology that has been adopted in this book, objects are Data Abstractions — they are encapsulated data structures whose interaction with the external world is entirely restricted to operations.

The underlying motivation that informs this exclusive dependence on objects as the artefacts manipulated by OOPls appears to have been derived largely from a recognition of the naturalness of Object-Oriented design, and particularly from the benefits that accrue from structuring an application program in terms of the objects of the application problem domain — a topic that was also discussed in Chapter 5. There is thus little alternative to the user of such a language but to adopt an Object-Oriented approach to design: there is simply no support for, say, functional decomposition or data analysis.

In most applications there is a requirement for the replication of objects: many cars, employees, aircraft etc., each of which provides the same sort of behaviour, realised as a set of operations, that its fellows provide, but with different responses to external stimuli in accordance with its individual history. In the terminology of earlier chapters, the satisfaction of this requirement for replication is achieved, in each case, by the use of an Abstract Data Type — i.e. a type whose instances are Data Abstractions, each exhibiting behaviour defined by an identical set of operations. In the MODULA-2 context, for example, a definition module may export an opaque type; when variables are declared as being of this type in external modules then the operations applying to the type are available to them.

This idea is extended and strengthened in Object-Oriented Languages, which are exclusively concerned with implementing Abstract Data Types — in other words, the only reason for the writing of 'code' in one of these languages is as part of the implementation of an Abstract Data Type. It is as though, to use an analogy, Ada was used only to provide the implementations of limited private types.

The conventional terminology used in this context uses *Class* to mean an implementation of an Abstract Data Type. A module in Object-Oriented language terms is a Class, but the idea is much more tightly defined than even the specialised usage found in MODULA-2. This is because there is a *one-to-one* relationship between classes and abstract data types — every class is an implementation of one Abstract Data Type. In MODULA-2, by contrast, a Module may export an opaque type that may be considered to be an Abstract Data Type. On the other hand such a Module may export several such types, or none at all.

10.2.1   Instantiation

The relationship between Objects and Classes is generally expressed in terms of *instantiation* — an object is an *instance* of a class and thus its attributes and operations, which are often called *methods* in the OOPl context, are determined by its class. The conceptual difference between Classes and Objects is basically a very clear one: a Class is an essentially *static* entity, a textual structure that may be thought of as a body of code that provides the implementation underlying the behaviour of its instances. An Object is a *dynamic* entity that is created at run-time and which can interact with other objects, in ways that are determined by its class. (There is a suggestive analogy with the distinction between 'program' and 'process', to which we shall return.)

As we shall see in the next Chapter, the clarity of this distinction becomes slightly obscured in some specific examples of OOPls, although its essential validity remains unchanged.

10.2.2   Classes and Types

The distinction between Objects and Classes is superficially similar to the distinction between variables and types in a conventional language. The similarity is described as 'superficial' because there is a subtle, but significant, distinction between Classes and types.

The flavour of this distinction can be gained from the fact that it is possible for two objects that are instances of different Classes to be of the same type. This is because 'type', in the sense of Abstract Data Type, denotes behaviour, defined over an operational interface. As we have seen in the last Chapter, the semantics of such a type may be defined independently of the underlying implementation, which is conceptually one of many possible models of the semantic specification. Thus, it would be quite possible to provide two distinct Classes, each supporting an interface with the semantics of the stack, to give an original example, using different implementations. Instances of these Classes would possess identical behaviour and so their types would be the same.

In practice, such alternative implementations are unlikely and the relationship between Class and type is generally one-to-one. The distinction between the two concepts is a significant one, however, particularly in (the many) OOPls that do not exhibit specific type declaration, where there is a strong temptation to regard them as identical.

10.2.3 Dynamic Binding of Names to Objects

As we have seen, the execution of a typical OOPl-written program is a very dynamic affair with objects being created (and destroyed) in a way that is generally unpredictable at the time that the corresponding code is actually written. But yet the program code must be written in terms of the manipulation of objects, using names to refer to them in a manner not unlike variable identifiers in a conventional programming language. This is not a new problem — Pascal, MODULA-2 and Ada all provide for the programming of dynamic structures, and similarly use a static colllection of names to provide references to such structures, using the device of *indirection*, or the use of pointers, to handle their dynamic nature. This approach is also widely employed in OOPls, where the binding of names to objects commonly involves *reference* or pointer values: each such name denoting a location that may contain a pointer to an Object. The use of this technique carries two important implications:

- Because the binding of names to objects is done at run-time (so-called 'late binding'), a name may reference many different objects during program execution. Indeed, this is necessary so that the dynamically-changing population of objects may be referenced by a static collection of names. This opens up the question of the types of the objects referenced by a name — can type checking be imposed in such a dynamic environment?

- The use of indirection necessitates care in both assignment and testing for equality, for essentially the same reasons that led to the incorpo-

ration of limited private types in Ada as discussed in Chapter 4 —
i.e. the assignment or equality testing of the pointer values denoted
directly by program names is generally not the required operation.

The issue, particularly, of the typing of OOPls is an important one to which
we shall return in the next Chapter.

Garbage Collection

As a result of this dynamic creation of objects it is generally impossible to
determine the memory occupancy that will be required during the running
of an OOPl 'program' (the reason for the inverted commas will be explained
shortly) simply by inspecting the 'code'. For this and other reasons it is
normally not the case that an OOPl requires just a conventional compiler,
relying on the operating system to take care of run-time occurrences. Instead, most OOPls are designed for, and indeed may only be used within, a
program environment, which provides a large variety of auxiliary services to
the OOPl user. The most basic of these is memory management — the allocation of memory to objects as they are created. Now it is true that several
conventional languages, including MODULA-2 and Ada, as we have seen,
provide for dynamic memory allocation. What they do not do (although the
Ada definition suggests that compiler implementors might provide such a
feature) is to *deallocate* memory — that is, make available for use again the
memory occupied by objects that are no longer required — *automatically*.
This feature, which is known as *Garbage Collection*, is almost a defining feature of OOPls, although at least one widely-used language does not provide
it. Curiously, garbage collection is a feature of one of the oldest programming languages in existence, LISP, and it is perhaps partially for this reason
that there are a number of LISP-based OOPls.

The discussion above raised the possibility of objects that become redun-
dant or unnecessary, and the obvious question is how this happens. The
answer involves the dynamic nature of the binding of names to objects in an
OOPl environment. This permits the binding of a name to an object to be
broken, typically by binding the name to another object. This process may
be repeated until no names at all are bound to the object, at which point
it becomes unusable, as there is no means of referring to it. The garbage
collection activity operates, therefore, by monitoring the binding of names
to each object; on the detecting of an object with no references to it, its
storage is returned to the common pool.

10.2.4 The Message-Passing Metaphor

In Chapter 5 the claim was made that behaviour, in a very general sense, is naturally described in terms of *stimulus* and *response* — " what does this object do if we do this to it?". The accessibility of this model has led to the adoption, in many Object-Oriented languages, of the *message-passing computational metaphor*, which views all computation, at a certain level of abstraction, as consisting solely of the passing of messages between objects. Any interaction of two objects, according to the metaphor, conforms with the pattern that the *sender* object sends a message to the *receiver* object, which returns a *response* to the sender.

As its name indicates, this model of computation is metaphorical — Objects in Object-Oriented environments are not generally the kind of entities that are capable of 'sending messages', a terminology that normally implies some form of distributed processing involving communication channels. Typically, the Objects of a program are implemented as structures residing within a common memory, while message-passing is realised as procedure calls. These implementation details are obscured, however, in those languages that support it, by the message-passing metaphor, which is intended to emphasise the independence of:

- **Objects** — as separate exhibitors of behaviour, responding to stimuli from other, similarly independent Objects.

- **Messages** — as possessing an existence separate from the Objects to which they are sent, and thus providing the basis for *inclusion polymorphism*, topic that will shortly be explored.

The immediately discernible effect of the metaphor is a notational one. The typical format of the messages that comprise the 'statements' of an OOPl program is:

```
receiver selector argument(s)
```

The semantics of this format are that *receiver* is the name of the object to which the message is sent. *Selector* defines the kind of message, i.e. it specifies the service that the sender wishes the receiver to perform, while the arguments, if present, may be regarded as the input data for the operation concerned. The values of arguments, of course, are objects.

The flavour of the use of this format can be brought out by considering a reasonably close Ada equivalent. In Ada terms an object is a variable of a private type. If we imagine an Ada package as follows:

```
Package A_Class is
--
        type Object is private;
--
        procedure reset(obj : in out object; size : integer);
        -- reset object parameter with specified size
--
--      rest of package
--
```

Then the following fragment might be found in another unit:

```
this_Obj : A_Class.Object:
begin
        A_Class.reset(this_Obj, 100);
--
```

By contrast, a typical 'message-passing' equivalent would be:

```
            this_obj reset(100)
```

The supporters of OOPls claim, with some justification, that this is a more natural representation; but it is only a matter of representation, after all. The significant difference is the primacy of the receiver Object in the message-passing format — it has a distinguished place at the start of the message rather than being just another parameter, as in the Ada version. Furthermore the class of which the receiver is an instantiation does not feature in the message, emphasising the position of the Object as the dynamic agent of computation, rather than the static code underlying its behaviour.

As we shall see in the next Chapter, the message-passing metaphor is supported with various degrees of fidelity by specific examples of OOPls. Probably the most complete and consistent realisation is to be found in Smalltalk, where even the summing operation represented by the arithmetic expression $3 + 1$ is interpreted as a message sent to the object "3", with the method selector "+" and argument "1", producing the response "4". (As Meyer has observed [7], this interpretation does not seem to possess any great advantage over the conventional arithmetic one.)

An interesting possibility is the transformation of the message-passing model from a metaphor into actuality in a parallel processing environment. In such a realisation, the operations of every object would comprise an independent *thread of control* or process, which is executed in parallel with the processes of all other objects in the system. At this level of realisation, objects are independently active and the execution of a service by an object on behalf of a client is not like a procedure call, where a single thread of control passes from the sender, through the code associated with the receiver, to return back to the sender, but the result of a message passed between two independent processes. Message-passing provides a very natural basis for programming parallel, multi-processor systems and, importantly, their simulation on single-processor systems, *without the need to change the code at the language level.* It was for this reason that message-passing was adopted as the mechanism for inter-task (i.e. inter-process) synchronisation in Ada.

In practical terms the realisation of the message-passing metaphor differs little from the interaction between Ada packages as recommended by the principles of Object-Oriented design. It reflects a philosophy that emphasises loose coupling between modules, with interaction restricted to the passing of data values. There is no support for 'transfer of control', global data or any other tight linkage.

The Current Object

A computation in an OOPl system consists therefore of a connected chain of messages, each message generally being sent by an object as part of its response to a message that it has received. At any particular time during the computation, therefore, there will be an object that is the 'most recent receiver' of a message. This object clearly has a special significance in the insantaneous state of the computation and is distinguished by a special name in many languages. This name — often *self* or *me* — is used when an object wishes to invoke one of its own methods. The semantics of message-passing require the object in such a case to send a message to itself, and so a name is required for this self-reference.

Main Programs

Readers familiar with conventional programming languages may well be puzzled as to how a system constructed within an Object-Oriented environment actually works. A system written even in MODULA-2 or Ada has a 'main program', no matter how trivial, which essentially provides the root of the calling chain that the execution of the program creates. In an Object-Oriented 'program' — the term seems hardly appropriate — this is carried to its logical conclusion: there is no 'main program', merely an interlinked collection of objects. Obviously there must be a way of setting the whole thing going — this is provided by an interface to the operating system that, for example, allows messages to be sent directly to an object from the keyboard, or some other type of user input.

The address space in which the objects of a system exist is a 'one-level' one in which they are all directly and equally visible, both to each other and to an external user: there is no requirement for import or context clauses.

10.2.5   Class Definitions

As is implied by the nature of the message-passing metaphor, the internal structure of an object, which is defined by its class, must be such as to enable it to respond to messages sent to it. The nature of this structure will come as no surprise after the lengthy discussions of encapsulating constructs in earlier chapters: a class possesses an *interface*, in which the *attributes* and *services* that it offers to the external world are defined, and an *implementation* part that encapsulates the code that supports this external interface. A variety of terminology is employed over the range of OOPls currently available to describe this structure. Classes define *Methods*, *Routines*, *features* or indeed *Operations*, in order to respond to messages from their *clients*. Additionally, completing the structure of the data abstraction that each class defines, a class will typically include an encapsulated data structure consisting of items variously called *Instance Variables*, *attributes* or *components*. These items are invariably instances of other classes — objects in other words. The set of objects that are instances of the same type all have the same set of instance variables. The values of the instance variables distinguish individual objects.

It is clear that the basic structure of the class closely resembles the corresponding structures — Packages and Library Modules — in Ada and MODULA-2, when these are used for implementing Abstract Data Types, in particular in its support for the separation of interface from implementation details. As we shall see in the comparison of a number of OOPls in the next Chapter, this basic concept appears in a variety of guises. The major variations lie in the area of encapsulation, while the essential attribute of data abstraction: the restriction of the manipulation of data items to operations only, is preserved generally.

Classes and Messages

The dichotomy between classes and objects gives rise to a conceptual problem when the creation of objects is considered. If, as has been maintained, every computation in an OOPl system is identified with message passing between objects, to what object is a message sent to cause the creation of a new object? Obviously the class of which the object is an instance must be involved, but how can a message be sent to a class — a static behavioural description? In less specialised terms, how can a static entity like a class take part in the run-time creation of dynamic entities like objects? The answer to this question is provided in different ways by the various OOPls that will be considered in the next Chapter.

10.3 Inheritance

The picture outlined so far lacks a highly important, some would say the most important, feature. This is the structure of relationships that exists between the classes in an Object-Oriented environment, which provides the basis for information sharing.

In discussing the Ada approach to program libraries, reuse, and so on, the point has been made that the language is quite neutral towards the semantics of the entities, particularly Abstract Data Types, that are implemented in it. It might well be envisaged that every Ada installation, indeed every Ada library, will possess a different set of units, reflecting the applications and interests of its users.

This picture is modified slightly if we adopt Booch's view, as expressed in *Software Components with Ada*, which holds that there is a fundamental set of components that will be applicable in *any* context, and so should be available to any Ada user. This is still a matter of choice, however: nothing in the language imposes this view. Furthermore, as we have seen, the nature of the language provides little positive support for the recognition of relationships between realisations of Abstract Data Types.

An alternative approach, one that is almost universally respected in Object-Oriented languages, is based on a perception that the recognition of relationships between Abstract Data Types, or the classes that implement them, can contribute powerfully towards two significant concerns in programming:

- Reuse

- Abstraction

10.3.1   Information Sharing and Reuse

As was briefly noted in the Introduction to this Chapter, information sharing permits the defining of one class in terms of one or more other classes already known to the system, so that only the differences exhibited by the new class need be defined. These differences will typically consist of additional methods, for which the implementations are supplied, comprising the complete definition of the new class.

The Information Sharing mechanism recognises the interdependencies between classes defined in this way, known as *programming-by-difference*, and merges the features of the pre-existing class(es) with the additional features of the new definition, thus re-using the pre-existing classes in a very direct fashion. As compared with the Ada model of software reuse, the Information Sharing approach is essentially orientated towards extensibility and incremental development in a way that the former cannot hope to match, because of its inflexibility.

10.3.2   Information Sharing and Abstraction

A great deal of this book has been related to abstraction, in the form of Data Abstraction: the replacing of implementation detail by well-defined, operational interfaces. As we have seen, the use of this technique has significance both for the structure of software and also for the intelligibility of the program code — in that this may be written in terms of the objects of the problem space, a technique that contributes benefits both to the writing and the subsequent maintenance of the code in question.

The recognition of relationships between objects, other and richer than 'interacts with', enables this kind of abstraction-raising to be carried further;

so that not only is the code written in terms of the manipulation of the objects of the problem-space, but also these manipulations can be defined in the most general way. The basis of this is a very characteristic mode of human thought: *classification* by recognising relationships, particularly resemblances, between objects.

This idea may be illustrated by a simple example. Suppose it is required to write a program dealing with geometric shapes — perhaps in order to optimise the cutting of such shapes from a piece of material so as to minimise waste. A small fragment of code calculates the total area of the set of shapes defined for the particular program run. We might imagine a pseudo-code version of this fragment as follows:

```
for_each SHAPE in BAG_OF_SHAPES
loop
        TOTAL_AREA := TOTAL_AREA + AREA_OF(SHAPE);
end loop;
```

We understand that the **for_each** construct is a slightly more advanced version of the Ada **for** construct, which combines an iterator with the loop so as to extract the members of the collection **BAG_OF_SHAPES** (a bag is a mathematical object like a set but which permits multiple instances of members) one at a time, the loop body being executed once for each member as the value of the loop variable **SHAPE**. We also assume that **BAG_OF_SHAPES** contains an arbitrary collection of different shapes: squares, polygons, ellipses and so on.

This fragment of pseudo-code is a close approximation to an informal version expressed along the lines of 'we take each shape in turn, find its area and add it to the total'. The human mind has no difficulty in coping with the idea of a generalised calculation like 'find the area of (any) geometrical shape', as represented by the **AREA_OF** operation, capable of determining the area of any kind of figure that has two-dimensional extension. It would be desirable, therefore, from the point-of-view of intelligibility, for an implementation of this design to exhibit a similar simplicity, deriving from the use of such an abstract operation.

In practice, it is rather difficult to realise this idea using a conventional language, even one as powerful as Ada, particularly if an Object-Oriented approach is used. One problem is that the different shapes that the program is required to accommodate would naturally be realised as different (abstract) types, and so there is the immediate difficulty of allowing SHAPE to assume different types during a single execution of the loop. A similar, and more serious, problem confronts the writer of the AREA_OF function, which is required to be invoked with actual parameters of different types. Ada's generic facility, as we saw in Chapter 8, is a static mechanism and is thus unable to cope with parameter types determined at run-time. The language rules permit the overloading of the AREA_OF function — i.e. the introduction of several functions with this name, distinguished by the parameter type: square, circle and so on. But Ada's overloading mechanism is similarly statically limited, and incapable of resolving the necessary association of function and parameter type at run-time.

The only possible solution to these problems, within the Ada context, is to implement the family of geometric shapes as a variant record type: a feature similar to the Pascal variant record feature. This provides for alternative structures to be defined for a record type, discriminated by a 'tag' field in the record, known as a *discriminant* in its Ada version. This feature would allow the declaration of a record type, say figure, with a discriminant of an enumerated type containing literals such as square, circle, rectangle... etc. The declaration of figure would include variants corresponding to each value of the discriminant type: the circle variant would possess fields containing data defining centre and radius, that for polygon vertices, and so on. Ada also permits the declaring of subtypes corresponding to the individual variants of such a type, and so it would be possible for SHAPE and the parameter of AREA_OF to be of type figure, while accepting objects of the variant subtypes corresponding to circle etc.

There are, however, a number of drawbacks to this solution, some serious enough to invalidate it completely. The variant structure would be 'hardwired' into the program, representing a high level of coupling. But the main problem arises from the status of subtypes in Ada — subtypes are not types, and are not capable of leading the kind of independent existence that would be required for them to be established as Abstract Data Types, private types in the Ada context, in a way that the use of an Object-Oriented approach requires.

The variant subtype idea does, however, suggest the kind of relationship between types that could support the abstraction that we are trying to achieve. What is required is the recognition of the 'shape subtypes', circle, square etc, as being types in their own right, while retaining their 'family resemblance' to the more general, higher-level type figure. This family relationship would permit the association of generalised, abstract operations such as

AREA_OF with the correspondingly generalised type `figure`, *whilst applying to all the shape subtypes.* More specific operations such as `radius_of` would apply only to specific shape subtypes: `circle` in this case.

10.3.3 The 'is a' Relationship

Both these applications of Information Sharing, reuse and abstraction, may be supported by various kinds of relationships between types. By far the most widely used, however, to such an extent that it is frequently cited as a defining characteristic of OOPls, is the *is a* relationship. This is the relationship recognised by the classical taxonomies of botany and zoology, and denotes the inclusion of a specialised species within a more generalised one. In the example used in the last section, the relationship is used to assert that, say, a polygon *is a* geometric figure, as also a circle *is a* geometric figure. Both these specialised shapes possess all the attributes possessed by the more general geometric figure, because of this relationship. The *is a* relationship is a transitive one — if the specialised shapes square and triangle are defined then both exhibit the relationship to polygon and, transitively, to geometric figure.

In the context of OOPls the *is a* relationship is commonly referred to as the *inherits* relationship, e.g. polygon inherits from geometric figure. The inherits terminology, with its suggestion of an active transmission of attributes, is perhaps more appropriate to the OOPl context. It must be admitted, though, that OOPl terminology is far from standardised, or even coherent. Inheritance is variously defined in terms of super and subclasses, parents and heirs, ancestors and descendants, and so on. In this and the next Chapter the terminology is used with little attempt at consistency, in order to prepare the reader for the mild anarchy prevailing in OOPs literature.

10.3.4 The Inheritance Mechanism

How, in practice, is inheritance realised as a programming feature? This involves typically both static, i.e. linguistic, and dynamic mechanisms. The former are straightforward enough: every class definition, either explicitly or implicitly, includes the name of its immediate parent, or superclass.(For the moment we will restrict our attentions to the possibility only of single superclasses.) The class that is the subject of the definition is then said to inherit from the nominated superclass, and to be an heir, or subclass of it. The transitive nature of inheritance means that 'chains' of classes can be linked together by the relationship. These structures, often called 'superclass chains' frequently, depending on the language, terminate at a single, most general class, known as *Object*, the whole collection forming a tree rooted on Object. Such a tree structure is commonly referred to as a *Class Hierarchy*.

The semantics of inheritance generally require a dynamic mechanism to perform so-called 'method binding' — the identification and execution of the appropriate code body on receipt of a messageby an object. The dynamic nature of method binding is necessary because the method selected by a message sent to an object may not be present in the class of the object, but in one of its ancestor classes. The mechanism operates by 'forwarding ' or 'promoting' the message up the superclass chain until the method is found, or the limit of the chain is reached. In the latter case an error condition, corresponding to a type clash in a conventional language, is generated, resulting in an error message along the lines of 'message not understood'.

10.3.5   Specialisation and Redefinition

The effect of the inheritance mechanism is to make available to an object the set of methods contained both in its class and all its ancestor classes. (As we shall see, *set* is used here in its mathematical sense that excludes duplication.) Each new subclass adds new methods, specialising the nature of the objects instantiated from it. Continuing the geometric figures example, the **polygon** class might well provide an iterator to allow the extraction of the vertices — the perimeter-defining points — for a polygon object. This would be an inappropriate operation for the more generalised **geometric_ figure**, which might include curved perimeter segments. In the same way the class **square**, inheriting from and specialising **polygon**, might provide methods relating to to the diagonal of a square object — a feature not generally found in polygons.

In general terms the relationship between classes established by the inheritance of generalised attributes from superclass to subclass means that:

> An instantiation of a class can always be used where an
> instantiation of one of its ancestor classes can be used.

This is simply an expression of the idea that if A 'is a' B, then A can do anything that B can do. In implementation terms this results from the inheritance, by A, of all B's methods. The reverse is not generally true, because the 'is a' relationship is not symmetrical.

This picture is slightly complicated by matters both practical and abstract. If we return to the AREA_OF operation — or rather message, to adopt the message-passing style — while we can imagine a corresponding generalised method included in the class **geometric_figure**, in practice the writing of such a method would be difficult. Also, it would be very inefficient to use such a general-purpose algorithm to calculate the areas of simple shapes such as circles or squares.

The avoidance of this sort of inefficiency (or even impossibility) is achieved by the *redefinition* of inherited methods within heir, or subclasses, thus preventing the promotion of the associated messages to high-level, generalised methods, which are then said to be *overridden* . In practice, the AREA_OF message would invoke methods contained in the specific shape classes, such as circle and square, each redefining the high-level method contained in geometric figure. In fact, there would be *no* algorithm for AREA_OF in geometric figure. The method would simply produce an error message, as it should never be invoked. The existence of the method has a symbolic significance only, to ensure that such a method is provided, by an appropriate redefinition, in all the descendants of the class.

As this example shows, information sharing may not always involve the sharing, and reuse, of method implementations: specifically when redefinition is employed. Redefinition is essentially an aid to the maintenance of abstraction, in the form of abstract, *polymorphic*, operations. As was discussed briefly in Chapter 8, polymorphic operations are capable of being applied to different types. In the OOP1 context the vehicle for polymorphism is the message — polymorphism refers to the ability of objects of different classes to respond to the same message, in the way exemplified by the AREA_OF message. This kind of polymorphism is conferred by the redefinition of high-level, abstract methods at the lower levels in the subtree of descendants: so-called 'polymorphic redefinition' . Its dependence on inheritance, the 'is a' relationship, is indicated by its name: *inclusion* polymorphism. The Information Sharing involved is restricted to the interface specification, and is effectively the imposition of a commitment on potential subclasses, so that abstraction can be related to classification.

A very common and useful, if somewhat mundane, example of inclusion polymorphism is the **print yourself** message, for which an abstract method is provided at the root of the class hierarchy and redefined in every class, so that any object will respond to it by printing out some representation of its structure.

Method Restriction

Method overriding by redefinition gives rise to the possibility of 'blanking out' inherited methods — by redefining them as null methods or error conditions. Indeed in some cases this may be difficult to avoid. Consider a queue class defined as a subclass of a linked-list class, not unlike the Ada example given in Chapter 8. There is little problem in adding methods to respond to Enqueue or Dequeue messages, and a method for Is_empty might well be included already in linked-list. However, the conventional operations for linked-lists include support for the ability to insert items *anywhere* into the sequential structure of the list, and methods for enabling this kind of insertion would be part of any useful linked-list class. Their use would not, however, be appropriate for a queue — insertion into a queue at any point other than at its 'end' would destroy the FIFO discipline. The queue class would therefore, presumably, override the offending methods so as to disable them. But in doing this we would have destroyed the 'is a' relationship! We could no longer guarantee that an instance of any subclass of linked-list could be used where any of *its* instances could be used, because such use might well depend on its 'free insertion' properties.

There is a range of responses to this problem. At one extreme is a robust attitude that simply accepts that the 'is a' relationship may be broken sometimes. This attitude is consistent with one of the two extremes of an increasingly well-defined polarisation that sees inheritance as, essentially, a vehicle for *code sharing* — the emphasis being placed on reuse rather than the more abstract virtues of polymorphism.

At the other extreme, as exemplified by Meyer [7], is the belief that 'a class may not reject its inheritance' — no inherited method may be blanked out, in other words. Certainly, polymorphism may be compromised if subclasses are allowed to 'reject their inheritance', but the example of the queue shows that this is sometimes difficult to avoid. The proponents of what might be called the strict view might well maintain that the problem is caused by an inappropriate inheritance — linked-lists are just the wrong kind of superclass for queues — but this seems difficult to justify. The example shows that inheritance may not provide the universal model for class relationships that it is often asserted to be, and, in any case, method overriding should be approached with care.

Clients and Heirs

The nature of inheritance means that any class potentially has two kinds of 'user': the *client* whose use is confined to the standard interface presented by the class to the world of external objects, and the *heir* who inherits from the class via the subclass relationship. The description above mentions operations, or methods, as the currency of inheritance and it is the case that this provides a realistic picture of the technique. It is also the case that a number of languages make accessible more than the methods of superclasses to their subclasses — some or all of the data structure defined in a class may also be made accessible: that is *directly* accessible via assignment. This, of course, destroys, or at least compromises, the encapsulation of a class in so far as its heirs are concerned.

There are two schools of thought on this matter. One holds that the tight coupling that is implied as between a class and its heirs is unacceptable in a software engineering environment. A change in the internal implementation of a class that changed the names or the use made of some of the instance variables would invalidate subclasses that accessed them. The other school holds that the relationship between a class and its heirs is, of necessity, an intimate one and that the implementor of a subclass must expect to be committed to the class involved, in the way that the implementor of a client would not.

The author's view, for what it is worth, is that the considerable persuasiveness with which the second approach is put forward cannot disguise the fact that it is really a piece of special pleading. However, the reader must make up his or her own mind, and it must be said that the particular nature of software development in the OOPs context makes the question far from black or white.

The inheritance mechanism supports an approach to software reuse that differs considerably from the conventional model exemplified by the Ada library approach. In the conventional model software components are black boxes — their internal features hidden from users either completely, or effectively. Even if a user can examine the code of an Ada library component it is completely inaccessible from the point of view of extension or modification. Indeed, as we have seen, it is not always possible to build on an existing component to create a more powerful, specialised component, without resorting to inelegant measures. By contrast, the use of inheritance frequently necessitates the visibility of the implementation of the existing component, or class. This is obviously necessary in the case where access is made, by name, to instance variables. It is also necessary in the majority of cases of redefinition, because the implementor must understand the code of the method that is redefined, if only to know that it *must* be redefined!

10.4   Program Development in an OOP Environment

The description given so far portrays a potential approach to the development of reusable software, based on a powerful set of related concepts including the superclass hierarchy and, particularly, the inheritance mechanism. This picture falls far short of the reality of actually using a mature Object-Oriented environment, of which Smalltalk provides the best example, because it fails to emphasise the established class structure that 'comes with' the more obvious system components as a compiler, the garbage collector, and so on. The purchaser of a Smalltalk system receives, in fact, a very large class structure, ready-made. The existence of this class structure, and its availability to the user, means that the software development process within such an environment is quite different from that found in traditional program development environments, even those supporting a 'component-oriented' language such as Ada, where there is no large scale *standard* library structure.

In an Object-Oriented environment a new application is developed by modifying the pre-existing class structure: typically by the addition of subclasses that specialise some of the existing classes, using a combination of new methods and redefined methods. It is clear in this context that the whole process of design and implementation, if it is to benefit from and exploit this potentially reusable software, must be informed by a detailed knowledge of what already exists in the class structure. The process of design, in fact, becomes largely a matter of *recognition* — of existing abstract data types, together with an educated knowledge of the possibilities of modifying existing classes to match the requirements of the application. In some respects, the skills involved seem more akin to those of a lawyer or a mediaeval scholar than the conventional view of the creative design engineer, although, in fact, 'creative design engineers' in, say, the electronics industry, rapidly acquire an encyclopaedic knowledge of catalogues of the components on which their designs depend.

10.4.1 Tools

The necessity for familiarity on the part of the designer/programmer with the class structure supported by the Object-Oriented environment being used would be a daunting task — sufficiently so as to be questionably practicable without the availability of powerful tools within the environment. These tools, commonly called *browsers*, permit the user to explore the structure via a highly responsive interactive interface, normally based on the use of windows and menus and dependent on pointing devices, usually mice, to mediate the interaction.

10.5 Summary

In this Chapter we have discussed the important characteristics of Object-Oriented languages. These have been discovered to be based on the essential feature of Data Abstraction, and its related concept, the Abstract Data Type, realised in terms of Objects — dynamic instantiations of Classes — with their independence emphasised by the message-passing metaphor. To Data Abstraction is added the new dimension of Information Sharing, so that relationships between Abstract Data Types may be recognised and exploited, both in the service of software reuse and in the raising of abstraction by the support of polymorphism. In the next Chapter the way in which these concepts are realised in specific examples of OOPls will be discussed.

Chapter 11

Object-Oriented Languages

11.1 Introduction

In the last Chapter the general characteristics of Object-Oriented languages were introduced in a manner that is generally non-specific to any particular language. In this Chapter the way in which these characteristics are exhibited by a number of specific languages is explored, with the intention not so much of providing an exhaustive 'manual' in each case, but of conveying the essential nature of each of the variations on the theme.

Despite the non-specific nature of the last Chapter, it is the case that much of its material applies directly to Smalltalk, as the result of the pervasive influence that Smalltalk has had on Object-Oriented culture, particularly in relation to terminology. The explosion of interest in Object-Oriented languages and environments that occurred during the nineteen eighties was undoubtedly initiated by Smalltalk, and it still commands an important position within the Object-Oriented world. Because of this importance it is appropriate to give a reasonably complete picture of Smalltalk, in its most widely-distributed variant Smalltalk 80, which can also then serve as a standard against which to compare other OOPls.

11.2   Smalltalk

11.2.1   Introduction

The first and important point to make about Smalltalk is that it is a *Programming Environment* that surrounds a language — the actual details of the language almost fade into insignificance against the other major features of the environment. These include a very highly developed interactive interface, characterised by the kind of window-driven facilities mentioned previously, and a very comprehensive *Class Hierarchy*, which is the result of years of accumulated development. Smalltalk exhibits all the characteristics identified previously as belonging to an Object-Oriented language: Data Abstraction, Dynamic Binding, Inheritance, Polymorphism and Message-Passing.

Many of Smalltalk's characteristics result from an overall aim to make program development a natural, free-flowing, incremental process, suited particularly to the rapid prototyping of software. The emphasis is on continuous, small-grained modification rather than the traditional coarse-grained, episodic life-cycle model. It is probably true to say that the Object-Oriented paradigm is seen as the means to achieve this overall aim rather than being the end in itself.

11.2.2   The Smalltalk System

In more specific terms, the Smalltalk system provides a 'single-mode' environment in which code input, translation and testing are performed in a highly interleaved manner. Each input, translate and test cycle typically involves only a few lines of text, by virtue of the system's support for *programming-by-difference* — the specialisation of existing classes in the hierarchy. The process is controlled by a unified interface to all the relevant system components, utilising a 'pointing' device such as a mouse.

Two major features of the system support this very dynamic environment:

- The code of the system is *interpreted* rather than being compiled. The system contains a translator, which is known as the compiler, but its function is a 'statement level' conversion of the source text into an intermediate format that can be executed by an interpreter. This means that 'compilation' is fast but that the ensuing execution is relatively slow — the appropriate trade-off for the rapid incremental development of prototype software. The more semantic features of compilation in its conventional sense are not supported, particularly type checking. In the Smalltalk context this means that no attempt is made to check that a method exists in the class of an object, or one of its ancestor classes, capable of responding to a message specified as being sent to it.

- A fundamental feature of the Smalltalk system which might be seen as necessitated either by the application of the Object-Oriented paradigm in a rigorous way, or by the requirements of the highly dynamic environment, is the fact that *everything* in the system is an object, including every member of the class hierarchy. This feature both provides an elegant solution to the conundrum of how essentially static classes may take part in the dynamic creation of objects, and contributes practically to the rapid response necessary for a system like Smalltalk to be usable.

As might be expected from the nature both of the Object-Oriented paradigm and these features of the Smalltalk system the language at the core of Smalltalk is somewhat unconventional.

11.2.3 The Smalltalk Language

The language used to write Smalltalk programs has comparatively few large structures: each program, or program increment, typically consists of some messages organised into methods within a class definition.

Messages

There are three variants of the message format: *unary*, *binary* and *keyword*, which are distinguished by the number of parameters that they require. A unary message consists of a single identifier (the term being used much as in any language) and requires no parameters, e.g: **tree isEmpty**, where **tree** is the receiver object of the message, which requests a Boolean response as to whether **tree** is empty. (The style of identifier used here, where words are run together with their initial letters capitalised, apart from the first word, is a standard Smalltalk convention.) A binary message takes one parameter: the 'other' parameter implied by *binary* is the receiver object. Characteristic binary messages are the equivalents of the arithmetic and relational operators in conventional languages. For example **total > 100**.

Keyword messages permit several parameters to be defined, each introduced by an identifier known as the keyword for the parameter. Conventionally, keywords are suffixed by a colon. For example:

symbolTable at:next put:variable

This is a characteristic form of message used to insert an item, in this case referenced by **variable**, into some kind of search structure object, here referenced by **symbolTable**, at a position indicated by **next**.

Assignments

One structure that is not a message is the assignment, which has a rather different role from that found in conventional languages. Essentially, assignment accomplishes the binding of a name — an identifier — to an object. We recall that the requirements for the handling of dynamic objects necessitate that such a binding is an indirect one, and that no copying of the object involved takes place, unlike assignment in a conventional language.

Assignment is frequently associated with object creation, either explicitly by the sending of a **new** message to the appropriate class (object), or implicitly, for example by the assignment of literal values. Examples:

symbolTable ← Dictionary new

where the name **symbolTable** is bound to the newly-created object of class **Dictionary**, a search structure providing keyed access.

vector ← #(65, 24, 26, 13)

which will create an array, referenced by the identifier **vector**, with the values shown in the square brackets.

As noted previously, there is no type-related variable declaration or type checking in Smalltalk, the class of the object referenced by an identifier is determined simply by the last assignment made to it. There is no restriction on the objects that an identifier may reference during execution.

Control Structures

Control structures in Smalltalk, as in other languages, provide for the execution of alternative or iterated pathways through the the code, depending on the values of *conditions*. The Smalltalk versions of the standard control structures, as might be expected, conform to the message-passing metaphor. A condition is evaluated by the sending of an appropriate message, perhaps the binary message <, and responds with an object denoted by one of the pseudo-variables *true* or *false*. (Pseudo-variables resemble ordinary variables except that their denotations are fixed and may not be changed.) The objects to which *true* and *false* are bound respond, for example, to the message **ifTrue:**, which takes a parameter in the form of a *block*. A block is a piece of program code delimited by square brackets, which is evaluated on receipt of a message, rather than when the execution sequence reaches it. The **ifTrue:** method provides such a message and thus causes the evaluation of the block parameter. Thus the Smalltalk equivalent of:

```
if  a > b
then a := a - b;
end if;
```

is:

$$a > b \ \textbf{ifTrue:}[a \leftarrow a - b]$$

When the **ifTrue:** message is sent to *false* then the parameter is not evaluated. The equivalent of the 'else' path of the conventional if statement is provided by the **ifFalse:** message, which causes its block parameter to be evaluated when it is sent to *false*.

A similar mechanism provides the Smalltalk equivalent of the *while* loop.

Classes

As remarked above, the standard way of 'writing Smalltalk programs' is by writing new class definitions in the form of subclasses related to the existing class hierarchy. The 'hook' that attaches such a class onto the hierarchy is an expression that heads its definition and specifies the immediate superclass, or parent, of the new class. For example, a class **Queue** would be defined as a child class of **LinkedList** by the expression:

LinkedList subclass: #Queue

Note that class names are conventionally started by a capital letter, and also that **Queue** is defined to be a unique name in the system, as it must be, by making it a *symbol* as indicated by the '#'.

The version of inheritance supported by the major versions of Smalltalk is that known as *Single* inheritance in which, as its name suggests, any class may have only one superclass. Only one expression such as that shown above may appear in a class definition, therefore.

Smalltalk terminology has already been introduced in the last chapter; to summarise: class definitions include *instance methods*, each of which is an operation associated with one of the *Messages* to which instances of the class respond. The data structure encapsulated by the class, at least in so far as its clients are concerned, comprises a set of *Instance Variables*, whose values survive the execution of individual methods. Individual methods may have *temporary* variables, the values of which are lost when control leaves the methods. The collection of methods and instance variables (and *Class Variables* q.v.) are known as the *Protocol* for the class.

The format of a class definition is not unlike that of a MODULA-2 Implementation Module or Ada Package Body, although with considerably less 'syntactic sugar' in the form of reserved words. (Generally, the Smalltalk language cannot be highly recommended either for its readability or self-documenting qualities.) The protocol for each method is preceded by the selector(s) of the message that invokes it, with identifiers for the formal parameters in binary or keyword messages. The following shows the protocol for a **factorial** method that might be added to a subclass of **Integer**.

```
factorial
"answer the factorial of the receiver"
        self > 0
                ifTrue: [↑ self * (self - 1) factorial]
        self = 0
                ifTrue: [↑ 1 ]
```

This short example illustrates a number of Smalltalk features. Comments are enclosed in double quotes. The entity **self** is the Smalltalk name, actually a pseudo-variable, for the 'receiver of the message', in this case an object that is an instance of **Integer**. If the value of the receiver object is greater than 0 then, because the priority of a unary message is greater than that of a binary, the **factorial** message is sent recursively to **(self - 1)** until this expression becomes 0, when the **Integer** object 1 is returned as the parameter to the first of the binary '*' messages that have been stacked up, causing the calculation of the factorial.

The ↑ symbol indicates the expression whose evaluation is returned as the response of the method. As can be seen, a method may contain several return expressions, the one that is executed being determined by the value of the condition and thus the path through the method.

In addition to the 'executable' code of messages and assignments, class definitions include data items in the form of Instance and Temporary Variables, both of which are classified as *private* in Smalltalk terminology, although, as we have seen, the Instance Variables of a class are directly accessible to its subclasses. Instance Variables and Temporary Variables are 'declared' by being listed at the head, respectively, of the class and method defnition to which they belong, between vertical bars in the case of Temporary Variables. Something of the flavour of a full class definition can be obtained from the (slightly amended and drastically truncated) protocol for class **Tree** shown in Figure 11.1.

No separate interface specification, along the lines of the Definition Module or Package Specification is required *as part of the language*, but is generated by the environment, which will produce a display of the messages to which each class responds.

Abstract Classes

In the last Chapter the concept of *inclusion polymorphism* was introduced as supporting the use of abstract operations, applicable to high-level classes and made available through polymorphic redefinition. This form of polymorphism is central to Smalltalk and is realised by the vehicle of Abstract Classes.

The classes in the regions of the hierarchy near to and including the root, naturally in view of the semantics of inheritance, are very generalised — to such an extent that they are not intended to support the creation of instances but to provide to, and impose on, their descendants a consistent set of methods. Such classes are known as *Abstract Classes*. A typical example of an Abstract class is *Magnitude*, which defines protocol for objects that can be compared or measured, including the relational operations such as = and <, realised as binary messages. The descendants of *Magnitude* include the numerical classes *integer* and *float* and also the class of ASCII characters *Char*. An example of polymorphic redefinition that is frequently given is the printOn message, which causes a textual representation of the receiver object to be output. This message is included in the protocol for *Object*,

Object subclass: #Tree
 instanceVariableNames 'root maxLevel avgLevel'
 classVariableNames "

 deleteLeft: aNode
   "Delete left offspring of aNode"
   |nodeToDelete|
   nodeToDelete ← aNode left.
   nodeToDelete left isNil ifTrue:[↑ aNode left: nodeToDelete right].
   nodeToDelete right isNil ifTrue:[↑ aNode left: nodeToDelete left].
   ↑aNode left: (self predecessorOf: nodeToDelete).

 predecessorOf: aNode
   "Replace aNode with its inorder predecessor"
   |predecessor|
   predecessor ← aNode predecessor.
   predecessor = aNode left ifFalse[
     aNode left right: predecessor left.
     predecessor left: aNode left].
   predecessor right: aNode right.
   ↑predecessor.

 insert: aNode
   "Insert based on key value in aNode subclass"
   |parent|
   self empty ifTrue: [↑self root: aNode].
   aNode key < parent key
     ifTrue:[parent left: aNode]
     ifFalse:[parent right: aNode].
   ↑self.

Figure 11.1: Part of the Protocol for Class **Tree**

the most abstract of all classes, being the root of the class hierarchy, and so a commitment to respond to it is placed on every class in the hierarchy. Obviously, the operations involved in producing the output vary greatly according to the nature of the class in question, and so each class *redefines* the protocol for this message so that the particular characteristics of the class are accommodated.

The methods included in an abstract class are present only to place a commitment on its descendants, and are not intended to be executed but to be redefined in each descendant. If a message selecting such a method actually reaches it then the result will be an error message produced by the execution of the method **subclassResponsibility**, which is also one of the methods exported by the class *Object* and is therefore inherited by all classes.

The redefinition of methods in Smalltalk is quite unconstrained — there is nothing to prevent, say, the redefinition of the + operation as 'minus', for example, foolish though this would be.

Classes as Objects

As we have seen, the consistency of the application of the Object-Oriented paradigm is carried through, in Smalltalk, to the extent that classes themselves are objects. The conceptual distinction between objects and classes is not lost by this arrangement, although it does lead to the possibility of confusion.

Classes are objects and so may respond to messages, by means of what are known as *Class methods*. The commonest example of a class method is **new**, which responds with a newly-created instance of the class. Class methods also characteristically provide information about the class; for example one might respond with the number of instances currently in existence.

A class may also declare *Class Variables*, which are accessible to all instances of the class. In a sense, class variables are global to instances, and represent a degradation of encapsulation. Their use is normally to hold constant data values with some fundamental relevance to the class and are obviously not *intended* to be used as global variables as such, although they are not protected by anything other than convention. A typical example of a class variable is **DaysInMonth** in the class **Date**, which defines protocol for the manipulation of dates. **DaysInMonth** is an array that contains the 12 values of the number of days in the months of the year.

Meta Classes

The fact that *everything* in a Smalltalk system is an object, including each of its classes, leads to a rather complex conceptual structure involving a new kind of entity — the *Meta Class*. As objects, classes are themselves instances of classes, which are distinguished by the special name *Meta class*. Every class in the hierarchy has a Meta class, which is created when the class is created. In a characteristically consistent way, meta classes are themselves instances of, in fact, only one class, thus the threatened infinite regress in which a class is an instance of a class, which is an instance of a class ... and so on, is short-circuited.

There seems little doubt that the existence of meta classes adds considerable complexity to the conceptual elegance of the basic class hierarchy model, which perhaps might have been avoided by abandoning the exclusive view of Smalltalk entities as being objects only. The insistence on regarding classes as objects certainly provides for consistency, specifically in the creation of instances where the create message is sent to the class in question. If classes were not objects then their ability to receive messages would require a special mechanism — but as there is a clear conceptual distinction between classes and objects this does not seem to present any great difficulty.

11.2.4   The Smalltalk Class Hierarchy

The Smalltalk class hierarchy is known as the *Image*, because of the fact that classes exist as objects within the memory occupied by the run-time system. By mid 1990 the Image contained over 200 classes. As described previously, the environment provides the *Browser* tool to enable the user to become familiar with the structure of the image. Physically, the browser appears as a window within which the class hierarchy, or the code of individual classes, may be scrolled. In addition to the Browser tool, the documentation of the Image is highly structured as an aid to the accessibility of its details.

This is not the place to give an exhaustive description of the Smalltalk Image but it will be useful to give a brief picture of its structure, together with some selected detail, particularly of how polymorphism is managed.

The structure of the Image may be categorised as follows:

- Magnitude Classes — These classes define objects that may be compared, measured, counted or arithmetically manipulated. They include numbers, characters, dates and times. They are the most commonly used classes.

- Collection Classes — The data structures used in Smalltalk are the collection classes, or are developed from them. They include arrays and dictionaries: structures indexed by alphanumeric key.

- Stream Classes — These classes are used in accessing external devices and files.

- Windows — Applications developed under Smalltalk are invariably window driven, and a number of related classes are provided to support this type of user interface.

- Graphics — The normal platform for Smalltalk is a workstation equipped with a high-resolution bit-mapped graphics display. The graphics classes enable the facilities of these displays to be exploited by Smalltalk users.

- Kernel Classes — provide the protocol for the internal operations intrinsic to Smalltalk such as the creation of subclasses and the operation of the inheritance mechanism.

- System Classes — encompass the operations involved in maintaining the Smalltalk Image.

- Interface Classes — provide facilities for communicating with the operating system, allowing 'call-outs' to non-Smalltalk code.

Of these categories the first three, with the addition of the class **boolean** which occupies a unique position in providing for alternative execution sequences, are the basis of what might be termed application programming in the conventional sense. The remaining classes are either concerned with the highly responsive Smalltalk user interface, replete with windows, pull-down menus, icons and so on, which is transferable, suitably modified, to applications, or with low-level features of the Smalltalk environment and its (operating system) environment. In passing we might note the unusually open nature of the environment, where all the system functions such as 'compilation' (actually interpretation) and the tools, such as the system browser, are accessible by the user.

The collection category, which is a complete subtree of the hierarchy rooted by the class **Collection**, is perhaps the most interesting from the point of

Collection
    Bag
    Set
        Dictionary
            IdentityDictionary
     SequenceableCollection
        ArrayedCollection
           Array
               LiteralArray
           String
           WordArray
        Interval
           LinkedList
           OrderedCollection

Figure 11.2: The Hierarchy Subtree based on **Collection**

view of application development. As remarked above, it is the repository
for the data structure classes provided in the Image and, as such, displays
the richness of the hierarchy. An outline of the subtree is shown in Figure 11.2, indicating the subclass relationship by indentation. The major
characteristics of the members of the subtree rooted on **Collection** are as
follows:

- **Collection** is an abstract superclass and thus does not have instances,
  but defines methods that are intended to be redefined in its subclasses.
  The essential nature of a collection is that it is a group of individuals, upon which structural relationships may be imposed. The main
  methods defined are **add:, remove:, includes:** and **do:** (the colon
  following the method selector means that a following parameter is required. In the first three cases the parameter specifies the object that
  is to be added to, removed from or whose presence is to be tested for
  in, the collection.) The method invoked by **do:** applies an operation
  to every member of a collection.

  Collection contains three class variables that define default maxima
  for the number of members in a collection, and the sizes of general
  object members and strings.

- **Set** and **Bag** are the most abstract of the subclasses of **Collection**, adding little additional protocol. They provide for *unordered* collections, and differ in that a **Set**, in conformity with the corresponding mathematical entity, contains no repeated members, while a **Bag** may contain repeated members. **Bag** accordingly provides a method that responds with the count of instances of a repeated member.
  A typical application for a set is to provide a 'coarse' recogniser for the reserved words of a language: the set is created containing the reserved words; as tokens are extracted they can be tested using the **includes:** method.

- **Dictionary** is a subclass of **Set**, which specialises its superclass by restricting members to **Associations**. An association is a pair of objects, in which the first is used to reference the second, in the manner of a key. The dictionary provides, therefore, an indexed structure that can be used in many applications that require data retrieval by key. Retrieval is supported by the **at:** method, which takes an object that is the first member of an association pair and returns the second member. An association may be updated by the **at: put:** method: the first parameter identifies the association and the second provides the new value for the second member.

- **SequenceableCollection** is an abstract superclass of classes that have members that possess a well-defined order, in other words in which it makes sense to refer to 'the first member', 'the next member' and so on.

- **ArrayedCollection** is a subclass of **SequenceableCollection** but is still an abstract superclass — of classes with external fixed-range integer keys. The subclasses **array** and **string** provide conventional, and highly comprehensive, support for these data structures. **ByteArray** is a specialised class whose members are defined as 8-bit fields and which is used in low-level applications involving machine code.
  WordArray also is used in low-level applications, particularly in accessing and changing bit maps used to store graphics display elements.

- **LinkedList** provides protocol supporting an abstract form of the linked list: abstract in the sense that no data fields are included in the nodes of the list, and that insertions may be made only at the ends of the list. The intention is that appropriate additions will be made in subclasses.

OrderedCollection is a class defining a structure whose members are ordered with reference to the sequence in which they are inserted or removed. Typical specialisations of **OrderedCollection** are stacks and queues .

11.2.5   The MVC Triad

No description of Smalltalk is complete without a mention of the Model View Controller Triad. The MVC triad is the basic structure for an application developed in the Smalltalk environment. The three components are:

- *The Model* — Is the data structure underlying the application, generally constructed from one or more collection classes. The model corresponds to what would be regarded as *the* application in a conventional development environment.

- *View* — Is a system component supporting the visual representation of the application during its activation, utilising the windowing facilities of the Smalltalk environment. There may well be several views for a particular implementation, corresponding to different user requirements.

- *Controller* — Controllers handle the user input to the application, which is mediated by a variety of interaction mechanisms such as pulldown menus, mouse and keyboard input. Again, there may be several controllers for a single application.

A considerable portion of the Smalltalk image is taken up with the support of the MVC Triad, which provides the user with the potential to create HCIs (Human Computer Interfaces) with a responsiveness and power matching that of the environment itself. On the other hand, the Triad is an undeniably complex affair, and it is probably true to say that the Smalltalk programmer, at least until a considerable degree of experience with it has been gained, spends more time wrestling with it than in indulging in the elegance of Object-Oriented software creation.

11.3   C++

Of all currently popular OOPls the one that seems likely to displace Smalltalk is C++, indeed in terms of installed systems C++ is probably more widely distributed. In some ways, however, the philosophies underlying the two languages are so different that it is difficult to view them as competing in any real sense.

The C++ language, and here it is reasonable to refer to the language rather than an environment, exhibits a somewhat minimalist approach to the Object-Oriented paradigm. C++ does not obviously support computation by message passing, nor is dynamic binding necessarily observed. Data abstraction and inheritance *are* supported, however. As is suggested by this combination of characteristics the language is intended to be used in the conventional mode of program development, with little support for the kind of dynamic incremental development that permeates Smalltalk.

11.3.1   Introduction

Apart from its popularity, C++ is of interest as being the most successful representative of a collection of languages that are Object-Oriented extensions of existing languages. C++ was developed as an extension of the C language, which commenced its career as the implementation language for the Unix operating system and has since, despite its considerable lack of suitability, become the standard applications language on PCs. Much of the motivation behind the development of C++ seems to have been to improve the known deficiencies of C, in the context of general applications programming, rather than to enter the Object-Oriented world. In some ways C++ might be thought of as possessing the same sort of relationship to C as does MODULA-2 to Pascal, although this comparison ignores the question of inheritance. As might be expected C++ is a compiled language, although often via a two-stage process in which the C++ source is translated into C, which is then compiled by a standard C compiler.

11.3.2   Information Hiding in C

The C language provides some support for data abstraction, although this is dependent on the particular implementation. The only program structure defined in the language is the *function*, which is a subprogram construct that may possess read-only parameters and generally returns a value via a **return** statement, in a way that is not too far removed from its Ada equivalent. The standard *implementations* of C recognise a higher level construct — the file — which is simply a file containing C source. Files

are compilation units, i.e. comprise the input to any particular run of the
compiler. Practical considerations, and those of good practice, require that
all but the smallest programs are compiled from several files, the executable
program being composed typically by the standard linker utility provided
by the operating system. However, this feature introduces the possibility of
errors, because C is not a secure language. C compilers, unlike their Ada
or MODULA-2 counterparts, are generally not capable of performing type
checking over separate compilations, i.e. across several files, and there is no
import or context clause feature to allow the dependencies between files to
be specified.

To a certain extent this shortcoming can be alleviated by the adoption of a
widely-used, although optional, checking technique. The linguistic feature
that enables this checking is somewhat similar to the Ada facility for separate
subprogram declarations, as utilised in package specifications, for example.
In C the distinction is made between the *definition* of, say, a function, which
includes the details of its implementation, and the *declaration* of the function,
which shows only its name and return and parameter types. A function
definition may appear only once within a program, but its declaration may
appear several times.

This distinction is utilised in a technique involving *header* files, which are
merged into source files by the compiler pre-processor under the control of the
`#include` directive. Header files conventionally contain only declarations
and may be used to define the interface to a 'module', as a set of function
declarations, the implementation of the 'module' being held in a separate file
as the corresponding collection of function definitions, the internal details
of which are hidden by the operation of C's scope rules. 'User modules' —
i.e. files containing calls to the interface functions — may then `include` the
interface definition, in the form of the header file, so that the compiler is
enabled to check that the invocations of the interface functions are correct,
thus simulating separate compilation . It should be noted, however, that this
technique is a recommended convention only, as indicated by the references
to 'module' above — the C compiler knows nothing of such a construct.

11.3.3   Classes

The major extension introduced into C++ is intended to overcome the shortcoming of this lack of a formally recognised module construct, with its defining characteristics of separation of interface definition and implementation,

```
struct int_stack {
                  int stack_array[100];
                  int TOS = 0;
                  void push(int i);
                  int  pop();
             };
```

Figure 11.3: An Integer Stack Type Declared as a Struct

and the encapsulated association of operations and data structure. The basis of the C++ extension over C is the use of the 'struct' feature, which corresponds to the Pascal or MODULA-2 record: a structure defining a composite type with heterogeneously typed 'slots' or fields, known as *members* in C. In addition to containing data items, structs may contain function members in the form of function declarations, and thus enable the packaging together of data structures and operations. For example, a struct containing the appropriate items to implement a stack type for stacks holding integer items might be defined as shown in Figure 11.3 Some explanatory notes might be in order here:

1. Structure defining brackets, corresponding to **begin** and **end**, in the 'structured' languages, are '{' and '}' in C/C++.

2. Types, such as int (integer), are placed before their objects in definitions and declarations.

3. Variables may be initialised in their definitions, as in the case of TOS.

4. Function definitions/declarations are typed, showing the type of the returned value. The type **void**, meaning no type at all, defines the type of a function that does not return a value.

5. The definitions of the functions push and pop are conceptually given elsewhere, and need not concern us. They are individually encapsulating, as are all C functions.

The declaration of the functions as members of the int_stack type means that they may be used only in conjunction with objects of the type. For example:

```
class   int_stack {
                 int stack_array[100];
                 int TOS = 0;
                 public:
                 void pusᵢ(int i);
                 int  pop();
            };
```

Figure 11.4: An Integer Stack Type Declared as a Class

```
{ int i;
  int_stack is;
       is.push(0);
       i = is.pop()i;
}
```

(Note the characteristic dotted notation for the selection of a struct/record member.)

In the context of encapsulation, the struct suffers from the serious defect that all its components are accessible to external functions and so, echoing a refrain from Chapter 3, the following would be perfectly acceptable:

```
int_stack is;
is.TOS = 99;
```

Once again the device of the 'syntactic wall' is called into play, with a developed version of the struct called the *class*, a choice of name that is, of course, highly significant. The class construct, which is marked by the reserved word class at its head, instead of struct, allows the contents of the struct/class to be divided into *private* and *public* parts, with properties that will come as no surprise to the reader. The members that are included within the private part are encapsulated, and may not be accessed directly from an ordinary external function. The public part, which follows the reserved word public: and extends to the end of the structure, contains the externally visible members, which will typically be functions that provide the operations by which the encapsulated data structure may be manipulated. A class for int_stack, with appropriate encapsulation, may therefore be defined as shown in Figure 11.4. As can be seen, the class structure does not support a 'pure' *documentary* separation of interface and implementation, in that the details of the encapsulated data structure are visible to the human reader, in much the same way as for an Ada private type declaration, and for much the same reason.

11.3.4 Object Creation and Destruction

The C++ class is, in a very real sense, a development of the C struct, which also forms part of C++ in accordance with the upward compatibility maintained between the two: any C program is also a C++ program. Specifically, a struct is equivalent to a class with the **public:** separator placed immediately after the opening '{'.

This means that objects — class instances — may be created, in the way shown in the example above, in the conventional way for any C variable. This is very similar to the mechanism in, say, Pascal: an amount of memory determined by the compiler is allocated on entry to the subprogram within which the variable is declared, the address of which is denoted by the variable for the duration of the period that execution remains in the subprogram. A variable used in this way is said to be 'statically bound' to the object.

The main drawback to this approach is that the facilities for the initialisation of objects created in this way are not adequate for the complexity of the data structures underlying many classes, nor is there any way that the compiler can ensure that an appropriate initialisation is carried out at object creation.

This drawback is overcome by the provision of an object creation mechanism that has the effect, where it is employed, of making C++ objects very similar to their equivalents in other OOPls, particularly in respect of name binding. This mechanism involves the inclusion, in a class definition, of one or more member functions that perform the creation and initialisation of objects of the class. These functions, which are known as *constructors*, are distinguished by possessing the same name as the class in which they are members; the constructor for a class is called automatically when the execution of the program reaches the point where an instance of the class is declared. Typically, a constructor utilises dynamic memory allocation for object creation, employing the standard system function **new** for this purpose. New operates in a manner that is very similar to its Ada namesake — it returns a *pointer* to the memory area allocated to the newly-created object — thus realising the indirect, late-binding of name to object identified previously as characteristic of the Object-Oriented paradigm. It should be noted, however, that the provision of constructors is optional, and thus so is the utilisation of late binding.

The handling of objects via pointers is very natural in C/C++ where, for example there is a close (not to say incestuous) relationship between pointers and arrays — the name of an array denotes a pointer to its first element. This leads to the writing of very terse, not always totally readable, code. Returning to the int_stack class, a constructor might be provided as follows:

```
class int_stack{
                int* stack_array;
                int* TOS;
              public:
                void push(int i);
                int  pop();
                int_stack(){TOS = stack_array = new int[100]};
            };
```

This example illustrates a number of points:

1. The '*' type derivation has the meaning of 'pointer to' the type to which it is appended. As a result of the intimate relationship between arrays and pointers noted above, an array *declaration*, which does not involve memory allocation, may be given as a declaration of a pointer to one of its elements, notionally the first.

2. This ability to reference the first element via a pointer, avoiding the need to use the conventional index notation, is complemented by a feature that allows subsequent elements to be accessed by incrementing the pointer to the first — a feature beloved of C programmers, which contributes much to C's reputation for readability.

3. The appearance of the int_stack constructor constitutes a *definition*, because the body of the function appears in the class declaration as the expression between the {} delimiters. In most cases the definition is too large to include in the class declaration, but in cases such as this there is little need for a separate definition. There is, however, an additional significance to function definitions of this type: such functions are implicitly understood to be *inline* functions, that is their code is executed by virtue of the fact that it is inserted into the program at the position of each call, rather than by invoking the function call

mechanism, with its inevitable overhead. Externally defined functions may also be explicitly declared as inline. This feature is characteristic of what can only be described as an obsession with efficiency that permeates the design of C++.

4. The body of the constructor consists of a multiple assignment ('=' is the assignment operator), which groups right, so that the **new** function is called first to create a dynamic object consisting of a 100-element integer array, to which is bound the name **stack_array**. Then the value involved, actually a pointer to the first element of this array, is assigned to TOS so that the **push** and **pop** operations may avail themselves of this direct pointer access to the elements of **stack_array**.

The operation of constructors is not restricted to the simple allocation of memory, and its associated initialisation, in this way; a common technique is to attach the newly created object onto a structure, such as a list or tree, so that it may be manipulated as one of a collection of objects of a particular class.

Object Destruction

The explicit creation of objects, possibly involving the manipulation of complex structures, carries with it at least the possibility of a requirement for the correspondingly explicit destruction of objects — if for no other reason than the desirability of returning the allocated memory to the free store by using the **delete** standard function: there is no automatic garbage collection in C++. In cases where creation has involved the linking of the object into a structure then obviously it will be necessary to delete it in a manner that respects the integrity of the structure. C++ therefore provides the facility to specify *destructor* member functions, which are distinguished by possessing the name of the class, prefixed by a tilde: '~'. If a destructor is defined for a class then it is called, implicitly, when execution reaches the end of the scope of the declaration of any instance of the class

'This'

The linking of objects into pointer-connected structures is facilitated by the existence of a value for every object denoted by the reserved identifier **this**, which is implicitly declared as a member of every class. **This** is a pointer to the object in which it occurs, and thus has some similarity to the Smalltalk pseudo-variable **self**.

Friends

A rather unusual feature of C++ is the existence of *friends*. These are functions that are not members of a class but which are nominated in its definition, and which are allowed access to the internal, private members of the class. This provides a controlled penetration of the encapsulation of the class and is intended to ease the introduction of Object-Oriented structures into existing systems. This is in line with the prevailing philosophy of the language, which has been described as avoiding culture shock to existing C programmers. Another facet of this philosophy is what has been described as an obsession with efficiency, which occasionally appears to conflict with Object-Oriented principles. The cause of this obsession appears to be a desire to prevent programmers avoiding the use of the Object-Oriented features of C++, because of their fear of incurring performance penalties, and merely using the C subset.

11.3.5   Inheritance

Inheritance in C++ is realised by the device of *derived classes*, whereby a class may be declared as being derived from, i.e. is a subclass of, another class, known as its *base* class. The inheritance relationship is shown by an indication that the derived class *is a* (subclass of) the base class by an expression of the form:

```
class derived : public base{
```

The significance of the reserved word `public` in this expression is that all the public members of the base class are available to users of the derived class.

An important feature of the C++ version of inheritance is that derived class members have no privileged access to the private members of the base class — unlike their equivalents in Smalltalk. C++, in other words, recognises no distinction, in this respect, between clients and heirs. It is possible for members of a derived class to be `friends` of the base class, and so have access to its private members, but because they would have to be nominated as such in

the base class this approach cannot support the kind of free, and unpremed-
itated, extensibility that is normally thought of as being characteristic of
the Object-Oriented paradigm. In this respect, C++ provides little more
support for extensibility than Ada, because of their common imposition of
'strict' encapsulation.

The syntactic structure shown above provides for the specification of only
one base class as C++ supports only single inheritance. C++ is not provided
with an imposing class hierarchy after the manner of Smalltalk. Doubtless
there will be a steady proliferation of class libraries as the language becomes
more widely used, but the absence of a standard environment will hinder
the general adoption of a standard class hierarchy.

11.3.6 Polymorphism

Polymorphism in C++ is supported by *Virtual Functions*, which are members of the base class, distinguished by the reserved word **virtual**. Virtual
functions may be redefined in derived classes, and thus enable polymorphic
redefinition. Some of the significance of the idea is lost, however, by the fact
that *only* virtual functions may be redefined. Thus the writers of derived
classes are dependent on the foresight of the base class designer in what
must be regarded as another facet of the rather inflexible characteristics of
the language.

Typing

As the examples have shown, C++, like its predecessor, is a statically-typed
language. Every program object is declared to have a type by source program
expressions, and their usage within the program is checked for consistency
by the compiler, as far as is possible. In this it is quite different from
Smalltalk where, as we have seen, there is no attempt to check statically
that a type clash — the sending of a message to an object that cannot
respond to it — cannot occur. In the OOPl context static type-checking
is intended to prevent this kind of error by detection at compile time, but
is complicated by inheritance and polymorphism. A full discussion of this
subject will be deferred until the next section, because C++, necessarily,
adopts C's approach to typing — C being characterised as a 'loosely typed'
language. Generally, this means that a value of one particular type may be
converted into any other, and thus a rigorous type discipline can always be

circumvented by the C++ programmer.

It is also the case that the C language subset of C++ allows for encapsulation to be destroyed by low level tricks — e.g. by accessing directly the memory addresses occupied by a class private part. Still, as Stroustrup, the designer of the language, remarks in his book [8], "this, of course, is cheating".

11.4   Statically and Strongly-Typed OOPLs

Despite its very considerable dynamic power, and the richness of the mature class hierarchy, Smalltalk has never found favour in what might be termed 'serious' software engineering. The reasons for this include the unavoidable inefficiency of interpreted systems, Smalltalk's nature as essentially a single-user system, but particularly the lack of strong typing reinforced by compiler checking. The possibility that a new operational circumstance might involve an untested message/object combination, resulting in nothing more constructive than an error message, is one that software engineering managers are commonly unwilling to contemplate. The major benefit of strong typing — the ability of the compiler to detect errors that, although syntactical in nature, frequently arise from errors in logic or design — is well-understood and there is considerable reluctance to abandon it. In the Object-Oriented context it is appropriate that the normally implied qualification 'statically' — meaning determined at compile time — is made explicit. In conventional languages, strong typing is invariably enforced statically. In Object-Oriented languages the dynamic nature of name-binding, and polymorphism, would appear to make static type checking at best difficult, at worst impossible. Before describing the approach adopted in several OOPls, it is as well to remind ourselves of what static type checking is intended to achieve in the Object-Oriented context. This may be stated as: it will never be the case, in a correctly compiled program, that a message will be sent to an object whose class, or whose ancestor classes, are incapable of responding to it.

The immediately obvious problem in achieving this intention is that if objects can be created and bound to names without constraint, there is no possibility that the compiler can check that the messages including such a name as the reference to the receiver object are appropriate. Clearly the possibility of static checking must depend on some form of restriction as to the nature of the objects that may be bound to each name. One approach would be to adopt strong typing in the manner of Pascal or Ada, and declare every name as being of a particular class; the compiler would then check that every object bound to a name was of the correct class. But this approach is too restrictive — it would preclude inclusion polymorphism because in, say, Ada terms a subclass of a class is of a different type from its parent, and so the operations exported from its parent may not be applied to its instances. How can we avoid throwing out the polymorphism baby with the type clash bathwater?

11.4.1 Static Typing and Inheritance

The two representatives of statically typed OOPs that will be considered — the OWL language developed by the Digital Equipment Corporation, and Eiffel, from Interactive Software Engineering Inc. — both adopt the same approach to the reconciliation of strong typing with inheritance. This is to extend the notion of *type compatibility*, which exists in Pascal, for example, in a limited form: integer subrange variables may be mixed with integer variables, and so on. This is permitted because all the operations that apply to integer values apply to integer subrange values.

Type compatibility, or *conformance* as it is known in this context, in the two OOPls is based on the principle of inheritance that a subclass may be used wherever its superclass may be used, but not vice versa. This is a consequence of the fact that the *is a* relationship that exists between a class and its parent is not generally symmetrical. If we imagine a class hierarchy including the class 'wheeled vehicle' with one of its many subclasses 'wheelbarrow', it is clear that every wheelbarrow *is a* wheeled vehicle, but that not every wheeled vehicle *is a* wheelbarrow.

Following this idea, a class is considered to be compatible with its parent, and indeed with all its ancestors, and therefore its instances may be used wherever instances of its ancestors are required. As we have seen, if the objective of statically-checked strong typing is to be achieved, type conformance must be observed in the binding of names to objects. This conformance is enforced by a modified version of the conventional variable declaration mechanism. Every name is declared as being associated with a specific class, which remains unchanged throughout the execution of the program. During the execution of the program a name may be bound to, or used to denote, several objects as the result of dynamic binding. The type compatibility rule means, however, that the objects to which an entity is bound must be instances either of its declared class, *or of subclasses of its declared class.* In this way, the possibility of an inappropriate message being sent to an object is prevented, because the instance of a subclass can always respond to any message to which an instance of its parent class can respond. At the same time inclusion polymorphism is not precluded. (It should be noted that this type system is dependent on the avoidance of method restriction — no class should be permitted to 'reject its inheritance', in other words.)

This approach to the reconciliation of static typing and inheritance resembles that found in C++. The very general facilities for type *coercion* supported by C++, however, make it impossible to characterise the language as *strongly-typed*.

11.4.2 Eiffel

Eiffel, which is associated very much with its designer Bertrand Meyer, represents a comprehensive reconciliation of the Object-Oriented paradigm with software engineering. In scope, Eiffel rivals Ada, although it does not possess constructs designed explicitly to support concurrency. Like Ada it provides for static parametric polymorphism in the form of generics, and also an exception mechanism. The system exhibits a conventional approach to compilation, as might be envisaged from its commitment to static type checking.

Class Defintions

The language provides much more syntactic sugar than either Smalltalk or C++ and supports readability to a level approaching that of Ada. Eiffel code is written exclusively to define classes, which are unambiguously described by Meyer as 'the implementations of Abstract Data Types'. There is no risk of confusion between classes and objects in Eiffel: classes are static code modules, objects exist only dynamically, at run-time. A class definition contains a number of *features*, some or all of which constitute the external interface of the class as indicated in an **export** list, much after the style of a MODULA-2 internal module. Features may be either *attributes* or *routines*. Attributes are data items, whose existence in an instance is much like that of the fields of a record — i.e. they are directly accessible by other objects, but in read-only mode. Write access to attributes is provided only to operations internal to the class, thus preserving encapsulation of a modified sort. The inclusion of attributes seems to be an attempt at a compromise to avoid the need for 'get' operations for each simple exported data item. Whether or not this justifies the complication necessarily incorporated into class interface designs is a moot point.

Routines are classified conventionally into procedures and functions. As might be expected, formal parameters and function results have declared types and substitution is governed by type conformance as described above — an object supplied as an actual parameter must be an instance of the class specified for the corresponding formal, or of one of its subclasses.

The meaning of the term 'type' is very close to that of 'class'; the difference between the two exists to permit generic classes to be distinguished from their instances, in the sense of generic instantiation, not object instantiation. When a class is created by compile-time substitution from a generic class, the result defines a type. Non-generic classes are indistinguishable from types.

Eiffel exhibits message-passing only at a notational level, with the message format 'object.message(parameters)'. This is relaxed further in the case of a set of basic types, including **integer** and **boolean**; expressions including them, particularly control expressions, may be written in a style that is recognisably similar to conventional languages. Eiffel implements dynamic name binding in a way that closely conforms to the Object-Oriented paradigm — names, or *entitities*, denote references to objects that have an uninitialised value of **void** when first declared, corresponding to **nil** in Pascal. Objects are created by invoking the **Create** routine on the entity, rather than the class, in a way that is rather reminiscent of the creation of dynamic objects in Pascal or MODULA-2.

An example of a simple class is shown in Figure 11.5. The 'LINKABLE' objects defined by the class are effectively nodes for linking into lists. The class is generic, with a generic formal parameter T that specifies the type of the data field in each LINKABLE node. The example is taken from a standard library that forms part of the Eiffel environment, which, although not as imposing as the Smalltalk image, nevertheless is a rich and evolving one.

Something of the difference in the flavour of Smalltalk and a strongly-typed language can be gleaned from considering the task of creating an array of objects of different classes. In Smalltalk arrays are simply indexed cell structures that are created without reference to the classes of the objects that will populate them. In Eiffel an array is created with a defined class for its elements. The rule of type conformance allows for objects of different classes

```
                --Linked list elements
     class LINKABLE [T] export
            value, change_value, change_right, put_between
     feature
            Create(Initial : T) is
                    -- Initialise with value Initial
            do value := Initial
            end - - Create

            change_value(new : T) is
                    - Assign value new to current element
            do value := new
            end - - change_value

            right :like Current - automatic declaration in subclass

            change_right(other : like Current) is
                    -- Put other to right of current element
            do right := other
            end - - change_right

            put_between(before, after : like Current) is
                    -- Insert current element between before and after
            do
                    if not before.Void then-- is before initialised?
                            before.change_right(current)
                    end
                    change_right(after);
            end - - put_between
     end - - class LINKABLE
```

Figure 11.5: The Eiffel Class LINKABLE

to be inserted into such an array, provided that these different classes are subclasses of the defined element class. The effect is to encourage more cohesion in the class hierarchy, and to impose considerably more discipline on the programmer.

Assertions

This imposition of cohesion within the class hierarchy is supported by another feature of Eiffel — the use of *assertions*. Assertions are logical expressions including program entities, that allow the programmer to define relationships between the values of the entities that must be true. Assertions are related to well-defined program structures such as statements, subprograms or, indeed, programs. There are several kinds of assertion, of which two are recognised as being particularly important in the Eiffel context:

- *Pre-conditions*, which precede their related program structure and define relationships between the input values which must be true if the execution of the structure is to be valid.

- *Post-conditions*, which follow their related program structure and which define the effect that the execution of the program structure has on program entities.

A simple example might be a square root function **sqroot**. The pre-condition restricts the values of the argument to positive values. The post-condition specifies that the result actually is the square root of the argument. In Eiffel the pre and post conditions are respectively introduced by the reserved words **require** and **ensure**, and so the code for the function might look as follows:

```
sqroot(I : integer): float;
require I >= 0
–
–     code for (say) Newton Raphson root algorithm
–     leaving the final value in result
ensure I = result²
```

Additionally, a different type of assertion called an *invariant*, which states a logical relation between program entities that must remain unchanged as the result of the program construct execution may be included.

Assertions used in this way are effectively specifying the semantics of the piece of program with which they are associated. Indeed, one of the important formal specification techniques, VDM ('Vienna Development Method'), uses pre and post conditions and invariants to define the semantics of programs.

(The reader may well be questioning the apparent abandonment of the algebraic specification technique, about which considerable claims were made in the last Chapter. The point is that algebraic specifications are particularly appropriate to the specification of abstract data types viewed *externally*, but here we are concerned with the specification of the operations viewed *internally*, where they must be considered independently. As we have seen, algebraic specifications define the semantics of operations by equating their composition, and so are not appropriate for specifying operations considered in isolation.)

In the context of OOPls, assertions provide a means by which the designer of a class can prevent others from destroying or distorting the semantics of the class during the process of redefining operations. This is because Eiffel requires that any assertions associated with an operation are valid for any redefinition of that operation in a subclass. In this way we can prevent the kind of idiocy referred to previously where 'plus' is redefined to mean 'minus'. This feature of Eiffel is a highly unusual one in any programming language — only the experimental language EUCLID appears to have provided for the incorporation of assertions — but its application to the problem of uncontrolled redefinition seems to be a particularly appropriate one. This is particularly true in relation to abstract classes, defined to impose semantics on their descendants; in Eiffel abstract classes are known as *deferred* classes — the implementations of their features being deferred to their subclasses.

This is also an important point when (inclusion) polymorphism is taken into account. The effect of polymorphism is to permit alternative implementations of an abstract operation, as created by redefinition, to be invoked according to the dynamic binding of the entity involved. To return to the example from the last Chapter: given a class called *Polygon* we may envisage a subclass *Rectangle*. Polygon exports an operation *perimeter* that returns the length of the perimeter of the Polygon object. The implementation of this operation provides for the full generality of polygonal shapes, with no effective limit on the number of sides, with a correspondingly (relatively) complex algorithm. In comparison, the algorithm for determining the perimeter of a rectangle is simple, and so it is appropriate that the perimeter

```
           P : Polygon;
           R : Rectangle;
   do
           R.Create; -- create a rectangle object bound to R
           P := R; -- dynamic binding of rectangle object
                   -- to entity P of static type polygon
           1 := P.perimeter; -- Polymorphic choice available
```

Figure 11.6: An Example of Dynamic Binding

operation is redefined in the rectangle subclass. The existence of these alternative implementations would impact on the example of dynamic binding shown in Figure 11.6 The effect of the dynamic binding of a rectangle object to the entity P will be to cause the invocation of the 'rectangular' perimeter operation on the right hand side of the assignment to 1, despite P's static type being Polygon. It is, therefore, highly desirable that the semantic properties of the perimeter operation are preserved in its redefinitions. (It should be noted that current versions of the Eiffel compiler are not able to check that assertions and invariants are satisfied by the code; an optional run-time check may be imposed, however.)

11.4.3 TRELLIS/OWL

This rather exotic title refers to a language (OWL) that is supported by an environment, with characteristic window facilities, called TRELLIS. The system was developed by the Digital Equipment Corporation for its internal use and is not, therefore, widely available, although it has been fairly extensively presented and discussed at conferences.

OWL is very similar to Eiffel, even to the extent of providing *components*, which are the equivalents of Eiffel's attributes. OWL ignores the term 'class' totally, using 'type' to refer to essentially the same concept, including generic types, which are referred to as *type generators*. Class definitions, or type definitions, possess a characteristic structure bracketed by **type_module** and containing, rather confusingly in the Eiffel context, *attributes* and *definitions*. Attributes specify such characteristics as whether the type is a **base** type, from which objects may be instantiated, or **abstract** types, which perform the same role as their Smalltalk namesakes. Definitions are of components or *operations*, which are categorised as procedures, functions and iterators, the latter providing the systematic access to a replicated structure as defined in Chapter 3.

A small but significant difference from Eiffel is that OWL provides the means for a class to protect its internal features from its subclasses. Eiffel adopts the Smalltalk view that subclasses, or heirs, are privileged in the sense that instance variables are visible to them. OWL permits the features internal to a type definition as being *private*, which means that they are not *subclass visible*, and may not be directly accessed.

Another, and perhaps deeper, difference concerns the question of type conformance in redefined routines. The Eiffel rule says that a routine contained in a class that redefines a routine of a superclass may redeclare the type of a corresponding parameter, provided the redeclaration is of a type that is a *subtype* of the type of the superclass routine parameter type. The OWL rule says that the redeclaration must be of a *supertype* of the superclass routine parameter type. This is not the place to conduct a detailed discussion of the type systems of the two languages. Suffice it to say that Eiffel's type system has been the subject of a number of critical articles, which have invoked a fine display of Meyer's considerable powers of polemical writing in justifying his approach.

11.5   Multiple Inheritance

By a coincidence that probably derives from their comparatively recent appearance on the OOPs scene both TRELLIS/OWL and Eiffel exhibit multiple inheritance — the ability of a class to inherit from more than one superclass. Given multiple inheritance, the class hierarchy takes the form of an acyclic directed graph rather than a tree.

The additional power that multiple inheritance bestows is qualitative rather than quantitative — the design of new classes is largely identified with the *combination* of the properties of several parents, rather than with the *specialisation* of one, although of course the latter technique is always available within an environment that supports multiple inheritance.

The characteristic example that is often given to illustrate multiple inheritance is the window — as found in many workstation user interface systems. A window possesses the attributes both of an output stream — textual and graphical data is written to it for display to the user — and also of a geometric figure, normally rectangular. With multiple inheritance, a window class may be defined by inheriting from appropriate parents: an output stream class and a rectangular figure class. The actual amount of additional code requiring to be written would be negligible. The corresponding implementation using only single inheritance would require the window class to inherit from either the output stream class or the rectangular figure class. Whichever is chosen, the operations of the other will have to be reimplemented as part of the window class.

The proponents of multiple inheritance maintain, with some justification, that it is 'true' inheritance and that single inheritance is too constraining to allow the full power of the technique to be deployed. The question might therefore reasonably be asked, why do not all OOPs support multiple inheritance?

The answer is that multiple inheritance involves a number of conceptual problems that have been perceived by some — namely the supporters of single inheritance — to have been sufficiently intractable to necessitate its rejection, albeit with reluctance. The supporters of multiple inheritance, on the other hand, claim that these problems are largely illusory. As might be expected, the truth seems to lie somewhere between these poles: the problems are not so great as to invalidate multiple inheritance, but they do introduce a certain unavoidable level of complexity.

The most obvious problem arises from the possibility that two (or more) of the parents of a class may have operations with the same name. Apart from the difficulty of unambiguously invoking on of the operations from within the descendant class, if the name is used by a client of the class, up which superclass chain does the inheritance mechanism go? The basic approach of both the representative languages is to regard name clashes as an error. TRELLIS/OWL simply places the responsibility for avoiding them on the programmer by the use of qualified names, of the form S'F, where S is the particular superclass from which the desired version is to be inherited. Eiffel adopts perhaps a more practically-oriented approach and recognises that it would be unreasonable to expect the parent classes of some projected new class to be rewritten because they possess a common operation name. Instead, Eiffel provides a renaming facility that allows such operations to be given new names for use both within the descendant class, and by its clients.

A more complex problem arises when the superclass chains form a class join — in other words, when the parents of a class have a common ancestor. This is of course always the case at the root of the hierarchy, but the problem is normally associated with common ancestors below the root level. The question arises as to whether an operation that has such a *repeated inheritance* is singular, i.e. the fact that two inheritance chains provide it to the class is ignored, or replicated, i.e. one copy being provided via each inheritance chain. This is irrelevant for an idempotent operation but not if the operation is affected by some internal state. In fact both possibilities are applicable, depending on the circumstances, and Eiffel recognises this fact. If such an operation, obtained by repeated inheritance from a common ancestor, is renamed in any of its inheritance chains, then it is treated as replicated; if it is not so renamed then it is treated as shared. The designers of OWL do not appear to have considered this possibility.

11.6 Summary

In this chapter we have described the salient features of a number of Object-Oriented languages, in terms of their realisation of the various characteristics of the Object-Oriented paradigm — inheritance, the message-passing metaphor, dynamic binding and polymorphism. The discussion has ranged from the archetypal OOPl, Smalltalk, to later developments in the field, notably Eiffel with its support both for static strong typing and multiple inheritance.

Chapter 12

Coda — Two Cultures?

The intention underlying the writing of this book was to provide, in a reasonably accessible way, an insight into the collection of interrelated concepts associated with, and including, data abstraction by a developmental treatment from comparatively simple and, it is hoped, familiar topics. We have covered a good deal of ground, and it would be appropriate to provide, as a kind of epilogue, a review attempting to take stock of where this development has led.

We started with a discussion of the design of large software systems, with a, perhaps unspoken, suggestion that some relevant prescriptions would be revealed in due course. In fact, as became clear in Chapter 3, a 'hidden agenda' was present from the start (it was, after all, heavily telegraphed by the title of the book) in the form of a preoccupation with what is really more a technique than a specific program structure: data abstraction. This concept, described in various ways, is essentially the bundling of data structure and operations, to form a unified, semi-independent object manipulated via an interface established for the purpose. As such it provides obvious and comprehensive support for the idea of 'black-box' software components that was arrived at in the discussion of software design in Chapter 1.

There will doubtless be many raised eyebrows at the intimate association of the term 'Design' with what is essentially a programming technique. There is a view of software design that sees it in lofty creative terms, far-removed from the sordid details of 'coding', and certainly not the sort of thing to be influenced by them. This view neglects the history of 'structured' programming, which, however ill-defined, is essentially concerned with the notion that program design should be influenced by language. In its initial phase, with Algol 60, the level at which this influence was exerted was at the statement level: 'programming in the small'. Later developments supported modularity and, eventually, data abstraction, with a progressive raising of the level of the design activity to which they were intended to relate. This is not to deny the existence of language-independent, high-level design, but as noted in Chapter 1 the very plasticity of software makes valid the adoption of structures relevant to apparently mundane issues such as maintenance, and so the support by languages of these kinds of structures renders them appropriate frameworks to which the design process may be related.

Given the validity of this view, the reader may be forgiven for assuming that the problems of the intractable nature of software design are solved — that the application of the well-understood principles of Object-Oriented design and subsequent Object-based software construction have reached a state of perfection from which no further advance is either necessary or possible.

This is, of course, a satirical suggestion. It is certainly true that a significant trend towards the general recognition of the validity of Object-Oriented techniques is visible, with even the mighty citadels of Structured Analysis and Design throwing open their gates to them. (Yourdon has decreed that Object-Oriented Design is the methodology of the future.) It is also true that there are still obvious areas for improvement and some still unsolved problems.

One general problem concerns the possibility of reconciling conventional analysis and design techniques, based on Data Flow Diagrams, with the Object-Oriented methodology. The desirability of such a reconciliation derives not so much from any shortcomings of Object-Oriented design, but from the fact that DFD-based techniques are the stock-in-trade of the vast majority of analysts and designers, and the tools that they use, thus representing a huge investment that cannot be lightly discarded. The search for a link between the two techniques has come to resemble that for the North-West passage, with very considerable financial rewards in sight for the successful discoverer. A number of papers have been published, notably by Ward [9] and Shumate [10], claiming to have uncovered the secret, but as yet there seems to be little agreement on a general method for going from structured analysis to Object-Oriented design.

Another question may be more immediately apparent to the reader, arising from the two linguistic contexts within which the discussion of Data Abstraction has been presented, which might be characterised as 'Ada' and 'OOPl'.

Are these to be regarded as competitors, or as stages along an evolutionary process with the latter superseding the former? As was discussed in earlier parts of the book, data abstraction brings benefits to software design from two perspectives:

- from the analytic perspective — in providing the appropriate entity for *modules*, meeting the criteria of low coupling and high cohesion.

- from the synthetic perspective — as a powerful basis for the modelling of the objects of the application, with all this means in terms of clarity of design and intelligibility of implementation.

It is also true to say that there are two discernibly different cultures in the Object-Oriented (using the term in its widest sense) community that are distinguished by the priority that each places on the perspectives listed above. These cultures are also associated with two different development pathways from the original structured programming language — Algol 60. On the one hand, the analytic culture, which is closely associated with Ada, displays the most direct pathway from the original objectives of structured programming, with its emphasis on security and data abstraction realised by 'iron-clad' encapsulation. On the other, the synthetic culture is associated with 'real' OOPls, with a common (but not exclusive) ancestry including SIMULA, an Algol 60 descendant. SIMULA has received a rather inadequate mention in this book. Its importance to this discussion is that, as its name suggests, it is a simulation language designed specifically for the modelling of real-world objects and events. SIMULA introduced both inheritance and data abstraction into programming languages with, significantly, the latter realised in a form that provides for the association of data structures and operations, but without encapsulation.

This is not, of course, to suggest that these categorisations possess anything approaching water-tightness. As was discussed in Chapter 5, Ada was certainly intended to be a design language, supporting very specifically an approach to design to which the term Object-Oriented is quite appropriate. At the same time there are several examples of statically-typed OOPls that are intended to be recognised as 'Software Engineering' languages. It is clear, however, that the two cultures exhibit quite strong *tendencies* towards the characteristics suggested above, with corresponding shortcomings resulting from the particular emphasis. More specifically:

- The analytical, 'strong encapsulation' model trades off flexibility for security. As we have seen in Chapter 8, Ada's support for reuse is limited because of the impenetrability of the package body. Extensibility can be provided generally only by very considerable visibility of the encapsulated features via the package specification, which then compromises the information hiding qualities of the unit.

The general lack of support for information sharing exhibited by this model effectively rules out any abstraction-raising through inclusion polymorphism.

- The synthetic model exhibits the trade-off with the balance tilted in the opposite direction — the visibility of instance variables commonly vouchsafed to subclasses provides a high level of extensibility, but represents a degree of coupling that may cause problems in a production environment. The heavy commitment to inheritance may itself be a mixed blessing, particularly in the case of single inheritance, as was intimated in the last Chapter.

It is certainly the case that, as far as the engineering of large software systems is concerned, Ada's track record is by far the most impressive — to such an extent that talk of 'superseding', or even 'competition', might be considered to be premature, to say the least. The factor that intrudes on this perception, however, is reuse, and the strength of support for what is widely recognised as a powerful mechanism that is provided by typical OOPls. Perhaps the clearest expression of this has appeared in the documentation produced in association with the **Ada 9X** project. Ada 9X is the provisional name given to the next official revision of the language, the '9X' indicating an intention, or at least a hope, that this will be established during the nineteen-nineties. The Ada 9X Requirements document [10] published in 1990 contains the following:

"**User Need U4.3-B: Programming by Adaption of Existing Units**: When adapting an existing package to new uses, programmers typically change just a few properties of the package. For example, the package might be adapted to new uses by adding several subprograms *or by modifying the implementation of an existing subprogram.*(Author's italics)... An increasing number of programmers want to program in this style... Ada 9X shall make it possible to define new declared entities whose properties are adapted from those of existing entities by the addition or modification of properties or operations in such a way that:

- the original entity's definition and implementation are not modified;

- the new entity (or instances thereof) can be used anywhere the original could be, in exactly the same way.

This is a very clear recommendation of 'programming-by-difference', and seems to be suggesting an evolution of the language towards a realisation of statically-typed inheritance very much along the lines of the Eiffel or OWL model. (We might also add C++ were it not for the loose-typing of the latter.)

The movement for convergence between the two cultures seems to be underway, therefore, with what appears to be a fairly comprehensive capitulation by the 'strict encapsulation' school. Yet, some doubts persist: is the trade-off between security and extensibility an inexorable law? Is there no compromise? It is clear that there is still considerable scope for innovation in the exploitation of data abstraction, particularly in respect of the association of the concept with those of extensibility and polymorphism. Whatever new developments transpire, it cannot be doubted that data abstraction will be a significant technique for the foreseeable future.

Bibliographic Notes

Chapter 1

The classical, and readable, work on the traumas and tribulations of software development is still Brooks' *The Mythical Man-Month: Essays on Software Engineering* (Addison-Wesley 1975). A more conventional text-book treatment may be found in Lamb, *Software Engineering: Planning for Change* (Prentice-Hall 1988).

Chapter 2

Myers' book, *Reliable Software through Composite Design* (Petrocelli-Charter 1975), from which much of the material of this Chapter is derived remains a useful, if slightly dated, text. Myer's categorisations of coupling and cohesion are frequently mentioned, without acknowledgement, for example in Steward, *Software Engineering with Systems Analysis and Design* (Brooks/Cole 1987).

Chapter 3

The terminology introduced in this Chapter is taken from [1] Liskov and Zilles, *Specification Techniques for Data Abstractions* (IEEE Transactions on Software Engineering, Vol. SE-1, 1975). This article is mainly concerned to compare a number of formal specification techniques, but also provides a useful overview of the data abstraction.

Chapter 4

There are numerous books on MODULA-2, many of which can be recommended, for example Sale, *MODULA-2 Discipline and Design* (Addison-Wesley 1986. Wirth's own book is rather terse for an introductory work, although his updated *Algorithms and Data Structures* (Prentice-Hall 1986), which uses MODULA-2 as its illustrative language, is a very useful book.

Chapter 5

Again, as might be expected, Ada has inspired a considerable volume of literature, of variable quality. For a straightforward introduction to the language it is difficult to beat *Programming in Ada* (Addison-Wesley 1984) by Barnes, who was one of Ada's designers. Booch, *Software Engineering with Ada*, (Benjamin/Cummings 1986), is a splendidly committed exposition, which attempts, with considerable success, to provide a 'top-down' view of the language in which, inevitably, some of the detail is obscured. The final arbiter on the language is the 'LRM' — *Reference Manual for the Ada Programming Language*, which is an ANSI standard: MIL-STD-1815. As the definition of a large and complex language the LRM is a considerable achievement, and any serious Ada programmer should possess a copy — most Ada compilers produce error messages that refer to the relevant sections of the LRM. It is published in the UK by Castle House.

Chapter 6

There is little to add to the acknowledgement in the text: Parnas' paper *On the Criteria to be used in Decomposing Systems into Modules* was published in the Communications of the ACM, Vol. 15, December 1972.

Chapter 7

Abbott's paper, *Program Design by Informal English Descriptions*, was published in The Communications of the ACM, Vol. 26, November 1983, and was closely related to Booch's book referred to above (in its first edition). It is certainly worth reading, if only to gain an appreciation of the complexities to which such an apparently simple approach can lead.

Neilson and Shumate [2], *Designing Large Real-Time Systems with Ada*, (Communications of the ACM, Vol. 30, August 1987), includes a consideration of the Booch methodology in the real-time context, and find it wanting. Their own methodology might be regarded as a modified version of Object-Oriented design, tailored specifically to real-time systems. Buhr, *System Design with Ada* (Prentice-Hall 1984), also adopts what might be termed a modified Object-Oriented approach.

A description of the technique of discovering Objects by identifying Agents of behaviour is given by Elizabeth Gibson in *Objects Born and Bred* (Byte Magazine October 1990)

Chapter 8

Software reuse has yet to become a popular topic outside the realm of research papers. The outstanding example is [3] Booch *Software Components in Ada*, (Benjamin/Cummings 1986), which is a worthy, although perhaps not totally compelling, attempt at a logically-derived taxonomy of reusable Ada components.

A polemical celebration of the potential of reusable software is given by Brad J Cox in *There is a Silver Bullet* (Byte Magazine, October 1990) and the ubiquitous Parnas has contributed to *Enhancing Reusability with Information Hiding* in Software Reusability: Concepts and Models eds. Biggerstaff and Perlis (Addison-Wesley 1989).

Chapter 9

The great populariser of algebraic specification is Guttag, in numerous papers, for example [4]*Abstract Data Types and the Development of Data Structures*, (Communications of the ACM, Vol. 20 June 1977). A more rigorous, and, perhaps, better written, collection of papers is provided by Goguen, of which the seminal *An Initial Algebra Approach to the Specification, Correctness and Implementation of Abstract Data Types*, [5] Goguen Thatcher and Wagner (Current Trends in Programming Methodology, ed. Yeh, Prentice-Hall 1978), is well worth reading.

A number of later publications provide more accessible treatments of the subject, for example Van Horebeek and Lewi *Algebraic Specifications in Software Engineering* (Springer-Verlag 1989).

A paper describing the generation of Ada packages from algebraic specifications is given in [6] Priestley *Implementing Structured Algebraic Specifications in Ada* (Proceedings of the 8th Ada UK Conference, Peter Peregrinus 1989).

Chapter 10

Until recently, the literature available in respect of Object-Oriented languages and techniques was restricted to language-specific books — concerned with Smalltalk or Eiffel for example — or the proceedings of the OOPSLA ('Object-Oriented Programming Systems, Languages and Applications') conferences that took place in a variety of desirable locations in the USA in the late 'eighties. This situation is changing, and a number of recent publications have started to fill this vacuum; for example Blair *et al* *Object-Oriented Languages, Systems and Applications* (Pitman 1991).

A discussion of the transformation of the traditional software development process effected by the characteristics of Object-Oriented environments is given in *Programmer as Reader* by Adele Goldberg, in *Information Processing 86*, ed. H J Kugler (North-Holland 1986).

Chapter 11

Bertrand Meyer's book [7] *Object-Oriented Software Construction* (Addison-Wesley 1988) is mainly concerned to provide an exposition of the Eiffel language, but it also contains an excellent introduction to Object-Oriented programming in general, including comparisons between Eiffel and other languages, including Ada. Perhaps not surprisingly, Meyer is slightly less than fair to Ada. By contrast, Stroustrup's book [8] *The C++ Programming Language* (Addison Wesley 1986) is very much more a language manual, in which concerns with efficiency are frequently allowed to obscure the main features. A more readable introduction to C++ is provided by Pinson and Wiener (Addison-Wesley 1987).

Smalltalk is well-served by a number of books written by members of its design team, notably Adele Goldberg and David Robson, *Smalltalk 80, The Language and its Implementation* (Addison Wesley 1983) and Adele Goldberg, *Smalltalk 80, The Interactive Programming Environment* (Addison Wesley 1983). Pinson and Wiener also provide a good introduction in *An Introduction to Object-Oriented Programming and Smalltalk* (Addison-Wesley 1988).

Chapter 12

Ward's paper [9] *How to Integrate Object Orientation with Structured Analysis and Design* appeared in IEEE Software March 1989; The main message of the paper is that Entity-Relation diagrams provide the link between the two methodologies. Shumate in [10] *Structured Analysis and Object-Oriented Design are Compatible* (Ada Letters May/June 1991) approaches the problem from the perspective of the design of real-time systems, and identifies objects with processes, derived by conventional structured analysis techniques.

Index